Real-Resumes for Aviation & Travel Jobs...
including real resumes used to change careers
and transfer skills to other industries

Anne McKinney, Editor

P R E P   P U B L I S H I N G

FAYETTEVILLE, NC

PREP Publishing
1110½ Hay Street
Fayetteville, NC 28305
(910) 483-6611

Library of Congress Cataloging-in-Publication Data

Real-resumes for aviation & travel jobs : including real resumes used to change careers and transfer skills to other industries / Anne McKinney editor.
     p. cm. -- (Real-resumes series)
   ISBN - 978-1475093346; 147509334   9 (trade pbk.)
   1. Résumés (Employment) 2. Airlines. 3. Travel agents. I. McKinney, Anne, 1948- II. Series.

  HF5383 .R3954 2002
  650.14'2--dc21   2002020595
                                               CIP

Printed in the United States of America

By PREP Publishing

Table of Contents

Welcome to the Real-Resumes Series. The Real-Resumes Series is a series of books which have been developed based on the experiences of real job hunters and which target specialized fields or types of resumes. As the editor of the series, I have carefully selected resumes and cover letters (with names and other key data disguised, of course) which have been used successfully in real job hunts. That's what we mean by "Real-Resumes." What you see in this book are *real* resumes and cover letters which helped real people get ahead in their careers.

The Real-Resumes Series is based on the work of the country's oldest resume-preparation company known as PREP Resumes. If you would like a free information packet describing the company's resume preparation services, call 910-483-6611 or write to PREP at 1110½ Hay Street, Fayetteville, NC 28305. If you have a job hunting experience you would like to share with our staff at the Real-Resumes Series, please contact us at preppub@aol.com or visit our website at http://www.prep-pub.com.

The resumes and cover letters in this book are designed to be of most value to people already in a job hunt or contemplating a career change. If we could give you one word of advice about your career, here's what we would say: Manage your career and don't stumble from job to job in an incoherent pattern. Try to find work that interests you, and then identify prosperous industries which need work performed of the type you want to do. Learn early in your working life that a great resume and cover letter can blow doors open for you and help you maximize your salary.

This book is dedicated to those seeking jobs in the aviation and travel fields. We hope the superior samples will help you manage your current job campaign and your career so that you will find work aligned to your career interests.

Real-Resumes for Aviation & Travel Jobs...
including real resumes used to change careers
and transfer skills to other industries

Anne McKinney, Editor

As the editor of this book, I would like to give you some tips on how to make the best use of the information you will find here. Because you are considering a career change, you already understand the concept of managing your career for maximum enjoyment and self-fulfillment. The purpose of this book is to provide expert tools and advice so that you *can* manage your career. Inside these pages you will find resumes and cover letters that will help you find not just a job but the type of work you want to do.

Overview of the Book

Every resume and cover letter in this book actually worked. And most of the resumes and cover letters have common features: most are one-page, most are in the chronological format, and most resumes are accompanied by a companion cover letter. In this section you will find helpful advice about job hunting. Step One begins with a discussion of why employers prefer the one-page, chronological resume. In Step Two you are introduced to the direct approach and to the proper format for a cover letter. In Step Three you learn the 14 main reasons why job hunters are not offered the jobs they want, and you learn the six key areas employers focus on when they interview you. Step Four gives nuts-and-bolts advice on how to handle the interview, send a follow-up letter after an interview, and negotiate your salary.

The cover letter plays such a critical role in a career change. You will learn from the experts how to format your cover letters and you will see suggested language to use in particular career-change situations. It has been said that "A picture is worth a thousand words" and, for that reason, you will see numerous examples of effective cover letters used by real individuals to change fields, functions, and industries.

The most important part of the book is the Real-Resumes section. Some of the individuals whose resumes and cover letters you see spent a lengthy career in an industry they loved. Then there are resumes and cover letters of people who wanted a change but who probably wanted to remain in their industry. Many of you will be especially interested by the resumes and cover letters of individuals who knew they definitely wanted a career change but had no idea what they wanted to do next. Other resumes and cover letters show individuals who knew they wanted to change fields and had a pretty good idea of what they wanted to do next.

Whatever your field, and whatever your circumstances, you'll find resumes and cover letters that will "show you the ropes" in terms of successfully changing jobs and switching careers.

Before you proceed further, think about why you picked up this book.
- Are you dissatisfied with the type of work you are now doing?
- Would you like to change careers, change companies, or change industries?
- Are you satisfied with your industry but not with your niche or function within it?
- Do you want to transfer your skills to a new product or service?
- Even if you have excelled in your field, have you "had enough"? Would you like the stimulation of a new challenge?
- Are you aware of the importance of a great cover letter but unsure of how to write one?
- Are you preparing to launch a second career after retirement?
- Have you been downsized, or do you anticipate becoming a victim of downsizing?
- Do you need expert advice on how to plan and implement a job campaign that will open the maximum number of doors?
- Do you want to make sure you handle an interview to your maximum advantage?

Introduction:
The Art of
Changing
Jobs...
and Finding
New Careers

- Would you like to master the techniques of negotiating salary and benefits?
- Do you want to learn the secrets and shortcuts of professional resume writers?

Using the Direct Approach

As you consider the possibility of a job hunt or career change, you need to be aware that most people end up having at least three distinctly different careers in their working lifetimes, and often those careers are different from each other. Yet people usually stumble through each job campaign, unsure of what they should be doing. Whether you find yourself voluntarily or unexpectedly in a job hunt, the direct approach is the job hunting strategy most likely to yield a full-time permanent job. The direct approach is an active, take-the-initiative style of job hunting in which you choose your next employer rather than relying on responding to ads, using employment agencies, or depending on other methods of finding jobs. You will learn how to use the direct approach in this book, and you will see that an effective cover letter is a critical ingredient in using the direct approach.

The "direct approach" is the style of job hunting most likely to yield the maximum number of job interviews.

Lack of Industry Experience Not a Major Barrier to Entering New Field

"Lack of experience" is often the last reason people are not offered jobs, according to the companies who do the hiring. If you are changing careers, you will be glad to learn that experienced professionals often are selling "potential" rather than experience in a job hunt. Companies look for personal qualities that they know tend to be present in their most effective professionals, such as communication skills, initiative, persistence, organizational and time management skills, and creativity. Frequently companies are trying to discover "personality type," "talent," "ability," "aptitude," and "potential" rather than seeking actual hands-on experience, so your resume should be designed to aggressively present your accomplishments. Attitude, enthusiasm, personality, and a track record of achievements in any type of work are the primary "indicators of success" which employers are seeking, and you will see numerous examples in this book of resumes written in an all-purpose fashion so that the professional can approach various industries and companies.

Using references in a skillful fashion in your job hunt will inspire confidence in prospective employers and help you "close the sale" after interviews.

The Art of Using References in a Job Hunt

You probably already know that you need to provide references during a job hunt, but you may not be sure of how and when to use references for maximum advantage. You can use references very creatively during a job hunt to call attention to your strengths and make yourself "stand out." Your references will rarely get you a job, no matter how impressive the names, but the way you use references can boost the employer's confidence in you and lead to a job offer in the least time.

You should ask from three to five people, including people who have supervised you, if you can use them as a reference during your job hunt. You may not be able to ask your current boss since your job hunt is probably confidential.

A common question in resume preparation is: "Do I need to put my references on my resume?" No, you don't. Even if you create a references page at the same time you prepare your resume, you don't need to mail, e-mail, or fax your references page with the resume and cover letter. Usually the potential employer is not interested in references until he meets you, so the earliest you need to have references ready is at the first interview. Obviously there are exceptions to this standard rule of thumb; sometimes an ad will ask you to send references with your first response. Wait until the employer requests references before providing them.

An excellent attention-getting technique is to take to the first interview not just a page of references (giving names, addresses, and telephone numbers) but an actual letter of reference written by someone who knows you well and who preferably has supervised or employed you. A professional way to close the first interview is to thank the interviewer, shake his or her hand, and then say you'd like to give him or her a copy of a letter of reference from a previous employer. Hopefully you already made a good impression during the interview, but you'll "close the sale" in a dynamic fashion if you leave a letter praising you and your accomplishments. For that reason, it's a good idea to ask supervisors during your final weeks in a job if they will provide you with a written letter of recommendation which you can use in future job hunts. Most employers will oblige, and you will have a letter that has a useful "shelf life" of many years. Such a letter often gives the prospective employer enough confidence in his opinion of you that he may forego checking out other references and decide to offer you the job on the spot or in the next few days.

With regard to references, it's best to provide the names and addresses of people who have supervised you or observed you in a work situation.

Whom should you ask to serve as references? References should be people who have known or supervised you in a professional, academic, or work situation. References with big titles, like school superintendent or congressman, are fine, but remind busy people when you get to the interview stage that they may be contacted soon. Make sure the busy official recognizes your name and has instant positive recall of you! If you're asked to provide references on a formal company application, you can simply transcribe names from your references list. In summary, follow this rule in using references: If you've got them, flaunt them! If you've obtained well-written letters of reference, make sure you find a polite way to push those references under the nose of the interviewer so he or she can hear someone other than you describing your strengths. Your references probably won't ever get you a job, but glowing letters of reference can give you credibility and visibility that can make you stand out among candidates with similar credentials and potential!

The approach taken by this book is to (1) help you master the proven best techniques of conducting a job hunt and (2) show you how to stand out in a job hunt through your resume, cover letter, interviewing skills, as well as the way in which you present your references and follow up on interviews. Now, the best way to "get in the mood" for writing your own resume and cover letter is to select samples from the Table of Contents that interest you and then read them. A great resume is a "photograph," usually on one page, of an individual. If you wish to seek professional advice in preparing your resume, you may contact one of the professional writers at Professional Resume & Employment Publishing (PREP) for a brief free consultation by calling 1-910-483-6611.

Part One: Some
Advice About
Your Job Hunt

What if you don't know what you want to do?

Your job hunt will be more comfortable if you can figure out what type of work you want to do. But you are not alone if you have no idea what you want to do next! You may have knowledge and skills in certain areas but want to get into another type of work. What *The Wall Street Journal* has discovered in its research on careers is that most of us end up having at least three distinctly different careers in our working lives; it seems that, even if we really like a particular kind of activity, twenty years of doing it is enough for most of us and we want to move on to something else!

Figure out what interests
you and you will hold the
key to a successful job
hunt and working career.
(And be prepared for your
interests to change over
time!)

That's why we strongly believe that you need to spend some time figuring out *what interests you* rather than taking an inventory of the skills you have. You may have skills that you simply don't want to use, but if you can build your career on the things that interest you, you will be more likely to be happy and satisfied in your job. Realize, too, that interests can change over time; the activities that interest you now may not be the ones that interested you years ago. For example, some professionals may decide that they've had enough of retail sales and want a job selling another product or service, even though they have earned a reputation for being an excellent retail manager. We strongly believe that interests rather than skills should be the determining factor in deciding what types of jobs you want to apply for and what directions you explore in your job hunt. Obviously one cannot be a lawyer without a law degree or a secretary without secretarial skills; but a professional can embark on a next career as a financial consultant, property manager, plant manager, production supervisor, retail manager, or other occupation if he/she has a strong interest in that type of work and can provide a resume that clearly demonstrates past excellent performance in *any* field and *potential* to excel in another field. As you will see later in this book, "lack of exact experience" is the last reason why people are turned down for the jobs they apply for.

How can you have a resume prepared if you don't know what you want to do?

You may be wondering how you can have a resume prepared if you don't know what you want to do next. The approach to resume writing which PREP, the country's oldest resume-preparation company, has used successfully for many years is to develop an "all-purpose" resume that translates your skills, experience, and accomplishments into language employers can understand. What most people need in a job hunt is a versatile resume that will allow them to apply for numerous types of jobs. For example, you may want to apply for a job in pharmaceutical sales but you may also want to have a resume that will be versatile enough for you to apply for jobs in the construction, financial services, or automotive industries.

"Lack of exact experience"
is the last reason people
are turned down for the
jobs for which they apply.

Based on more than **20 years** of serving job hunters, we at PREP have found that your best approach to job hunting is **an all-purpose resume** and **specific cover letters tailored to specific fields** rather than using the approach of trying to create different resumes for every job. If you are remaining in your field, you may not even need more than one "all-purpose" cover letter, although the cover letter rather than the resume is the place to communicate your interest in a narrow or specific field. An all-purpose resume and cover letter that translate your experience and accomplishments into plain English are the tools that will maximize the number of doors which open for you while permitting you to "fish" in the widest range of job areas.

Your resume will provide the script for your job interview.
When you get down to it, your resume has a simple job to do: Its purpose is to blow as many doors open as possible and to make as many people as possible want to meet you. So a well-written resume that really "sells" you is a key that will create opportunities for you in a job hunt.

This statistic explains why: The typical newspaper advertisement for a job opening receives more than 245 replies. And normally only 10 or 12 will be invited to an interview.

But here's another purpose of the resume: it provides the "script" the employer uses when he interviews you. If your resume has been written in such a way that your strengths and achievements are revealed, that's what you'll end up talking about at the job interview. Since the resume will govern what you get asked about at your interviews, you can't overestimate the importance of making sure your resume makes you look and sound as good as you are.

Your resume is the "script" for your job interviews. Make sure you put on your resume what you want to talk about or be asked about at the job interview.

So what is a "good" resume?
Very literally, your resume should motivate the person reading it to dial the phone number or e-mail the screen name you have put on the resume. When you are relocating, you should put a local phone number on your resume if your physical address is several states away; employers are more likely to dial a local telephone number than a long-distance number when they're looking for potential employees.

If you have a resume already, look at it objectively. Is it a limp, colorless "laundry list" of your job titles and duties? Or does it "paint a picture" of your skills, abilities, and accomplishments in a way that would make someone want to meet you? Can people understand what you're saying? If you are attempting to change fields or industries, can potential employers see that your skills and knowledge are transferable to other environments? For example, have you described accomplishments which reveal your problem-solving abilities or communication skills?

The one-page resume in chronological format is the format preferred by most employers.

How long should your resume be?
One page, maybe two. Usually only people in the academic community have a resume (which they usually call a *curriculum vitae*) longer than one or two pages. Remember that your resume is almost always accompanied by a cover letter, and a potential employer does not want to read more than two or three pages about a total stranger in order to decide if he wants to meet that person! Besides, don't forget that the more you tell someone about yourself, the more opportunity you are providing for the employer to screen you out at the "first-cut" stage. A resume should be concise and exciting and designed to make the reader want to meet you in person!

Should resumes be functional or chronological?
Employers almost always prefer a chronological resume; in other words, an employer will find a resume easier to read if it is immediately apparent what your current or most recent job is, what you did before that, and so forth, in reverse chronological order. A resume that goes back in detail for the last ten years of employment will generally satisfy the employer's curiosity about your background. Employment more than ten years old can be shown even more briefly in an "Other Experience" section at the end of your "Experience" section. Remember that your intention is not to tell everything you've done but to "hit the high points" and especially impress the employer with what you learned, contributed, or accomplished in each job you describe.

Once you get your resume, what do you do with it?

You will be using your resume to answer ads, as a tool to use in talking with friends and relatives about your job search, and, most importantly, in using the "direct approach" described in this book.

When you mail your resume, always send a "cover letter."

A "cover letter," sometimes called a "resume letter" or "letter of interest," is a letter that accompanies and introduces your resume. Your cover letter is a way of personalizing the resume by sending it to the specific person you think you might want to work for at each company. Your cover letter should contain a few highlights from your resume—just enough to make someone want to meet you. Cover letters should always be typed or word processed on a computer—never handwritten.

Never mail or fax your resume without a cover letter.

1. Learn the art of answering ads.

There is an "art," part of which can be learned, in using your "bestselling" resume to reply to advertisements.

Sometimes an exciting job lurks behind a boring ad that someone dictated in a hurry, so reply to any ad that interests you. Don't worry that you aren't "25 years old with an MBA" like the ad asks for. Employers will always make compromises in their requirements if they think you're the "best fit" overall.

What about ads that ask for "salary requirements?"

What if the ad you're answering asks for "salary requirements?" The first rule is to avoid committing yourself in writing at that point to a specific salary. You don't want to "lock yourself in."

What if the ad asks for your "salary requirements?"

There are two ways to handle the ad that asks for "salary requirements."

First, you can ignore that part of the ad and accompany your resume with a cover letter that focuses on "selling" you, your abilities, and even some of your philosophy about work or your field. You may include a sentence in your cover letter like this: "I can provide excellent personal and professional references at your request, and I would be delighted to share the private details of my salary history with you in person."

Second, if you feel you must give some kind of number, just state a range in your cover letter that includes your medical, dental, other benefits, and expected bonuses. You might state, for example, "My current compensation, including benefits and bonuses, is in the range of $30,000-$40,000."

Analyze the ad and "tailor" yourself to it.

When you're replying to ads, a finely tailored cover letter is an important tool in getting your resume noticed and read. On the next page is a cover letter which has been "tailored to fit" a specific ad. Notice the "art" used by PREP writers of analyzing the ad's main requirements and then writing the letter so that the person's background, work habits, and interests seem "tailor-made" to the company's needs. Use this cover letter as a model when you prepare your own reply to ads.

Date

Exact Name of Person
Title or Position
Name of Company
Address (number and street)
Address (city, state, and ZIP)

Dear Exact Name of Person (or Sir or Madam if answering a blind ad):

I would appreciate an opportunity to talk with you soon about how I could contribute to your organization through my experience in the travel industry and my reputation as a gracious individual with excellent customer service and problem-solving skills.

As a Travel Consultant with International Travel in Atlanta, GA, I have built a diverse clientele through my knowledge and my ability to courteously deal with people. Since graduating from Atlanta Travel School, I have continued to attend regular annual training in the use of the SABRE system as well as programs to familiarize individuals with the nearly limitless travel options and opportunities.

I have an aptitude for easily learning new computer programs and am familiar with Apollo and System One as well as SABRE. As you will see from my enclosed resume, I am familiar with all aspects of arranging transportation by air, land, and sea including the details of arranging business travel, cruises, and trips to popular vacation destinations throughout the world.

You would find me in person to be a congenial and poised person who is accustomed to dealing with people and developing travel plans to suit their style and tastes. In my experience, a satisfied customer nearly always returns for repeat business, and I am proud of the track record of satisfied customers I have established. Although I am highly regarded in my current job and am regarded as a valuable asset to the business, I would like to join a travel agency which is aggressive in its orientation to be the best.I am a high-powered, highly motivated individual and would have much to offer an organization that is determined to be the travel agency of choice in our area.

I hope you will welcome my call soon to arrange a brief meeting to discuss your current and future needs and how I might serve them. Thank you in advance for your time.

Sincerely,

Glory Anne Honore

Alternate last paragraph:
I hope you will call or write me soon to suggest a time convenient for us to meet and discuss your current and future needs and how I might serve them. Thank you in advance for your time.

Employers are trying to identify the individual who wants the job they are filling. Don't be afraid to express your enthusiasm in the cover letter!

2. Talk to friends and relatives.

Don't be shy about telling your friends and relatives the kind of job you're looking for. Looking for the job you want involves using your network of contacts, so tell people what you're looking for. They may be able to make introductions and help set up interviews.

About 25% of all interviews are set up through "who you know," so don't ignore this approach.

3. Finally, and most importantly, use the "direct approach."

The "direct approach" is a strategy in which you choose your next employer.

More than 50% of all job interviews are set up by the "direct approach." That means you actually mail, e-mail, or fax a resume and a cover letter to a company you think might be interesting to work for.

To whom do you write?

In general, you should write directly to the *exact name* of the person who would be hiring you: say, the vice-president of marketing or data processing. If you're in doubt about to whom to address the letter, address it to the president by name and he or she will make sure it gets forwarded to the right person within the company who has hiring authority in your area.

How do you find the names of potential employers?

You're not alone if you feel that the biggest problem in your job search is finding the right names at the companies you want to contact. But you can usually figure out the names of companies you want to approach by deciding first if your job hunt is primarily geography-driven or industry-driven.

In a **geography-driven job hunt,** you could select a list of, say, 50 companies you want to contact **by location** from the lists that the U.S. Chambers of Commerce publish yearly of their "major area employers." There are hundreds of local Chambers of Commerce across America, and most of them will have an 800 number which you can find through 1-800-555-1212. If you and your family think Atlanta, Dallas, Ft. Lauderdale, and Virginia Beach might be nice places to live, for example, you could contact the Chamber of Commerce in those cities and ask how you can obtain a copy of their list of major employers. Your nearest library will have the book which lists the addresses of all chambers.

In an **industry-driven job hunt,** and if you are willing to relocate, you will be identifying the companies which you find most attractive in the industry in which you want to work. When you select a list of companies to contact **by industry,** you can find the right person to write and the address of firms by industrial category in *Standard and Poor's, Moody's,* and other excellent books in public libraries. Many Web sites also provide contact information.

Many people feel it's a good investment to actually call the company to either find out or double-check the name of the person to whom they want to send a resume and cover letter. It's important to do as much as you feasibly can to assure that the letter gets to the right person in the company.

On-line research will be the best way for many people to locate organizations to which they wish to send their resume. It is outside the scope of this book to teach Internet research skills, but librarians are often useful in this area.

What's the correct way to follow up on a resume you send?

There is a polite way to be aggressively interested in a company during your job hunt. It is ideal to end the cover letter accompanying your resume by saying, "I hope you'll welcome my call next week when I try to arrange a brief meeting at your convenience to discuss your current and future needs and how I might serve them." Keep it low key, and just ask for a "brief meeting," not an interview. Employers want people who show a determined interest in working with them, so don't be shy about following up on the resume and cover letter you've mailed.

It pays to be aware of the 14 most common pitfalls for job hunters.

STEP THREE: Preparing for Interviews

But a resume and cover letter by themselves can't get you the job you want. You need to "prep" yourself before the interview. Step Three in your job campaign is "Preparing for Interviews." First, let's look at interviewing from the hiring organization's point of view.

What are the biggest "turnoffs" for potential employers?

One of the ways to help yourself perform well at an interview is to look at the main reasons why organizations *don't* hire the people they interview, according to those who do the interviewing.

Notice that "lack of appropriate background" (or lack of experience) is the *last* reason for not being offered the job.

The 14 Most Common Reasons Job Hunters Are Not Offered Jobs (according to the companies who do the interviewing and hiring):

1. Low level of accomplishment
2. Poor attitude, lack of self-confidence
3. Lack of goals/objectives
4. Lack of enthusiasm
5. Lack of interest in the company's business
6. Inability to sell or express yourself
7. Unrealistic salary demands
8. Poor appearance
9. Lack of maturity, no leadership potential
10. Lack of extracurricular activities
11. Lack of preparation for the interview, no knowledge about company
12. Objecting to travel
13. Excessive interest in security and benefits
14. Inappropriate background

Department of Labor studies have proven that smart, "prepared" job hunters can increase their beginning salary while getting a job in *half* the time it normally takes. (4½ months is the average national length of a job search.) Here, from PREP, are some questions that can prepare you to find a job faster.

Are you in the "right" frame of mind?

It seems unfair that we have to look for a job just when we're lowest in morale. Don't worry *too* much if you're nervous before interviews. You're supposed to be a little nervous, especially if the job means a lot to you. But the best way to kill unnecessary fears about job hunting is through 1) making sure you have a great resume and 2) preparing yourself for the interview. Here are three main areas you need to think about before each interview.

Do you know what the company does?
Don't walk into an interview giving the impression that, "If this is Tuesday, this must be General Motors."

Research the company before you go to interviews.

Find out before the interview what the company's main product or service is. Where is the company heading? Is it in a "growth" or declining industry? (Answers to these questions may influence whether or not you want to work there!)

Information about what the company does is in annual reports, in newspaper and magazine articles, and on the Internet. If you're not yet skilled at Internet research, just visit your nearest library and ask the reference librarian to guide you to printed materials on the company.

Do you know what you want to do for the company?
Before the interview, try to decide how you see yourself fitting into the company. Remember, "lack of exact background" the company wants is usually the last reason people are not offered jobs.

Understand before you go to each interview that the burden will be on you to "sell" the interviewer on why you're the best person for the job and the company.

How will you answer the critical interview questions?
Put yourself in the interviewer's position and think about the questions you're most likely to be asked. Here are some of the most commonly asked interview questions:

Anticipate the questions you will be asked at the interview, and prepare your responses in advance.

Q: *"What are your greatest strengths?"*

A: Don't say you've never thought about it! Go into an interview knowing the three main impressions you want to leave about yourself, such as "I'm hard-working, loyal, and an imaginative cost-cutter."

Q: *"What are your greatest weaknesses?"*

A: Don't confess that you're lazy or have trouble meeting deadlines! Confessing that you tend to be a "workaholic" or "tend to be a perfectionist and sometimes get frustrated when others don't share my high standards" will make your prospective employer see a "weakness" that he likes. Name a weakness that your interviewer will perceive as a strength.

Q: *"What are your long-range goals?"*

A: If you're interviewing with Microsoft, don't say you want to work for IBM in five years! Say your long-range goal is to be *with* the company, contributing to its goals and success.

Q: *"What motivates you to do your best work?"*

A: Don't get dollar signs in your eyes here! "A challenge" is not a bad answer, but it's a little cliched. Saying something like "troubleshooting" or "solving a tough problem" is more interesting and specific. Give an example if you can.

Q: "What do you know about this organization?"

A: Don't say you never heard of it until they asked you to the interview! Name an interesting, positive thing you learned about the company recently from your research. Remember, company executives can sometimes feel rather "maternal" about the company they serve. Don't get onto a negative area of the company if you can think of positive facts you can bring up. Of course, if you learned in your research that the company's sales seem to be taking a nose-dive, or that the company president is being prosecuted for taking bribes, you might politely ask your interviewer to tell you something that could help you better understand what you've been reading. Those are the kinds of company facts that can help you determine whether or not you want to work there.

Q: "Why should I hire you?"

A: "I'm unemployed and available" is the wrong answer here! Get back to your strengths and say that you believe the organization could benefit by a loyal, hard-working cost-cutter like yourself.

In conclusion, you should decide in advance, before you go to the interview, how you will answer each of these commonly asked questions. Have some practice interviews with a friend to role-play and build your confidence.

STEP FOUR: Handling the Interview and Negotiating Salary

Now you're ready for Step Four: actually handling the interview successfully and effectively. Remember, the purpose of an interview is to get a job offer.

Eight "do's" for the interview

According to leading U.S. companies, there are eight key areas in interviewing success. You can fail at an interview if you mishandle just one area.

1. **Do wear appropriate clothes.**
   You can never go wrong by wearing a suit to an interview.

2. **Do be well groomed.**
   Don't overlook the obvious things like having clean hair, clothes, and fingernails for the interview.

3. **Do give a firm handshake.**
   You'll have to shake hands twice in most interviews: first, before you sit down, and second, when you leave the interview. Limp handshakes turn most people off.

4. **Do smile and show a sense of humor.**
   Interviewers are looking for people who would be nice to work with, so don't be so somber that you don't smile. In fact, research shows that people who smile at interviews are perceived as more intelligent. So, smile!

5. **Do be enthusiastic.**
   Employers say they are "turned off" by lifeless, unenthusiastic job hunters who show no special interest in that company. The best way to show some enthusiasm for the employer's operation is to find out about the business beforehand.

Go to an interview prepared to tell the company why it should hire you.

A smile at an interview makes the employer perceive of you as intelligent!

6. Do show you are flexible and adaptable.

An employer is looking for someone who can contribute to his organization in a flexible, adaptable way. No matter what skills and training you have, employers know every new employee must go through initiation and training on the company's turf. Certainly show pride in your past accomplishments in a specific, factual way ("I saved my last employer $50.00 a week by a new cost-cutting measure I developed"). But don't come across as though there's nothing about the job you couldn't easily handle.

7. Do ask intelligent questions about the employer's business.

An employer is hiring someone because of certain business needs. Show interest in those needs. Asking questions to get a better idea of the employer's needs will help you "stand out" from other candidates interviewing for the job.

8. Do "take charge" when the interviewer "falls down" on the job.

Go into every interview knowing the three or four points about yourself you want the interviewer to remember. And be prepared to take an active part in leading the discussion if the interviewer's "canned approach" does not permit you to display your "strong suit." You can't always depend on the interviewer's asking you the "right" questions so you can stress your strengths and accomplishments.

Employers are seeking people with good attitudes whom they can train and coach to do things their way.

An important "don't": Don't ask questions about salary or benefits at the first interview. Employers don't take warmly to people who look at their organization as just a place to satisfy salary and benefit needs. Don't risk making a negative impression by appearing greedy or self-serving. The place to discuss salary and benefits is normally at the second interview, and the employer will bring it up. Then you can ask questions without appearing excessively interested in what the organization can do for you.

Now..negotiating your salary

Even if an ad requests that you communicate your "salary requirement" or "salary history," you should avoid providing those numbers in your initial cover letter. You can usually say something like this: "I would be delighted to discuss the private details of my salary history with you in person."

Once you're at the interview, you must avoid even appearing *interested* in salary before you are offered the job. Make sure you've "sold" yourself before talking salary. First show you're the "best fit" for the employer and then you'll be in a stronger position from which to negotiate salary. **Never** bring up the subject of salary yourself. Employers say there's no way you can avoid looking greedy if you bring up the issue of salary and benefits before the company has identified you as its "best fit."

Don't appear excessively interested in salary and benefits at the interview.

Interviewers sometimes throw out a salary figure at the first interview to see if you'll accept it. You may not want to commit yourself if you think you will be able to negotiate a better deal later on. Get back to finding out more about the job. This lets the interviewer know you're interested primarily in the job and not the salary.

When the organization brings up salary, it may say something like this: "Well, Mary, we think you'd make a good candidate for this job. What kind of salary are we talking about?" You may not want to name a number here, either. Give the ball back to the interviewer. Act as though you hadn't given the subject of salary much thought and respond something like this: "Ah, Mr. Jones, I wonder if you'd be kind enough to tell me what salary you had in mind when you advertised the job?" Or ... "What is the range you have in mind?"

Don't worry, if the interviewer names a figure that you think is too low, you can say so without turning down the job or locking yourself into a rigid position. The point here is to negotiate for yourself as well as you can. You might reply to a number named by the interviewer that you think is low by saying something like this: "Well, Mr. Lee, the job interests me very much, and I think I'd certainly enjoy working with you. But, frankly, I was thinking of something a little higher than that." That leaves the ball in your interviewer's court again, and you haven't turned down the job either, in case it turns out that the interviewer can't increase the offer and you still want the job.

Salary negotiation can be tricky.

Last, send a follow-up letter.

Mail, e-mail, or fax a letter right after the interview telling your interviewer you enjoyed the meeting and are certain (if you are) that you are the "best fit" for the job. The people interviewing you will probably have an attitude described as either "professionally loyal" to their companies, or "maternal and proprietary" if the interviewer also owns the company. In either case, they are looking for people who want to work for *that* company in particular. The follow-up letter you send might be just the deciding factor in your favor if the employer is trying to choose between you and someone else. You will see an example of a follow-up letter on page 16.

A follow-up letter can help the employer choose between you and another qualified candidate.

A cover letter is an essential part of a job hunt or career change.

Many people are aware of the importance of having a great resume, but most people in a job hunt don't realize just how important a cover letter can be. The purpose of the cover letter, sometimes called a **"letter of interest,"** is to introduce your resume to prospective employers. The cover letter is often the critical ingredient in a job hunt because the cover letter allows you to say a lot of things that just don't "fit" on the resume. For example, you can emphasize your commitment to a new field and stress your related talents. The cover letter also gives you a chance to stress outstanding character and personal values. On the next two pages you will see examples of very effective cover letters.

A cover letter is an essential part of a career change.

Please do not attempt to implement a career change without a cover letter such as the ones you see in Part Two of this book.

Special help for those in career change

We want to emphasize again that, especially in a career change, the cover letter is very important and can help you "build a bridge" to a new career. A creative and appealing cover letter can begin the process of encouraging the potential employer to imagine you in an industry other than the one in which you have worked.

As a special help to those in career change, there are resumes and cover letters included in this book which show valuable techniques and tips you should use when changing fields or industries. The resumes and cover letters of career changers are identified in the table of contents as "Career Change" and you will see the "Career Change" label on cover letters in Part Two where the individuals are changing careers.

Date

**Addressing the Cover
Letter:** Get the exact
name of the person to
whom you are writing. This
makes your approach
personal.

Exact Name of Person
Title or Position
Name of Company
Address (number and street)
Address (city, state, and zip)

Dear Exact Name of Person (or Sir or Madam if answering a blind ad):

I would appreciate an opportunity to talk with you soon about how I could contribute to your organization through my extensive experience in aviation operations worldwide. I offer a reputation as a highly skilled troubleshooter and mechanic with excellent supervisory abilities.

Second Paragraph: You
have a chance to talk
about whatever you feel is
your most distinguishing
feature.

With approximately four years of experience with the UH-60 Blackhawk utility helicopter and another 3-1/2 years with the AH-1 Cobra, I am recognized as a dedicated professional. Now in the process of completing my FAA Airframe and Power Plant License, I am licensed to operate heavy machinery used to remove aircraft blades and engines. I have logged 600 flight hours as a Crew Chief in multi-engine, rotary-wing aircraft and 100 hours as an Instructor.

Third Paragraph: You
bring up your next most
distinguishing qualities and
try to
sell yourself.

I have been honored with numerous medals and awards in recognition of my accomplishments and abilities. In my current assignment as a UH-60 Dedicated Crew Chief, I was singled out by the organization's commander as his Crew Chief and chosen for special UN peacekeeping missions.

Fourth Paragraph: Here
you have another
opportunity to reveal
qualities or achievements
which will impress your
future employer.

Through my extensive experience, I would be a valuable asset to any government contractor who can use a knowledgeable troubleshooter and aircraft mechanic who has lived and worked in international settings and is familiar with the unique needs of the military aviation community.

Final Paragraph: She
asks the employer to
contact her. Make sure
your reader knows what
the "next step" is.

I hope you will welcome my call soon to arrange a brief meeting to discuss your current and future needs and how I might serve them. Thank you in advance for your time.

Sincerely,

Janet A. Rjewuna

**Alternate Final
Paragraph:** It's more
aggressive (but not too
aggressive) to let the
employer know that you
will be calling him or her.
Don't be afraid to be
persistent. Employers are
looking for people who
know what they want to
do.

Alternate last paragraph:
I hope you will call or write me soon to suggest a time convenient for us to meet and discuss your current and future needs and how I might serve them. Thank you in advance for your time.

Date

Exact Name of Person
Title or Position
Name of Company
Address (no., street)
Address (city, state, zip)

Dear Exact Name of Person (or Dear Sir or Madam if answering a blind ad):

I would appreciate an opportunity to talk with you soon about how I could contribute to your organization through my versatile management skills and technical knowledge.

Management and leadership ability
My management and leadership skills were tested in numerous "hotseat" positions which I held while serving my country in the U.S. Army. After excelling in the rigorous Air Traffic Control School which has a failure rate of nearly 50%, I was selected for jobs which involved supervising people working on shifts at air traffic control facilities in the U.S. and overseas. While managing a multinational work force in Korea, I became known for my skill as a supervisor in working with employees from different racial, ethnic, cultural, and economic backgrounds. "Attention to detail" is second nature to me, since I have been accustomed to working in environments in which there was "no room for error" because a careless mistake could cost human lives and multimillion-dollar assets. As a management philosophy, I believe in "leadership by example" and I am proud that I have helped many young soldiers turn their lives around and become hard-working go-getters.

Transportation industry knowledge
As you will see from my resume, I have become knowledgeable about how people and parcels get moved by aircraft in the safest and fastest way. In a "track record" of progression from radar controller to air traffic control supervisor, I was responsible for "life or death" decisions related to the air transportation of people and products.

Telecommunications industry skills and knowledge
I offer extensive knowledge of telecommunications and computer equipment. I have become skilled in maintaining various types of communications equipment including interphone systems. I am knowledgeable of COMSEC equipment.

I would appreciate an opportunity to discuss your current and future needs and how I might serve them. Thank you in advance for your time.

Sincerely yours,

Victor Plant

CC: Michael Reardon

Date
Three blank spaces

Address

Salutation
One blank space

Body

cc: Indicates you are sending a copy of the letter to someone

Date

Exact Name of Person
Title or Position
Name of Company
Address (number and street)
Address (city, state, and zip)

Dear Exact Name:

I am writing to express my appreciation for the time you spent with me on 9 December, and I want to let you know that I am sincerely interested in the position of Airport Manager which you described.

I feel confident that I could skillfully interact with your 60-person work force in order to assure expert management of your private airport. I want you to know, too, that I would not consider relocating to Salt Lake City to be a hardship! It is certainly one of the most beautiful areas I have ever seen.

As you described to me what you are looking for in a manager, I had a sense of "déjà vu" because my current boss was in a similar position when I went to work for him. He needed someone to come in and be his "right arm" and take on an increasing amount of his management responsibilities so that he could be freed up to do other things. I have played a key role in the growth and profitability of his aviation transport business, and he has come to depend on my sound financial and business advice as much as my day-to-day management skills. Since Christmas is the busiest time of the year in his private contracting business, I feel that I could not leave him during that time. I could certainly make myself available by mid-January.

It would be a pleasure to work for a successful individual such as yourself, and I feel I could contribute significantly to your business not only through my management and business background but also through my strong qualities of loyalty, reliability, and trustworthiness. I look forward to hearing from you at your convenience.

Yours sincerely,

Jacob Evangelisto

In this section, you will find resumes and cover letters of aviation and travel industry professionals—and of people who want to work in those fields. How do they differ from other job hunters? Why should there be a book dedicated to people seeking jobs in these areas? Based on more than 20 years of experience in working with job hunters, this editor is convinced that resumes and cover letters which "speak the lingo" of the field you wish to enter will communicate more effectively than language which is not industry specific. This book is designed to help people (1) who are seeking to prepare their own resumes and (2) who wish to use as models "real" resumes of individuals who have successfully launched careers in the police, law enforcement, or security field or who have advanced in the field. You will see a wide range of experience levels reflected in the resumes in this book. Some of the resumes and cover letters were used by individuals seeking to enter the field; others were used successfully by senior professionals to advance in the field.

Newcomers to an industry sometimes have advantages over more experienced professionals. In a job hunt, junior professionals can have an advantage over their more experienced counterparts. Prospective employers often view the less experienced workers as "more trainable" and "more coachable" than their seniors. This means that the mature professional who has already excelled in a first career can, with credibility, "change careers" and transfer skills to other industries.

Newcomers to the field may have disadvantages compared to their seniors. Almost by definition, the inexperienced professional—the young person who has recently earned a college degree, or the individual who has recently received certifications respected by the industry—is less tested and less experienced than senior managers, so the resume and cover letter of the inexperienced professional may often have to "sell" his or her potential to do something he or she has never done before. Lack of experience in the field she wants to enter can be a stumbling block to the junior manager, but remember that many employers believe that someone who has excelled in anything—academics, for example—can excel in many other fields.

Some advice to inexperienced professionals...
If senior professionals could give junior professionals a piece of advice about careers, here's what they would say: Manage your career and don't stumble from job to job in an incoherent pattern. Try to find work that interests you, and then identify prosperous industries which need work performed of the type you want to do. Learn early in your working life that a great resume and cover letter can blow doors open for you and help you maximize your salary.

Special help for career changers...
For those changing careers, you will find useful the resumes and cover letters marked "Career Change" on the following pages. You can also consult the Table of Contents for page numbers of resumes and cover letters showing career changers.

Aviation and travel industry professionals might be said to "talk funny." They talk in lingo specific to their field, and you will find helpful examples throughout this book.

Delta Airlines
ATTN: Mike Smith
P.O. Box 777
Rogers, AR 72756

AVIATOR   Dear Mr. Smith:

I am responding to your advertisement for a Customer Service Representative. I would appreciate an opportunity to talk with you soon about how I could contribute to your organization through my experience in managing human, financial, and physical assets.

With a B.S. degree in mathematics and strong computer operation skills, I have excelled in "hotseat" jobs while serving my country as an Air Force officer. I was continuously handpicked for jobs which required exceptional strategic planning, troubleshooting, problem-solving, and decision-making abilities. In one job I built "from scratch" a new command-and-control facility which improved the efficient functioning of a 2,000-person aviation community. In several jobs I used my computer knowledge to develop spreadsheet and database applications that reduced errors, improved equipment maintenance, and reduced variable operating costs.

Because most of my jobs required me to make critical decisions daily while coordinating multimillion-dollar resources, I have acquired valuable skills and instincts related to strategic planning and operations management. I have come to believe strongly that attitude rather than ability is the main predictor of employee performance.

I am in the process of relocating to northwest Arkansas near my extended family, and I am interested in discussing with you the possibility of putting my proven management and customer service skills to work for your company.

I hope you will write or call me soon to suggest a time when we might meet to discuss your current and future needs and how I might serve them. I can provide outstanding personal and professional references including my present and previous two immediate supervisors.

You would, I am certain, find me to be an exceptionally talented problem solver and opportunity finder who offers a proven "track record" of improving efficiency and reducing costs in every job I have held.

Yours sincerely,

Arnold C. Lanely

ARNOLD C. LANELY

1110½ Hay Street, Fayetteville, NC 28305   •   preppub@aol.com   •   (910) 483-6611

OBJECTIVE

To benefit an organization that can use a creative problem solver with strong math and computer operations skills along with a talent for training and scheduling human resources in a way that maximizes quality and efficiency.

EDUCATION

B.S. degree in Mathematics, McPherson College, McPherson, KS.

COMPUTERS

Proficient with software including Word, PowerPoint, and other software.

EXPERIENCE

AVIATOR. Piedmont Air, Richmond, VA (2000-present). While flying a corporate jet throughout the U.S. and Caribbean, have used my knowledge of Lotus 1-2-3 to write computer programs that compute weight and balance data and calculate distance, time, and fuel requirements.
- Increased operational efficiency through the computer templates I created.

AVIATOR. U.S. Air Force, Ft. Bragg, NC (1998-00). At the world's largest U.S. military base, excelled in scheduling and coordinating multimillion-dollar assets and human resources; continuously found innovative ways to overcome personnel problems and equipment shortages.
- Developed a database application to track maintenance history and pinpoint recurring deviations.
- Dramatically decreased scheduling errors through a scheduler checklist I developed which is still in use today.

OPERATIONS OFFICER. U.S.A.F., Nellis AFB, NV (1995-98). Was rapidly promoted to positions of increasing responsibility in managing/ scheduling pilots and aircraft; was regarded by the chief executive officer as "the man who can fix it" when any kind of operational problem arose.

GENERAL MANAGER. U.S.A.F., Pope AFB, NC (1992-95). Was handpicked for this essentially entrepreneurial job which involved building "from scratch" and then managing a new command-and-control facility that was the critical "nerve center" used to facilitate the smooth functioning of a 2,000-person aviation community.
- Helped design the facility, selected communications equipment, and wrote "quick reaction" checklists and operating policies.
- With the help of a programmer, authored a computer program that improved efficiency of the chief executive and his staff during crisis situations.

CONTROLLER/SERVICE OPERATIONS MANAGER. U.S.A.F., Pope AFB, NC (1990-92). Excelled in a "no-room-for-error" job at one of the nation's busiest airlift hubs; coordinated resources for launching aircraft and responding to aircraft mishaps while managing this busy command center with 40 telephone lines and numerous radios.

SCHEDULER/PILOT. U.S.A.F., Pope AFB, NC and Japan (1985-90). Refined my planning and organizational skills in a job scheduling the training and work assignments of 40 pilots.
- Became comfortable operating in a hectic environment in which deadlines, priorities, goals, and problems changed hour by hour.

PERSONAL

Excellent personal and professional references on request.

Date

Exact Name of Person
Title or Position
Name of Company
Address (no., street)
Address (city, state, zip)

AIR MARSHAL
This versatile individual wants to offer his aviation experience and law enforcement background to the federal government in the role of Air Marshal.

Dear Exact Name of Person (or Dear Sir or Madam if answering a blind ad):

I would appreciate an opportunity to talk with you soon about how I could contribute to your organization through my practical experience in both aviation and law enforcement. I am particularly interested in the position as Air Marshal.

As you will see from my resume, I offer a record of exceptional performance during 9 1/2 years with the New York Police Department. During my years of service as a Police Officer in this city of approximately 750,000 people, I earned the respect of my superiors, peers, and members of the community for my dedication to excellence in every aspect of my responsibilities. I was often singled out for difficult and sensitive assignments in recognition of my exceptional communication skills and ability to deal with any situation through my fair but firm manner. During one eight-month period, I worked as an Undercover Narcotics Enforcement Officer, and I participated in activities which resulted in closing 25 inner-city drug houses.

I have demonstrated that I work well under pressure, can follow directions from superiors and official guidelines, and also use my own common sense and intelligence to take charge and make decisions. Additionally I offer excellent public relations abilities and understand the importance of maintaining a strong community presence.

I left the law enforcement field to try to reach another of my career goals and completed rigorous training to become a U.S. Army warrant officer aviator. Literally tens of thousands of applications are received each year and only 750 of the most highly qualified applicants are chosen for this training program. I am very proud to have completed this training and earned a position as a helicopter pilot and military officer.

I feel that through my success in these demanding roles, I have proven my adaptability and versatility. Both professions require a person to think on his feet and handle crisis situations on a daily basis. I feel that I offer a unique mix of abilities which could make me a valuable addition to an organization such as yours.

I hope you will welcome my call soon to arrange a brief meeting at your convenience to discuss your current and future needs and how I might serve them. Thank you in advance for your time.

Sincerely yours,

Thomas E. Onslow

THOMAS E. ONSLOW

1110½ Hay Street, Fayetteville, NC 28305 • preppub@aol.com • (910) 483-6611

OBJECTIVE To offer my exceptional communication and motivational skills to an organization that can use a mature professional who has excelled in the demanding fields of law enforcement and aviation through demonstrated intellectual skills and an aggressive, enthusiastic personality.

EXPERIENCE **AVIATOR/TRAINING PILOT** and **OPERATIONS MANAGER**. Department of Defense, Washington, DC (2000-present). Am excelling as a professional aviator operating a million-dollar aircraft: plan, coordinate, and carry out assigned missions as the senior member of an air crew operating under an 18-hour notice as part of the rapid deployment forces.
- Chosen to train and supervise a 16-person Nuclear/Biological/Chemical (NBC) defense team; provided specialized proficiency training to a 45-person company, earning commendable — the highest possible — ratings in two consecutive inspections.
- Oversee the physical security for $20 million worth of equipment.

Served with distinction as a Police Officer known for my common sense approach and high moral values. Was effective in relating to people from diverse ethnic and cultural backgrounds by taking charge when the situation demanded, New York, NY:
POLICE OFFICER. (1995-00). Often singled out for highly sensitive and particularly demanding jobs, handled a range of activities including accident and crime investigations, enforcement of state and local laws, domestic dispute response and intervention, and "first responder" for first aid and emergency situations.
- Applied my public speaking skills while representing the department when giving testimony in criminal and traffic court.
- Received special recognition for saving the life of a man whose clothing caught fire in his yard — smothered the flames and treated him for shock until the ambulance arrived.
- Contributed to the police department's public image while coaching neighborhood youth in Police Athletic League competition.

UNDERCOVER NARCOTICS ENFORCEMENT OFFICER. (1990-95). Handpicked for this sensitive assignment, spent approximately eight months on teams which executed search warrants resulting in the shut down of more than 25 inner-city drug houses.
- Received training in specialized techniques which included "sting" operations, the use of personal listening devices (wires), undercover narcotics purchases, and surveillance.
- Developed cases through informants and received additional training in chemical testing from the state's crime lab.

EDUCATION & TRAINING B.S., Criminal Justice, Mount Senario College, Ladysmith, WI, 1989.
- Graduated *magna cum laude* with a 3.89 GPA: refined my time-management skills attending college full time while holding a demanding job as a police officer.

LICENSES & SPECIAL SKILLS FAA Commercial Pilot license, rotorcraft helicopter/ instrument helicopter.
"Law Enforcement Officer" certification, Wisconsin Law Enforcement Standards Board, 1995.
Am an experienced field training officer and undercover narcotics agent familiar with surveillance, search warrants, sting operations, and undercover purchases from suspects.
Qualified as an Expert with the M-16 rifle and 9mm pistol.

PERSONAL Offer approximately 900 accident-free flight hours in the UH-1H Iroquois (Bell Huey) and in the Cessna 150 with 300 hours as pilot-in-command. Have a Secret security clearance. Honed public speaking skills on award-winning high school debate and forensics teams.

Captain Ed Smith
Chief Pilot
Delta Airlines
123 Midway Lane
Atlanta, GA 77777

COMMERCIAL PILOT

Dear Captain Smith:

With the enclosed resume, I would like to make you aware of my interest in becoming associated with Delta Airlines as a pilot.

Currently I am flying for Delta Airlines, out of Atlanta. As a native Georgian, I am interested in offering my abilities to a carrier with a strong presence in that state.

I am interested particularly in Delta because I have observed its expanding presence in the aviation industry and am aware of its reputation for excellence. I would like to be a part of the company and feel I could become a quality member of a quality organization.

I hope I will have the opportunity to meet with you in person to discuss my interest in Delta, and I hope you will contact me if my experience and skills are of interest to you.

Sincerely,

Anthony Mark Cummings

ANTHONY MARK CUMMINGS

1110½ Hay Street, Fayetteville, NC 28305   •   preppub@aol.com   •   (910) 483-6611

OBJECTIVE: Career Pilot Employment

FLIGHT RATINGS: Commercial Pilot: Airplane SEL/MEL; Instrument
Medical Certificate: FAA Class I
ATP Written, FEX Written

FLIGHT TIMES: TOTAL 4018

Pilot-In-Command.....................1781	Jet..317	Actual Instruments................. 230
Second-In-Command...............2170	Multiengine............................2221	Simulated Instruments..............81
Instructor...................................10	Single Engine.........................1787	CrossCountry......................... 3179
Turboprop....................................18	Simulator.................................106	Night.....................................609

FLIGHT EXPERIENCE:

COMMUTER PILOT

2000- Present	Piedmont Airlines Raleigh, NC	First Officer: CL-65/E-120 Part 121 Scheduled air carrier operating throughout the eastern U.S. and parts of the midwest.

CORPORATE PILOT

1998 - 2000	U.S. Airlines New York, NY	Reserve Copilot: CE-500 Part 91 corporate flight operations throughout eastern U.S.
OCT 98 - Sept 99	Crank Aviation Service Atlanta, GA	Reserve Copilot: AC69-840 and CE-550 corporate flight operations throughout continental U.S.

FLIGHT INSTRUCTOR

SEP 96 - Sept 99	Merced Aviation Merced, CA	Single-engine flight instruction under Part 61 at the Merced Airport
JUL 97 - AUG 97	FDA Aviation Atlanta, GA	Photography pilot for the Agricultural Stabilization Conservation Service
JUN 96 - SEP 96	Bright Tours, Inc Southport, GA	Flight Instructor; Air Tour Pilot; Southport Airport
APR 96 - JUN 96	Carleton Air Service Atlanta, GA	Flight Instructor at the Gloria Airport

WORK EXPERIENCE:

BANK LOAN OFFICER

SEP 91 - JAN 95	Georgia Savings Bank Mercer, GA	Loan Officer and Branch Security Officer.

Prior to SEP 91	Continuous employment with wholesale beer distributor as a merchandiser, driver/salesman, night check-in attendant, and warehouse attendant while completing my college education.

EDUCATION: **B.A. DEGREE in Business Administration**, Mercer College, Mercer, GA, 1991

Exact Name of Person
Exact Title
Name of Company
Exact Address
City, state zip

COMMERCIAL PILOT

Dear Exact Name:

With the enclosed resume, I would like to make you aware of my interest in becoming associated with your airline as a Commercial Pilot.

Currently employed as a Pilot for a North Carolina company, I am an FAA licensed Airline Transport Pilot with more than 5,200 flight hours. In my previous position, I worked as Chief Pilot for a California airline which provided charter services for executives in the banking, entertainment, insurance, and other industries. On several occasions, I have handled simultaneous "office" and administrative duties while also working as a pilot for chartered flights. In my first "real" job after earning my college degree in Aviation Administration, I worked for two years in an administrative role for the Federal Aviation Administration.

You would find me in person to be a congenial individual who excels in establishing warm and effective working relationships. I am a nonsmoker and nondrinker, and I can pass the most rigorous background investigation.

Please contact me if you can use my considerable aviation skills and experience. I can provide outstanding references at the appropriate time.

Sincerely,

Gilbert W. Smith

GILBERT W. SMITH

1110½ Hay Street, Fayetteville, NC 28305   •   preppub@aol.com   •   (910) 483-6611

OBJECTIVE

To apply my outstanding managerial abilities to an organization in need of a mature professional accustomed to working under deadlines and pressure, dealing with executive clients through communication and interpersonal abilities, and scheduling and planning operations.

LICENSE

Skilled in avionics and the proper use of telecommunications equipment, am an FAA-licensed Airline Transport Pilot with more than 5,200 flight hours.

EDUCATION

B.S., Aviation Administration, Fairfield University, Fairfield, CT, 1985.

EXPERIENCE

FLIGHT COORDINATOR/SCHEDULER and **PILOT**. Air Transport, Inc., Greensboro, NC (2000-present). Arrange the details of ground transportation and accommodations for numerous corporate executives who were air charter clients; transported important aircraft parts.
- Excel in maintaining professional relations with high-level executives while ensuring their flights and other arrangements were complete and comfortable.
- Apply my attention to the details of flight scheduling and planning.

OPERATIONS MANAGER and **CHIEF PILOT**. Howard Aviation, Santa Cruz, CA (1998-99). Gained a broad background in sales, inventory control, and financial operations while controlling the charter operations for seven executive aircraft.
- Represented the company to decision-makers in the entertainment, insurance, legal, and banking industries.
- "Sold" services through my knowledge and communication skills and the company's location which, in many cases, reduced flight time for entertainment business clients.

PILOT. Charter Associates, Rockford, IL (1990-97). Ensured the airworthiness of aircraft used to fly scheduled commuter and charter trips.
- Controlled the transfer of critical materials from branch banks to headquarters.

EXECUTIVE PLACEMENT RECRUITER and **PILOT**. The Waters Group and Tops Personnel, Charlotte, NC (1988-90). Combined communication and "sales" skills successfully recruiting, interviewing, and placing job candidates in executive positions in printing, electronics, and industry.
- Placed personnel in entry- to executive-level positions through knowledge and awareness of company needs and a "knack" for finding the right person for the job.
- Refined my time management abilities while, simultaneously with my recruiting activities, maintaining aircraft and acting as senior pilot for corporate flights.

ADMINISTRATIVE ASSISTANT. Federal Aviation Administration, Washington, DC (1985-88). After graduating from college, worked for the FAA in an administrative position which allowed me to become acquainted with the internal workings of the nation's main aviation regulatory organization

SPECIAL SKILLS

Offer extensive experience in office operations including bookkeeping, preparing financial sheets, and payroll; have limited knowledge of using computers for recordkeeping.

PERSONAL

Offer strengths including scheduling and planning skills. Easily develop good working relationships with all types of people. Am accustomed to working long, irregular hours.

Exact Name of Person
Title or Position
Name of Company
Address (no., street)
Address (city, state, zip)

HELICOPTER INSTRUCTOR PILOT

Dear Exact Name of Person (or Dear Sir or Madam if answering a blind ad):

Can you use an experienced professional aviator who offers more than 1,700 hours of flight time, a license as an aviation mechanic, and outstanding leadership and management abilities?

Prior to my current position as an Instructor Pilot with a civilian organization, I became one of the U.S. Army's youngest OH-58 helicopter instructor pilots. I built a "track record" of accomplishments while achieving the instructor pilot rating within four years of my graduation from flight school.

I have flown more than 1,700 accident-free hours with one actual in-flight engine failure and numerous other emergencies and have had no injuries to crew members or damage to equipment. My additional experience includes extensive amounts of time spent in developing and conducting training programs which led to commendable ratings and in important upgrades of the flight status of less experienced pilots.

With the proven ability to handle pressure, rapidly changing priorities, and emergencies I offer the flying skills and experience that would make me a productive member of your organization.

I hope you will welcome my call soon to arrange a brief meeting at your convenience to discuss your current and future needs and how I might serve them. Thank you in advance for your time.

Sincerely yours,

Aaron N. Heisman

Alternate last paragraph:
I hope you will call or write soon to suggest a time convenient for us to meet and discuss your current and future needs and how I might serve them. Thank you in advance for your time.

AARON N. HEISMAN

1110½ Hay Street, Fayetteville, NC 28305   •   preppub@aol.com   •   (910) 483-6611

OBJECTIVE

To benefit an organization in need of a professional aviator who offers a combination of mechanical, flight, and instructional skills along with outstanding motivational, communication, and management abilities.

LICENSES

FAA Commercial Pilot license, instrument, including rotorcraft and rotorcraft helicopter. **FAA Airframe and Power Plant mechanic license.**

AIRCRAFT EXPERTISE

Am experienced in flying aircraft including the Bell 206 (OH-58A, C, and A720) as well as the Bell 205 (UH-1H).

- Offer 1,700 total flight hours broken down as follows:

pilot-in-command: 1,300	second-in-command: 400	
night vision goggle: 300+	rotary-wing: 1,700	turbine: 1,650
single-engine: 1,700	simulator: 100	instructor: 370

EXPERIENCE

INSTRUCTOR PILOT. Merced Charter Air, Conway, AR (2002-present). Managed the training of 15 aviators by providing a continuing course of classroom and hands-on training including ensuring their technical and tactical knowledge met official government standards through constant evaluations and upgrades of procedures.

- Implemented updates to training which gave executives more leeway in maximizing personnel assets by standardizing performance guidelines.
- Guided personnel from training status to "fully mission capable" pilots in four months.

HELICOPTER INSTRUCTOR PILOT. U.S. Army, Korea (1999-02). Officially evaluated as a "dynamic, energetic team player . . . whose professionalism places him well above his peers," trained and managed a minimum of eight aeroscout and attack helicopter pilots while orienting them on situations unique to the demilitarized zone.

- Completed 536 hours of mountain flying and was selected to instruct special procedures including full touchdown emergency landings.
- Received commendable ratings on the quality of air crew training accomplished during a major inspection of aviation resources management.
- Established an effective training cycle which allowed three pilots with low readiness levels to attain pilot-in-command status in two months.

AEROSCOUT HELICOPTER PILOT. U.S. Army, Ft. Ord, CA (1996-99). Earned a reputation as an adaptable professional who can "think on his feet" while handling flight time and air crew management responsibilities.

- Controlled maintenance and security for a $1 million inventory of night vision goggles.
- Expanded my knowledge of crime prevention and security procedures after being selected to control these areas; established procedural changes resulting in a 100% rating.
- Displayed my expertise in an emergency landing following an engine failure: landed an OH-58 helicopter over power lines and on a slope.

EDUCATION & TRAINING

A.A., **Aviation Maintenance**, Riverside Community College, Riverside, CA, 1995.
Excelled in training including the 1,500 credit-hour helicopter commercial instrument flight school and the 480-hour instructor pilot course.

PERSONAL

Hold a Secret security clearance. Am very proud of my accomplishments in consistently receiving evaluations as "one of the very best young instructor pilots in the U.S. Army."

Date

Exact Name of Person
Title or Position
Name of Company
Address (no., street)
Address (city, state, zip)

**INSTRUCTOR PILOT
& FLIGHT EXAMINER**

Dear Exact Name of Person (or Dear Sir or Madam if answering a blind ad):

I would appreciate an opportunity to talk with you soon about how I could benefit your organization through my extensive management experience as well as my special knowledge and abilities in operations, training, administration, safety and risk management, and standardization.

In my current position with an air ambulance company, I manage the scheduling of aircraft and air crews who are responding to emergencies worldwide. Since the organization works under contract with numerous government agencies, I have worked with organizations including the Drug Enforcement Administration in providing medical evacuation during drug sweeps. I am an FAA-licensed Commercial Pilot with 7,130 hours of flight time.

In previous experience in the U.S. Army as a chief warrant officer, I advanced in a "track record" of exceptional performance which has been recognized with medals including two Bronze Stars, a Silver Star, and the Distinguished Flying Cross as well as more than 40 achievement and commendation medals.

Widely recognized as a decisive leader who can be counted on to make difficult decisions under pressure, I have controlled multimillion-dollar budgets, planned large-scale international projects, and gained the respect of my peers and superiors for my leadership skills.

I hope you will welcome my call soon to arrange a brief meeting at your convenience to discuss your current and future needs and how I might serve them. Thank you in advance for your time.

Sincerely yours,

Gideon McCarthy

Alternate last paragraph:
I hope you will call or write soon to suggest a time convenient for us to meet and discuss your current and future needs and how I might serve them. Thank you in advance for your time.

GIDEON MCCARTHY

1110½ Hay Street, Fayetteville, NC 28305   •   preppub@aol.com   •   (910) 483-6611

OBJECTIVE

To contribute through my highly-refined problem-solving, communication, and leadership abilities which have been thoroughly tested in a distinguished career as a military officer.

LICENSE

FAA-licensed Commercial Pilot with 7,130 hours of flight time.
Offer strong understanding of FAA, OSHA, and ICAO (international aviation) regulations.

EDUCATION & TRAINING

M.S., Management and Operations, Embry-Riddle Aeronautical University, Daytona Beach, FL; will receive degree June 2003.
B.S. and **A.S** degrees, **Aviation Business Management**, Embry-Riddle, 1989 and 1988.
Excelled in more than 18 months of advanced training for military executives.

EXPERIENCE

INSTRUCTOR PILOT & FLIGHT EXAMINER. Air Ambulance, Inc., Dalton, GA (1998-present). "Juggle" the demands of multiple critical roles by scheduling aircraft/air crews, training and evaluating instructor pilots, ensuring safety standards, and piloting a $9.5 million helicopter in a 24-hour-a-day, seven-day-a-week air ambulance company with 44 aircraft in four states.
- Wrote standard operating procedures (SOP's) on training and standardization which received "commendable" ratings and are currently used at eight companies worldwide.
- Consistently brought flight hours program in under budget while maintaining "the highest standards" in a unit which flew 20,000 hours in seven years with **no** accidents.
- Was handpicked to provide the DEA (Drug Enforcement Administration) with medical support/evacuation during a drug interdiction "sweep" in Santa Fe, NM.
- Coordinated with law enforcement, fire, and medical personnel while providing the only air ambulance coverage in the first 15 days after a hurricane ravaged Miami, FL.

TRAINING STANDARDIZATION MANAGER. Arrow Air, Inc., Savannah, GA (1992-97). Traveled to Savannah to establish this company's operation "from scratch"; managed operations as the company grew from 2 to 16 aircraft in a 90-day period.
- Developed the standard operating procedures used by 10 organizations.
- Trained 12 instructor pilots who in turn refreshed pilot training and accomplished all assigned missions with no losses while supporting the needs of the military engaged in the war in the Middle East.
- Designed a 27-acre heliport which was completed nearly a month ahead of schedule.

FLIGHT EXAMINER and **STANDARDIZATION MANAGER.** On-Time Air Services, Frankfort, KY (1990-91). "Turned around" an aircraft company with the worst safety record in Kentucky.
- Updated operating procedures to bring them in line with government standards.
- Reduced expenses 9%.

After previously excelling as a pilot, instructor pilot, operations manager, and airfield manager, U.S. Army locations worldwide, advanced in leadership roles at Ft. Dix, NJ:
Served as **DIRECTOR OF FLIGHT STANDARDS** (1987-89) and as a **PILOT** (1984-86).

COMPUTERS

Am familiar with IBM computer operations and various software programs.

PERSONAL

Have been awarded the Silver Star, Distinguished Flying Cross, and two Bronze Star medals for heroism/exceptional service in combat in Vietnam and Saudi Arabia. Will relocate.

Exact Name of Person
Title or Position
Name of Company
Address (number and street)
Address (city, state, and zip)

**ROTARY-WING
PILOT**

Dear Exact Name of Person (or Dear Sir or Madam if answering a blind ad):

With the enclosed resume, I would like to make you aware of my interest in utilizing my aviation expertise for the benefit of your organization.

A graduate of the U.S. Military Academy at West Point, I served my country for over 25 years in the U.S. Army while advancing to the rank of Colonel. I hold a Commercial Pilot license—Rotorcraft - Helicopter Instrument and Airplane Multi-engine Land Instrument. In more than 19 years as an aviator, I have over 4,390 flight hours in 26 different aircraft, with 1,500+ as pilot-in-command.

My recent flight experience is as a PA-31 Cheyenne pilot and UH-60 helicopter pilot providing executive transport. This assignment followed two years of tactical aviation piloting both the OH-58D and UH-60 helicopters. I have served as a Special Operations Pilot (MH-60, MH-6, and AH-6 helicopters) and as an Experimental Test Pilot at the U.S. Navy Test Pilot School. I have been trained twice at Flight Safety International in both Piper Cheyenne and Piper Seminole Airplanes. I offer extensive experience in night vision goggle flight, mountain flight, overwater/shipboard operations, and helicopter external load operations.

Throughout my flying career, I have become known for my emphasis on safety, quality control, and strong interpersonal skills. In one assignment, I was specially selected to take over the management of a multinational staff after a fatal friendly fire incident between Air Force and Army aircraft. I provided leadership to a demoralized organization while making changes to assure the safety of flight operations in the war zone of Iraq.

If you can use an experienced pilot with extensive management experience, I would be pleased to make myself available at your convenience so that we could talk about your needs and how I might serve them. I can provide outstanding references at the appropriate time. Thank you in advance for your consideration.

Yours sincerely,

David Figeroa

DAVID FIGEROA

1110½ Hay Street, Fayetteville, NC 28305　　•　　preppub@aol.com　　•　　(910) 483-6611

OBJECTIVE:　　Career Pilot Employment

FLIGHT RATINGS: Commercial Pilot: Rotorcraft - Helicopter Instrument, Airplane Multi-Engine Land Instrument; Medical Certificate: FAA Class I; ATP Written

TOTAL FLIGHT TIME: 4390

Pilot-In-Command	2500	Helicopter	3142	Airplane	246
Instruments	264	Helicopter Turbine	3120	Multiengine	230
Night	930	Multi-engine Helicopter	903	Multi-engine Turbine Airplane	118
Simulator	320	Single-engine Helicopter	2239	Jet	14

AIRCRAFT FLOWN:　　PA-31 Cheyenne, PA-44 Seminole, MH/UH-60 (SK-70), OH-58D (BH-406), AH-1G/S (BH-209), MH/AH-6 (MD-530), CH-47 B,C,D (BV-234), CH-46 (BV-107), OV-1B, Beech Baron, UH-1 (BH-212), TH-55 (Sweitzer 300), T-38, A-37, U-6A, P-3, BK-117, SH-3D, CH-53, C-172, PA-28

FLIGHT EXPERIENCE:

ROTARY- & FIXED-WING PILOT
JUL 01 - PRESENT　　　　Department of Defense　　　Classified locations
Pilot: UH-60 and **PA-31**
Piper Cheyenne. Served as a **rotary-and fixed-wing pilot**

ROTARY-WING PILOT
JUN 99 - JUN 01　　　　U.S. Army　　　　　Europe
Pilot: OH-58D and **UH-60L.** Served as a **rotary-wing pilot** while also supervising 1,300 personnel, a 20,000-hour flight program, a $31 million budget, and overseeing the security, maintenance, and repair of 96 aircraft.

ROTARY-WING PILOT
NOV 93 - JUN 95　　　　U.S. Army　　　　　Asia
Pilot: UH-60 and **OH-58A.** Extensive **NVG** and **mountain flight** experience; supervised 650 personnel and managed the maintenance of 62 aircraft.

ROTARY-WING PILOT　　　　　　　　　　　　　Europe
FEB 91 - OCT 93　　　　U.S. Army
Pilot: UH-60 and **MH-6**; extensive **NVG** and **shipboard flight** experience. Conducted engineering test flights and flew combat missions in the Persian Gulf.

ROTARY- & FIXED-WING PILOT
APR 89 - JUN 90　　　　U.S. Navy Test Pilot School　　Hawaii
Experimental Test Pilot under training: **UH-60, CH-46, OH-58A Helicopters** and **OV-1B Multi-engine Turboprop Airplane**. Additional flight experience in more than 11 other fixed- and rotary-wing aircraft as part of a rigorous engineering test pilot program.

ROTARY-WING PILOT　　　　　　　　　　　　　Korea
SEPT 80 - JUN 89　　　　U.S. Army
Pilot: UH-1, OH- 58A/C, and **AH-1**. Qualified Korean **DMZ pilot**, extensive **mountain flight** experience.

Date

Mr. John J. Smith
Chief Pilot
Sikorsky Aircraft
6900 Main Street
Stratford, CT 06601-1381

TEST PILOT   Dear Mr. Smith:

I am sending my resume as we discussed when we spoke on the phone recently. As I told you then I am very interested in receiving your consideration for a position as a test pilot with Sikorsky. I am confident that I offer the enthusiasm, technical skills, and abilities you are looking for in candidates for this position.

In my current position as a UH-60 Maintenance Test Pilot and Pilot in Command with the Department of Defense, I have logged more than 1,300.5 accident-free flight hours with experience in three aircraft: UH-1H, UH-60A, and UH-60L helicopters. I am pursuing a Master of Aeronautical Science degree program while excelling in a profession which requires frequent travel worldwide in order to provide support for the war against terrorism.

In previous experience with the U.S. Army, I rose to the rank of Warrant Officer while earning widespread respect for my problem-solving and decision-making skills. I am familiar with the process of fielding new equipment into the military's inventory, and I believe I could profitably apply that knowledge to benefit Sikorsky as a test pilot. You will notice from my resume that in 1996 I completed Sikorsky's rigorous training program related to Advanced Fault Isolation.

I hope this resume will answer your questions about my qualifications and background. I hope you will call or write me soon to suggest a time convenient for us to meet and further discuss your current and future needs and how I might serve them. Thank you in advance for your time.

Sincerely,

Forrest J. Rancher

FORREST J. RANCHER

1110½ Hay Street, Fayetteville, NC 28305   •   preppub@aol.com   •   (910) 483-6611

OBJECTIVE   To apply my technical skills as a test pilot as well as my experience in aircraft maintenance management to an organization that can use a talented professional who has excelled through superior analytical, problem-solving, and motivational skills.

FLIGHT   Have logged more than 1,300 accident-free flight hours with experience in aircraft including
EXPERIENCE

   Bell UH-1H   **Sikorsky UH-60A/S70**   **Sikorsky UH-60L/S70**

   Hold qualifications in special areas including the following:

   ESSS/ERFS and MP   mountain and desert operations
   heads-up display   rappelling
   dust and snow operations   ASET II
   aviator air crew coordination training   paradrop
   water bucket   SPIES operations

   As of July 2002. had logged the following totals of flight hours:

   total: 1,300   pilot-in-command: 500   night vision goggles: 182.8

EDUCATION   Currently enrolled in a **Master of Aeronautical Science** program with Embry-Riddle Aeronautical University, have completed two courses with a perfect 4.0 GPA while concentrating in Advanced Aerodynamics and Aircraft and Spacecraft Development.
B.A., Geology, Triton College, River Grove, IL.

TRAINING   Completed extensive training including the following courses and programs:

   UH-60 Maintenance Test Pilot — 1996   Aviation Maintenance Manager — 1995
   Warrant Officer Basic — 1990   IERW — 1991
   Sikorsky Advanced Fault Isolation — 1996
   Aircraft Survivability Equipment Electronic Warfare Officer — 1993

EXPERIENCE   **UH-60 MAINTENANCE TEST PILOT.** Department of Defense, Ft. Stewart, GA (2001-present). Managed, maintained, and scheduled eight UH-60L helicopters in an aviation company which supports the military's no-notice worldwide deployment mission.

*   Ensured all maintenance functions are performed in accordance with applicable technical manuals and regulations as a technical inspector and maintenance test pilot.
*   Performed UH-60 troubleshooting and test flights to ensure all helicopter systems met operational and airworthiness standards with a constant emphasis on safety.
*   Became the battalion's only NVG qualified test pilot; passed my maintenance test pilot check ride in one flight.

   PILOT-IN-COMMAND. Department of Defense, Korea (1998-00). Officially cited for my "incredible knowledge" and "totally exceptional performance" as a UH-60 helicopter Pilot-in-Command in the assault helicopter company 12 miles from the demilitarized zone.

*   Entrusted with maintaining the highest standards of proficiency, flew under diverse conditions including any time of day or night under instrument flight conditions and with night-vision goggles in one of the military's most demanding flying environments.

   UH-1H PILOT. U.S. Army, Ft. Bragg, NC (1990-97). Was described in official performance reports as a "masterful technician" with the ability to remain in control under stress and tense situations in an air assault company which supported the 18th Airborne Corps' 18-hour, no-notice worldwide deployment mission.

PERSONAL   Attended college on a full academic scholarship; played four years of varsity football.

Exact Name of Person
Exact Title
Exact Name of Company
Address
City, State, Zip

TEST PILOT   Dear Exact Name of Person (or Dear Sir or Madam if answering a blind ad):

With this letter and the enclosed resume, I would like to express my interest in exploring employment opportunities with your organization.

As you will see, I am currently serving as a rotary-wing aircraft pilot. With in excess of 1,542 hours of total flight time and more than 880 as pilot in command, I have built a reputation as a meticulous and detail-oriented professional. I have consistently been evaluated as one who sets the standards for others.

I have logged more than 584 hours of night flight, and I offer a proven ability to pilot aircraft safely in the most hazardous circumstances, including combat. As a pilot and as an officer, I am widely recognized for my ability to make the split-second decisions which translate into safe mission accomplishments under the pressure of life-or-death situations.

Having completed extensive training with an emphasis on technical and managerial skills, I am qualified as a UH-60 Maintenance Test Pilot, Aviation Maintenance Manager, and Aircraft Survivability Equipment Trainer. I am a graduate of training programs including Airborne School, Ranger School, SERE training, and the Special Forces Qualification Course. I hold a Top Secret SCI security clearance and a current passport.

If you can use an experienced rotorcraft pilot with well-developed leadership abilities, I hope you will call or write me soon to suggest a time when we might have a brief discussion of how I could contribute to your organization. I can provide excellent professional and personal references at the appropriate time.

Sincerely,

Frank Borbon

FRANK BORBON

1110½ Hay Street, Fayetteville, NC 28305   •   preppub@aol.com   •   (910) 483-6611

OBJECTIVE	To offer technical skills as a flight officer/rotary-wing pilot to an organization that can use a dedicated professional known for unlimited potential, initiative, and integrity.

EDUCATION, TRAINING, & TECHNICAL EXPERTISE	**A.S. degree in Liberal Arts,** Webster University, Webster, MO, 1992
	Completed **extensive technical and management training** which included:
	    UH-60 Maintenance Test Pilot Course, Ft. Rucker, AL.
	    Aviation Maintenance Manager Course, Ft. Rucker, AL.
	Hold **certifications, ratings, and qualifications** which include the following:
	    Commercial Privileges: Rotorcraft–Helicopter and Instrument–Helicopter
	    FAA First Class Medical Certificate:

Flight hours: Total time: 1,542	Instrument: 111
Pilot in Command: 880	Simulator: 124
Rotary-wing multiengine: 1,404	Night: 584
Rotary-wing turbine: 1,542	Rotary-wing single-engine: 137

CLEARANCE	**Top Secret with SCI** security clearance
EXPERIENCE	**UH-60A TEST PILOT.** Sikorsky Helicopters, Inc. Sterling, CT (2000-present). Officially evaluated for "flawless performance … truly exceptional" am Test Pilot for a fleet of 15 UH-60A Black Hawk helicopters. Travel worldwide to provide troubleshooting and problem solving to military organizations involved in the global fight against terrorism.

- On worldwide troubleshooting assignments, direct the effective employment of aircraft under all modes of flight to include instrument meteorological conditions, map of the earth, and night vision goggle.
- On a formal performance evaluation, was commended for my "mission-first state of mind" and described as "a skilled aviator who continues to excel and outperform his peers."
- During a special project at the Joint Readiness Training Center (JRTC,) directed a training project and made a decision to launch a MEDEVAC aircraft that saved the life of a soldier.

Was widely recognized as a top-notch pilot while advancing to the rank of Chief Warrant Officer Two (CW2) in the U.S. Army:
FLIGHT OPERATIONS MANAGER & MH-60L PILOT. Ft. Kobbe, Panama (1995-00). Applied skills with state-of-the-art avionics and navigation systems to provide infiltration/ exfiltration operations in support of various missions vital to national security throughout Central and South America.

- Served as Company Flight Operations Officer and Fully Mission-Qualified Pilot assigned to the only forward deployed company of a Special Operations Aviation Regiment (Airborne). Responsible for precision navigation using state-of-the-art avionics and navigation systems under day, night vision goggle, and Forward Looking Infrared flight profiles.

UH-60L HELICOPTER PILOT. Ft. Rucker, AL (1988-95). Built a reputation as a professional who quickly adjusted to changes, provided meticulous attention to detail, and could be counted on to plan and carry out flight missions no matter how difficult.

- Was evaluated in writing as "a leader among his peers."

Exact Name of Person
Exact Title
Exact Name of Company
Address
City, State, Zip

**SIMULATOR PILOT
INSTRUCTOR**

Dear Exact Name of Person (or Dear Sir or Madam if answering a blind ad):

    With the enclosed resume, I would like to introduce you to my extensive and varied experience related to flight operations and training and to my expert knowledge of both the military and civilian aviation environments.

    As you will see from my resume, I am a retired Air Force brigadier general with in excess of 6,500 flying hours and am licensed by the FAA as an Airline Transport Pilot and Certified Flight Instructor. More recently I have been applying my knowledge as a Flight Simulator Pilot Instructor at the Delta Airlines Flight Academy in Atlanta. In this capacity, I oversee all phases of flight training for MD-80 captains and first officers during their initial and annual recurring training as well as when remedial training is needed. Additionally, I serve as the standardization evaluator for a staff of 22 simulator instructors as well as making recommendations on changes to the program's training plans.

    During a distinguished career with the U.S. Air Force which included tours as a U-2 pilot flying missions over both North and South Vietnam, I went on to earn rapid advancement ahead of my peers as a Pilot, Staff Officer, Wing Commander, and eventually Division Commander. I hold FAA-type ratings in the following aircraft: DC-9, B-707, B-720, and N-265. I have also been qualified in the F-84, RB-47, and U-2 aircraft. During my three years as Executive Director of the Civil Air Patrol, I also flew numerous models of Cessna, Mooney, Piper, Beech, and Rockwell civilian aircraft.

    Throughout my career, I have been handpicked for highly visible roles in organizations where technical knowledge of aircraft operations has been combined with managerial skills, the ability to foresee future needs and plan for them, and a talent for making sound decisions. I have played a very real role in making decisions which resulted in successful modernization of multimillion-dollar aviation assets.

    I have made the decision to relocate to Arizona, and since Delta Airlines does not have any job opportunities in that area for someone with my particular abilities and background, I will be searching for new opportunities in your area. If your organization can benefit from the abilities I offer and from my wide-ranging knowledge of aviation, I hope you will write or call me soon to suggest a time when we might meet to discuss your needs and goals and how my background might serve them.

    Sincerely,

Henry Livingstone

HENRY LIVINGSTONE

1110½ Hay Street, Fayetteville, NC 28305   •   preppub@aol.com   •   (910) 483-6611

OBJECTIVE

To offer a distinguished background and knowledge of flight operations and training to an organization that can benefit from my expertise in civilian and military aviation as well as from instructional, leadership, and managerial skills refined as a senior military officer.

EDUCATION & TRAINING

Graduate School of Management for Senior Executives, Hope College, Holland, MI.
M.S., Counseling and Guidance, Michigan State University, East Lansing, MI.
B.S., Business Administration and Management, University of Michigan, Flint, MI.
Completed programs for military executives including the graduate-level Air War College and Air Command and Staff College.
Excelled in technical programs including Instrument Pilot Instructor School, Information Systems Management, Systems Acquisition, Flight Instructors School, and Pilot Training.

EXPERIENCE

SIMULATOR PILOT INSTRUCTOR. Delta Airlines Flight Academy, Atlanta, GA (2000-present). Provide leadership and instruction for MD-80 aircraft captains and first officers while carrying out all phases of initial training, annual recurring training, and remedial training at the Delta Airlines Flight Academy.

- Apply my expert knowledge after being selected from among 22 qualified professionals as the standardization evaluator for a staff of simulator instructors.
- Ensure all proposals for changes or new training plans are accurate and comply with all applicable FAA and corporate regulations and guidelines.
- Utilize my background as a pilot and instructor pilot while making recommendations on checking and examining flight crewmembers.
- Am relied on to provide reasoned and sound advice when making suggestions on issues which impact on the safety and efficiency of crew members.
- Provide assistance during the development of changes and additions to the flight instruction program as new technology results in upgrades.

Highlight of prior military experience: Served in a distinguished career in the U.S. Air Force and retired with the rank of brigadier general, an accomplishment reserved for only 0.5% of senior officers:

DIVISION COMMANDER, WING COMMANDER, STAFF OFFICER, AND PILOT. (1980-00). Retired from the USAF in 2000 after holding a final assignment as Executive Director of the largest aeromedevac organization in the world, which capped off a career as a command pilot with more than 6,500 flying hours.

- Directly supervised thousands of people and millions of dollars in an organization which enjoyed rapid growth to 300 offices and 65,000 members while controlling a $10.5 million operating budget.
- Was the recipient of numerous prestigious awards and medals including the Distinguished Service Medal, Legion of Merit, Distinguished Flying Cross, Meritorious Service Medal, and Air Medal.
- As Wing Commander at Andersen AFB, Guam, was credited with diplomatic and problem-solving skills which allowed a sensitive international incident to be effectively resolved.
- Became known as an articulate, intelligent communicator and talented manager of resources while maintaining cooperation with representatives of public and private organizations, including the Departments of State, Labor, Defense, and Justice.
- Directed a $98 million typhoon-damage recovery program to include orchestrating efforts to restore utility services and provide food and shelter for thousands of people.

PERSONAL

Relocating to Arizona. Held a Top Secret/SBI clearance. Will travel in my job.

Exact Name of Person
Exact Title
Exact Name of Company
Address
City, State, Zip

AIRFIELD MANAGER

Dear Exact Name of Person (or Dear Sir or Madam if answering a blind ad):

I would appreciate an opportunity to talk with you soon about how I could contribute to your organization through the application of the human, material, and fiscal resource management abilities I am refining while earning rapid advancement as a military officer.

As you will see from my enclosed resume, I am presently the manager of a Texas airfield which serves both a nearby military post and the civilian community of Dallas-Ft. Worth. One of the most critical aspects of this job is public relations—developing and maintaining open lines of communication with a variety of representatives from throughout the community. In this job I am involved in such diverse activities as developing funding plans and controlling a $500,000 annual operating budget as well as supervising a diverse workforce in air traffic control, refueling, weather, and crash/rescue support activities.

In prior positions, I have worked for the Department of Defense as well as for major commercial airplane manufacturers. I am considered a security expert and have devised airport security plans which are considered models.

While building a reputation as a calm and resourceful problem solver with sound judgment, I previously excelled as a fixed and rotary-wing pilot while serving in the U.S. Army, I attracted the attention and respect of my superiors for my managerial skills and was selected for highly visible management positions. Since then, I have built a track record of outstanding results in every position, whether developing and overseeing training programs, managing maintenance operations, and implementing physical security programs.

If you can use an experienced and mature professional with a talent for maximizing resources, I assure you in advance that I could rapidly become an asset to your organization. Please call or write me soon to suggest a convenient time for us to meet and discuss my qualifications and how I could contribute to your organization. Thank you in advance.

Sincerely,

Jillian McKenzie

JILLIAN MCKENZIE

1110½ Hay Street, Fayetteville, NC 28305   •   preppub@aol.com   •   (910) 483-6611

OBJECTIVE   To offer exceptional communication and organizational skills displayed while managing human, material, and fiscal resources along with the ability to rapidly assimilate large amounts of information, remain calm under pressure, and resolve conflicts and problems.

EDUCATION   Am pursuing a Master of Aeronautical Science degree, University of San Diego, San Diego,
& TRAINING   CA; degree expected in August 2003.
B.S. in Aeronautical Studies, University of North Dakota, Grand Forks, 1993.
Completed junior college-level studies in Norwegian, Sagavol Folk School, Gvarv, Norway.

EXPERIENCE   **AIRFIELD MANAGER.** Department of Defense, Dallas-Ft. Worth Airfield, Dallas, TX (2001-present). Manage air traffic control and airfield operations for a joint military and civilian airfield while supervising 35 employees involved in supporting refueling, weather, and crash/rescue support activities.

- Control a $500,000 annual budget; am currently developing an external funding plan for staffing air traffic controllers from all military services, the city, and the National Guard.
- Developed strong and positive public relations with city officials and am on the Airport Commission Board.

TRAINING AND OPERATIONS INSPECTOR. Department of Defense, O'Hare Airport, Chicago, IL (1999-01). Earned respect for my problem-solving and communication skills.

OPERATIONS MANAGER. Lockheed Corporation, Riverside, CA (1996-99). Was credited with bringing about improvements in every area of operations for this aircraft manufacturer while controlling a $5 million inventory of equipment.

- Totally revitalized an inventory control system which had previously lost as much as $200,000 worth of equipment.
- Established "tough and realistic" training programs while emphasizing the importance of individual counseling and guidance in a diverse workforce.

SECURITY TRAINING MANAGER. Lockheed Corporation, Riverside, CA (1993-95). Was recruited for this position because of my "brilliant" performance while planning, coordinating, and monitoring training for a 35-person security staff.

- Was cited for my ability to translate concepts into clear and concise instructions.

SECURITY CHIEF. Boeing Aircraft, Los Angeles, CA (1990-93). After accepting the challenge of this difficult and complex job with no formal training, excelled at providing the leadership and guidance which allowed the organization to exceed standards for its physical security program.

AVIATION MAINTENANCE MANAGER. Sikorsky, Pasadena, CA (1985-90). Directed maintenance, security, and accountability for helicopters and equipment valued in excess of $33 million.

- Earned praise from observers/inspectors and gained recognition as developing and managing "the best ever seen" maintenance program.

PERSONAL   Honored as **Flight School Distinguished Graduate**, have logged over 1,200 flight hours. Entrusted with a **Top Secret** security clearance. Am familiar with Microsoft Office Suite.

Ms. Julienne Smith, Recruiter
Personnel Office
City of San Miguel
San Miguel Avenue
San Miguel, CA 28301

AIRPORT DIRECTOR   Dear Ms. Smith:

I would like to place my name in consideration for the job of Airport Director, and I am enclosing a resume as well as an application for employment with the city.

As you will see from my resume, after graduating from West Point I earned promotion to the rank of lieutenant colonel while specializing in the aviation management field.

In my current job as Deputy Director and Chief of the Test Division, I have been overseeing the testing of aviation assets. I am constantly managing multiple projects while controlling a $5 million budget and supervising 70 people. I am leading a team conducting operational testing to determine if the new Air Force C-17 aircraft fulfills Army requirements, and recommendations of my team will play a key role in military procurement decisions.

In my previous job as Director of Aviation Resource Management, I was the top strategic advisor to the commanding general on all decisions involving resources of an Aviation Center and Aviation Branch while also overseeing the $400 million operating budget of a military community. In a prior job, I functioned as Director of Aviation Support and Airport Services for an airborne aviation organization. Equipment I controlled included 118 helicopters, 307 vehicles, and 700 pieces of ground support equipment.

I have acted as airport director on numerous occasions. In my current job I have acted as airport director during field testing of aircraft and other equipment. In prior jobs I operated airports during Operations Desert Shield/Desert Storm. I designed and built an operational airfield and base camp in the middle of the Saudi Arabian desert. On numerous occasions as special projects have required, I have supervised the construction and management of airport operations. I am accustomed to operating by the "attention to detail" philosophy and am well known for my perfect safety record and aggressive commitment to Total Quality Management.

When the time comes for you to select a group of qualified candidates to interview for this position, I hope you will let me show you in person that I am the resourceful operations manager, skillful comptroller, astute strategic planner, and talented personnel manager you are seeking.

Sincerely yours,

Phil C. Flier

PHIL C. FLIER

1110½ Hay Street, Fayetteville, NC 28305　　•　　preppub@aol.com　　•　　(910) 483-6611

OBJECTIVE　　To serve the City of San Miguel as its Airport Director through my experience in managing airport operations, optimizing the use of aviation resources, planning and administering budgets of all sizes, and building teams of highly skilled and motivated employees dedicated to the highest standards in areas that include safety and customer satisfaction.

EDUCATION　　**B.S., Engineering,** The U.S. Military Academy at West Point, West Point, NY, 1984. Completed programs for military executives including the graduate-level Air War College and Air Command and Staff College.

SAFETY RECORD & CAREER SUMMARY　　Am a 40-year-old lieutenant colonel and West Point graduate with experience in planning and managing programs related to aircraft operations, equipment testing, building and field maintenance, regulatory compliance, and airport construction; have achieved a perfect safety record and am known for innovative approaches to instilling safety attitudes in employees.

EXPERIENCE　　**DEPUTY DIRECTOR** and **CHIEF, TEST DIVISION.** U.S. Army, Campbell, KY (2000-present). Was handpicked for this sought-after job as second-in-command of a 120-person organization which specializes in testing aircraft, airborne, and special operations equipment; as chief tester, currently testing C-17 aircraft to see if they can fulfill Army requirements.

- Manage multiple projects at all times while controlling a $5 million budget, directly supervising 70 people, and determining the use of $20 million in equipment.
- Am currently leading the Army team conducting operational testing to determine if the new Air Force C-17 aircraft fulfills Army requirements; my team's recommendations will significantly impact procurement decisions for these aircraft.
- Acted as **Airport Director** during field testing of aircraft and other equipment.

DIRECTOR OF AVIATION RESOURCE MANAGEMENT. U.S. Army, Ft. Hood, TX (1998-00). Was the top strategic advisor to the commanding general of this military base on all decisions concerning the management of resources of the Aviation Center and the Aviation Branch; as comptroller, was also directly responsible for planning and administering this community's operating budget of $400 million and workforce allocations of 7,000 military and civilian personnel.

- Planned, programmed, and executed all funding required to operate and maintain the five major airfields and 20 stagefields.
- Formulated strategy for the use of human resources through management studies, cost analyses, and productivity improvement initiatives.
- Implemented numerous special projects designed to reduce overhead and variable costs; decreased maintenance/training costs while boosting maintenance and training results.

DIRECTOR OF AVIATION SUPPORT AND AIRPORT SERVICES. U.S. Army, Ft. Sill, OK (1996-97). Directed support services and activities in these functional areas:

logistics supply	ground and aviation	facilities use
transportation	dining services	construction

- Controlled equipment valued at more than $1 billion which included 118 helicopters, 307 vehicles, 700 pieces of ground support equipment, and other assets.
- Prepared cost analyses and estimates for use in planning, programming, and budgeting.
- Managed an innovative rebuild program for ground handling equipment and forklifts.

AVIATION COMPANY COMMANDER. U.S. Army, the Middle East (1988-95). Controlled $40 million in property while providing support to 11 nations including the U.S.

City of New Orleans
Personnel Department
445 Orleans Avenue
New Orleans, LA 88301-5537

AIRPORT OPERATIONS ASSISTANT

Dear Sir or Madam:

I am sending a resume and formal application in order to initiate the process of applying for the position of Airport Operations Assistant for the City of New Orleans.

You will see from my resume that I offer experience in assuming responsibility for airport services and activities. In my current job I wear "two hats," one as a pilot and the other as the manager of communications, security, and construction at Baltimore International Airport.

In a previous job I managed all services and activities at a busy airlift center. I hired and trained personnel, scheduled and budgeted for runway and facilities construction, supervised air traffic control, and managed the supply of petroleum, oil, and lubricants. I am known for my Total Quality Management approach and for my relentless insistence on safety first, last, and always.

In addition to my management and operations experience, I also offer "the eyes and instincts of a pilot," since I am a commercially licensed pilot. In one previous position, I managed a training program for commercial pilots while flying numerous aircraft as captain. I offer expert knowledge of safety and regulatory policies promulgated by the FAA and international regulations.

You would find me to be a top-notch professional who would enjoy helping the City of New Orleans maintain and improve its reputation for airport service, safety, and efficiency. I am certain I have much to offer you, and I will be glad to provide excellent references, including from my current employer. I also speak, read, and write Spanish fluently, which comes in handy in many airport situations.

I hope you will call or write me soon to suggest a time convenient for us to meet and discuss your current and future needs and how I might serve them. Thank you in advance for your time.

Sincerely yours,

Scott M. Zucker

SCOTT M. ZUCKER

1110½ Hay Street, Fayetteville, NC 28305 • preppub@aol.com • (910) 483-6611

OBJECTIVE

To contribute to an organization that can use a resourceful manager who offers extensive operations management and problem-solving skills along with a proven ability to train and motivate workers and transform human resources into highly productive teams.

EDUCATION

Bachelor of Science degree, **cum laude**, Embry Riddle Aeronautical University, 1983.
Associate of Science degree, **with honors**, Embry Riddle Aeronautical University, 1981.
Completed extensive engineering, technical, and management training as a military officer.

COMPUTERS

Knowledgeable of software including Windows, WordPerfect, and Word

EXPERIENCE

SPECIAL PROJECTS OFFICER/PILOT. American Aviation Services, Baltimore International Airport, MD (2000-present). Am handling special projects, including construction projects, intended to improve customer service and work flow while overseeing numerous details of airport security; also routinely act as captain of large, category-type aircraft for passenger transport throughout the U.S.

OPERATIONS AND TRAINING SUPERVISOR. American Aviation Services, Baltimore, MD (1995-99). Coordinated maintenance, scheduling, and training activities in support of multiple airline pilot training programs; directed the training and proficiency evaluations of pilots.
- Became known as a resourceful problem solver and achieved a perfect safety record for the pilot training program.

PROGRAM MANAGER & STRATEGIC PLANNER. United Airlines, Washington, DC (1992-94). While managing a training program for pilots and evaluating their proficiency, tested and integrated into operations advanced new communications equipment including radio and television monitoring devices.

ENGINEERING & TECHNICAL SERVICES CONSULTANT. Midway Airport, Chicago, IL (1985-91). Instructed management on how to organize and manage human resources and physical aviation assets to assure smooth operations and a timely completion of an airfield which provides overflow services for O'Hare Airport.
- Advised on matters ranging from airport construction, to equipment maintenance, to personnel selection and training.

Highlights of U.S. Army experience:
AIRPORT ASSISTANT OPERATIONS OFFICER. Handled a variety of activities and projects related to maintaining efficiency and high morale in an airport in Korea; interviewed and hired Korean nationals for non-sensitive areas, and supervised air traffic control personnel.
- Scheduled and budgeted for runway and facilities construction.

LICENSES

Hold FAA Commercial Pilot license

PERSONAL

Can provide outstanding personal and professional references. Am respected for my ability to motivate others to excel in diverse areas of responsibility. Am known as a hard worker who believes in leadership by example. Am accustomed to working in aviation environments in which there is "no room for error" because one mistake could cost lives and assets.

Exact Name of Person
Exact Title of Person
Exact Name of Organization
Street Address or Box Number
City, State zip

AIRPORT
OPERATIONS
MANAGER

Dear Exact Name (or Dear Sir or Madam if answering a blind ad):

I would appreciate an opportunity to talk with you soon about how I could contribute to your organization through my background related to safety management.

As you will see from my resume, I have developed successful safety and accident prevention programs which have been hailed as "models" and which produced perfect safety records. I have also taken over the management of busy, accident-prone operations in harsh environments and transformed them into top-notch activities.

In one job I established safety programs for a school/training center while managing those safety programs in an experimental and testing environment which included special electronic aircraft. I have played a key role as a member of accident investigation boards, and I have excelled in training and developing other safety professionals.

You would certainly find me to be a congenial professional with very strong abilities related to finance and budgeting as well as personnel supervision. I have held a Top Secret security clearance with SBI, and I am skilled in using Word and PowerPoint software.

I hope you will write or call me soon to suggest a time when we might meet to discuss your current and future needs and how I might meet them. Thank you in advance for your time.

Yours sincerely,

Andrea S. Rooney

Alternate last paragraph:
I hope you will welcome my call soon when I try to arrange a brief meeting with you to discuss your current and future needs and how I might serve them. Thank you in advance for your time.

ANDREA S. ROONEY

1110½ Hay Street, Fayetteville, NC 28305   •   preppub@aol.com   •   (910) 483-6611

OBJECTIVE

To contribute to an organization that can use a versatile manager who offers extensive experience in the occupational safety field along with exceptionally strong skills related to budgeting, personnel supervision, as well as safety management and inspection.

EDUCATION & TECHNICAL TRAINING

Completing **Master of Aeronautical Science (M.A.S.) degree**, Embry Riddle Aeronautical University; degree to be awarded in 2003.

Earned **Bachelor of Science (B.S.) degree in Professional Aeronautics**, Embry Riddle Aeronautical University, Daytona Beach, 1993.

As a Chief Warrant Officer, completed extensive technical training related to accident investigation, safety management, OSHA, as well as occupational and aeronautical safety.

EXPERIENCE

AIRPORT OPERATIONS MANAGER. New Haven Airport, New Haven, CT (2002-present). Developed and implemented a safety and accident prevention program that is hailed as a "model"; supervised a staff of 27 personnel working in an air traffic control (ATC) facility.
- Maintained a perfect safety record of "no accidents/no incidents."

AIRPORT OPERATIONS MANAGER. Raytheon, Inc., Nome, AK (2000-01). In the harsh arctic environment of Alaska, was assigned management of an airfield which had suffered safety mishaps; completely revised operational procedures for the ATC facility and flight dispatch operations; led this busy, accident-prone airfield to achieve a perfect safety record.

SAFETY MANAGER. Boeing Aircraft, Los Angeles, CA (1998-99). Formulated safety policies and procedures for this major aviation organization and participated in two major aircraft accident investigations while excelling as safety manager.
- Was commended on my excellent training and development of other safety personnel.

FIRST-LINE SUPERVISOR. Allen Aircraft, Fairfield, CT (1996-97). In an essentially entrepreneurial role, directed the "start up" of a new aviation organization; routinely briefed visiting executives and VIP's on the organization's strategies and tactics.
- Controlled $36 million in aircraft/assets, motivated people toward a common goal.

SAFETY OFFICER. Flight Training Center & School, San Diego, CA (1992-95). Established safety programs for a school/training center which had 15 special electronic aircraft; learned to manage safety in an experimental and testing environment.
- Conducted safety surveys; coordinated monthly safety meetings and semiannual safety audits/inspections.
- Wrote the school's first aviation accident prevention plan.
- Trained 36 pilots on EH-60 electronics systems.

PERSONNEL ADMINISTRATOR. Boeing Aircraft, Los Angeles, CA (1988-91). Gained skills in personnel administration while directing hiring of personnel to staff the safety department; participated in safety investigations.

Other experience: Earned a reputation as an outstanding writer, manager, problem-solver, and strategic thinker in earlier "building block" jobs.

PERSONAL

Top Secret security clearance with SBI. Skilled in using various computer software. Offer extensive OSHA knowledge and experience. Hold a Commercial FAA Rotary Wing Multi-Engine Instrument pilot license. Emergency Medical Technician (EMT) trained.

Exact Name of Person
Exact Title
Exact Name of Company
Address
City, State, Zip

AIRPORT MANAGER

Dear Exact Name of Person (or Dear Sir or Madam if answering a blind ad):

With the enclosed resume, I would like to introduce you to my extensive experience related to flight operations/training and airport management as well as my expert knowledge of aviation environments.

As you will see from my resume, with in excess of 3,282 flying hours, I am licensed by the FAA as a Commercial Pilot, airplane single- and multi-engine land and instrument. In my current job as Airport Manager at Grand Rapids Airport, I manage the airfield complex, intelligence processing, maintenance analysis, weapons and HAZMAT handling, and air traffic controller training while also overseeing a weather station with 35 personnel.

In previous positions, I excelled as an F-15 Flight Commander and Quality Assurance Evaluator. Safety and quality assurance have always been foremost throughout my flying career, and I developed the first-ever programming training program at Lockheed Corporation which resulted in a drastic reduction of errors. Well known for my ability to handle multiple simultaneous priorities, I once created a tracking system to keep 45 major projects on time and within budget.

In a prior job at the Department of Defense, I was named Deputy Director for Current Operations, and in that capacity I served as a liaison with the military services, Department of State, and Joint Chiefs of Staff in the process of reviewing operations plans and formulating military plans in response to worldwide events. Not only in that job but also in others, I have earned respect for my strong written and oral communication skills as well as for my ability to utilize technology to produce what one boss described as "Hollywood-quality media presentations."

Although I have been strongly encouraged to remain at Grand Rapids Airport and assured of continued advancement, I have decided to explore other opportunities. I can provide outstanding personal and professional references. If my skills and talents interest you, I hope you will contact me to suggest a time when we might meet to discuss your needs. Thank you in advance for your time.

Sincerely,

Pedro Gonzalez

PEDRO GONZALEZ

1110½ Hay Street, Fayetteville, NC 28305　　•　　preppub@aol.com　　•　　(910) 483-6611

OBJECTIVE

To offer expertise related to airport operations management to an organization that can utilize a top-notch pilot and executive who has built a distinguished career as a military officer known for possessing a creative, detail-oriented, and approachable leadership style.

EDUCATION & EXECUTIVE TRAINING

Earned three degrees from Embry-Riddle Aeronautical University, Daytona Beach, FL: **M.S.** in Aeronautical Science; **B.S.** in Aeronautical Science; **A.S.** in Aviation Management. Excelled in more than 2,000 hours of advanced management and flight training programs.

EXPERIENCE

AIRPORT MANAGER. Grand Rapids Airport, Grand Rapids, MI (2000-present). Providing what one senior executive described as "awesome leadership" despite severe personnel shortages, oversee support for a 12,000-flying hour program.
- Manage the airfield complex, intelligence, maintenance analysis, air traffic controller (ATC) training, and a weather station with approximately 35 personnel.
- Coordinate air space issues with the FAA and with other users in this ATC complex; maintain an exceptional safety record.
- Established a team which improved data accuracy and integrity of five million CAMS (Core Automated Maintenance System) aircraft and maintenance records worldwide for an "amazing" 35% increase in accuracy rates and 50% reduction in processing time.

DIRECTOR OF OPERATIONS. Department of Defense, Miami, FL (1998-00). Was recruited to lead a diverse organization with serious problems; significantly revamped this severely substandard 26-aircraft, 35-instructor pilot, and 7,400-flying hour program.
- Safely relocated $900 million in aircraft during two separate hurricane evacuations.

F-15 FLIGHT COMMANDER & QUALITY ASSURANCE EVALUATOR. Lockheed Corp., Riverside, CA (1995-98). Conducted academic and simulator training for 200 pilots while supervising eight civilian managers and 10 mid-level managers.
- Worked with 34 contractors and created a tracking system for 45 major projects.
- Developed the first-ever programming training program which drastically reduced errors.

DEPUTY DIRECTOR FOR CURRENT OPERATIONS & CONSULTANT. Department of Defense, Washington, DC (1992-94). Handpicked to serve as a liaison with the military services, Department of State, and Joint Chiefs of Staff, reviewed operations plans and formulated military plans of action in response to world events which might call for U.S. involvement.
- Provided materials for briefings presented to the U.S. President and Congress and was cited as "brilliant...articulate... the absolute consummate professional."

FLIGHT COMMANDER, FLIGHT EXAMINER, & ASSISTANT OPERATIONS CHIEF. Lockheed Corp., Riverside, CA (1985-91). In this multi-duty position, demonstrated my aviation expertise and ability to manage multiple priorities.
- While conducting long-range planning and supervision of 22 F-15 aircraft, supervised 30 instructor pilots and 60 upgrading pilots yearly, and designed a multimillion-dollar program involving 4,752 sorties and 5,988 hours of flying time.

Highlights of earlier experience: F-15 Pilot, Flight Commander, and Instructor Pilot.

PERSONAL

FAA Commercial Pilot license, airplane single- and multi-engine land and instrument with more than 3,282.7 hours. Top Secret (SBI) security clearance. Excellent references.

AIRPORT MANAGER

Dear Sir or Madam:

I would appreciate an opportunity to talk with you soon about how I could contribute to your organization through my background which includes approximately 12 years in airfield management.

As you will see from my resume, I have gained experience in working with flight plans, FAA and military air traffic control regulations, airway systems, and all other aspects of airfield management. In the aftermath of the terrorist attack on the U.S. on September 11, 2001, I made major changes in airport security which have been adopted by airports all over the world.

During this period I was awarded two achievement medals, a commendation medal, an outstanding unit award, and the Humanitarian Service Medal. My reputation has consistently included praise for my adaptability, willingness to work long hours without complaint, cheerful and pleasant personality, and leadership skills.

My experience encompasses all aspects of flight data and air operations such as processing international, civil, and local flight plans; presenting briefings to air crew members on runway, flight, and weather conditions; and ordering, maintaining, and distributing flight publications.

I feel that through my history of finding ways to streamline and improve operational procedures and my reputation as a dependable and enthusiastic professional, I could make valuable contributions to your organization.

I hope you will call or write me soon to suggest a time convenient for us to meet and discuss your current and future needs and how I might serve them. Thank you in advance for your time.

Sincerely yours,

Arthur C. Glancy

ARTHUR C. GLANCY

1110½ Hay Street, Fayetteville, NC 28305　•　preppub@aol.com　•　(910) 483-6611

OBJECTIVE　To apply my expertise and experience in the area of airfield operations to an organization that can use an adaptable and dependable professional who can handle pressure and emergencies, lead employees to outstanding results.

EXPERIENCE　**AIRPORT MANAGER..** Dulles International Airport, Washington, DC (2001-present). Implemented improvements in operational procedures in the flight control center of a major airport while coordinating air traffic with the FAA (Federal Aviation Administration) using the FAA Service B computer system to plan domestic and international flights.
- Reduced time required for distributing publications by 60% and gained 50% more work space through a renovation project.

SUPERVISORY AIRFIELD MANAGEMENT SPECIALIST. Cape Canaveral, FL (1998-00). Earned a reputation as an exceptional performer with superior technical knowledge in a position which covered responsibilities ranging from inspecting flight facilities, to processing flight data, to reviewing flight data, to providing support for space shuttle launches.
- Expertly processed more than 2,500 international and domestic flight plans in two years.
- Played an important role in coordinating the evacuation of multimillion-dollar NASA, Department of State, and rescue squadron aircraft during Hurricane Andrew.

OPERATIONS SUPERVISOR. Gray's Air School, Los Angeles, CA (1995-97). Handled major operational areas simultaneously: managed a $250,000 inventory of simulators used to provide realistic training for air crews and served as primary contact for emergency responses to aircraft incidents and accidents.

FLIGHT OPERATIONS SUPERVISOR. Los Angeles Airport, CA, (1990-94). Planned and coordinated airfield operations; used my technical knowledge and communication skills to rewrite standard operating procedures for flightline activities and general operations.

AIRFIELD DISPATCHER. Clark Airfield, Columbus, OH (1986-90). Involved in checking and transmitting flight plans, coordinating air traffic information, responding to aircraft declaring emergencies, and dispensing information about weather conditions and training exercises.

EDUCATION & TRAINING
B.S. in Resource Management, Community College of the Air Force, 1989.
Received FAA certification in Airway Science.
Excelled in numerous training programs in airfield management and leadership.

SPECIAL KNOWLEDGE
Offer experience with the following computer hardware, software, and operating systems:

COMED system	Alden systems	FAA "B" circuit computer terminal
Data Products 8500 printer	GTE modem	pilot-to-dispatch radios
Western Union 8100 keyboard display terminal		Model 43 teleprinter
Sun type 4 and 5 keyboards		P3120 Marathon hard disc drive
Racal Milgo 24 LSI modem		
Automated Weather Distribution System (AWDS)		

Coordinated servicing and flight planning for ten space shuttle launches, most types of Army helicopters and a wide range of aircraft.

PERSONAL　Am known for my honesty and strong work ethic. Have frequently been described as a team player who can be counted on. Volunteer often for community improvement projects.

Exact Name of Person
Exact Title of Person
Exact Name of Organization
Address
City, State zip

**AIRPORT
OPERATIONS
MANAGER**

Here you see a resume and cover letter of an individual who seeks to change careers from aviation into a sales or marketing activity. Employers often assume that "the past is the best predictor of the future." In other words, if you have excelled in one field, you probably have a good chance of succeeding in another field if you decide to do so. A cover letter can help to establish your "credibility" in a career change and it can encourage the potential employer to think of you in words other than the job titles shown on your resume.

Dear Exact Name (or Dear Sir or Madam if answering a blind ad);

With the enclosed resume, I would like to make you aware of my interest in utilizing my outstanding sales, marketing, communication, and management skills for the benefit of your organization.

Although I most recently have been working in the aviation industry and am excelling in my current position, I have decided to embark on a radical career change. I have a strong desire to work in a professional position in which I can combine my extroverted personality and "natural" sales ability with my customer relations and problem-solving ability.

My recent experience in airport management, air traffic control, and in piloting advanced attack aircraft may not appear relevant to your needs, but my stable work history also includes several jobs which, I believe, illustrate my versatility. In one job I excelled as a Juvenile Counselor and thoroughly enjoyed the experience of providing a strong role model for troubled youth who had essentially been kicked out of their homes and labeled as "uncontrollable." In another job in California, I was part of the movie-making industry as I worked as a double for Mel Gibson. I also worked previously as a professional model. A wine expert and gourmet cook, I grew up in an Italian family which was in the restaurant business so I learned customer service at a young age!

In my current job involved in managing people and key areas related to airport management at one of the military's busiest airlift centers, I am continually using my problem-solving and decision-making skills. I am confident that my management ability, resourcefulness, and ability to relate effectively to others are qualities which could transfer to any field. In one of my jobs in the aviation industry, I managed a $3.5 million budget with outstanding results, and I offer a strong bottom-line orientation.

If you can use a highly motivated self-starter known for unlimited personal initiative and a creative problem-solving style, I hope you will contact me to suggest a time when we might meet to discuss your needs. I am single and would relocate and travel extensively as your needs require, and I can provide outstanding references at the appropriate time. Thank you in advance for your consideration.

Yours sincerely,

James Brown

JAMES BROWN

1110½ Hay Street, Fayetteville, NC 28305 • preppub@aol.com • (910) 483-6611

OBJECTIVE

To benefit an organization that can use an outgoing professional with excellent sales and marketing skills who has excelled in executive positions through applying my strong problem-solving, decision-making, communication, and management skills.

EDUCATION

Earned **A.A.S. degree in Logistics Management**, Community College of the Air Force, 1989; and an **A.A.S. degree in Liberal Arts**, Texas Central University, 1988.
Completed Pilot training; graduated **with honors,** top 10% of my class, 1991.
Excelled in executive development programs for military officers.

EXPERIENCE

AIRPORT OPERATIONS MANAGER. Department of Defense, Neilson AFB, CA (2000-present). At one of the nation's busiest airlift hubs, am making significant contributions to efficiency and safety through my managerial abilities and interpersonal skills.
- Reduced personnel costs by 35% while resolving critical staffing issues.
- Supervise airport management personnel; through my background as a pilot, have strengthened the knowledge of airfield management staff and increased their understanding of aircrew concerns; through my staff development expertise, morale is at an all-time high.
- Coordinate responses to flight emergencies, ground accidents, and contingency operations; am known for my ability to remain calm in a crisis.
- Simultaneously from 1991-present, have served in the Reserves as an **Attack Flight Pilot** and **Utility Pilot**, flying some of the world's most advanced aircraft.

RESOURCE MANAGER. Department of Defense, Los Alamitos, CA (1990-99). Managed a $3.5 million budget while coordinating the utilization of human and aviation assets for specific flights on flight schedules.
- Learned to make decisions among competing priorities as I managed a multimillion-dollar budget divided into six sections and subdivided into 34 sub areas in each section.
- Performed liaison with numerous state and federal agencies including the California Drug Team Task Force.
- Became skilled in managing multiple priorities in changing circumstances.

JUVENILE COUNSELOR. Concord Training School, Concord, SC (1989-90). At a school for troubled youth whose families could not control or provide for them, worked with teenagers and helped them develop realistic long-range and short-term goals for their lives.
- Thoroughly enjoyed providing a positive role model for children, and according to statistics, was more successful than most counselors in this job: my success rate for repeat offenders was 50%, which was better than my fellow counselors.

QUALITY CONTROL INSPECTOR. U.S. Air Force, Pope AFB, NC (1983-89). Performed in-flight, pre-flight, and post-flight checks in a role similar to that of an Inspector; acted as the technical expert during ground and in-flight emergencies.
- Supervised loading of passengers and cargo; accountable for the safety of all.

Other experience and skills:
- **Movie acting**: For one year, worked as a double for Mel Gibson.
- **Modeling:** Was a professional model.
- **Gourmet cooking:** Learned to cook growing up in an Italian family in the restaurant business; have expert knowledge related to fine wines and gourmet cooking.

PERSONAL

Am known for my ability to relate easily to others and to establish trust. Single. Would relocate and/or travel extensively according to my employer's needs.

Mr. Bill Smith
Brooks Executive Center
334 Executive Drive
Chicago, IL 88990

Dear Bill:

With the enclosed resume, I would like to make you aware of my interest in exploring opportunities with your organization and introduce you to my extensive abilities, talents, and skills. I am interested in acting as a consultant to you in situations which require an air traffic control expert who can identify the root causes of complex ATC mishaps and testify in a persuasive manner in a courtroom.

Extensive experience in investigating ATC mishaps and incidents
As a widely acknowledged expert in aviation safety, I have served as a consultant for incidents which included these: the crash of Algerian flight 395; a mishap involving a Blackhawk helicopter which was "hot refueling"; and an incident when a C-47 lost an engine and 19 members of the Bright Star air show team were killed.

Vast knowledge related to managing ATC operations
As you will see from my enclosed resume, I am recognized as an expert in managing high-stress operations where decisions must be made instantly in life-or-death situations. As a senior supervisory air traffic controller, flight instructor and evaluator, and pilot, I have become recognized as an authority in these areas. With an educational background which includes an M.B.A. and a bachelor's degree in Professional Aeronautics, I am able to make quick decisions while determining the best solutions to problems. During my more-than-30 years in air traffic control environments, I trained in excess of 1,000 professionals and am have been responsible for the training of more ATC personnel than anyone else in the country. My communication and human resource management skills are top-notch.

Numerous certifications and credentials
In addition to my years of service to the U.S. Government, I performed earlier service as an Air Force ATC. I am certified as an Advanced Ground Instructor, Instrument Ground Instructor, Flight Instructor, and Pilot with Multiengine Land Commercial Privileges as well as in rotary-wing aircraft.

If you can use an articulate, aggressive, mature, and educated professional who is considered one of the nation's foremost experts on air traffic control investigations and operations, I hope you will call me soon to discuss how I could serve your needs as a consultant.

Yours sincerely,

Patrick O. Jennings

PATRICK O. JENNINGS

1110½ Hay Street, Fayetteville, NC 28305   •   preppub@aol.com   •   (910) 483-6611

OBJECTIVE   To serve as a consultant for a legal firm which can benefit from my expertise as an air traffic controller with more than 30 years of in-depth knowledge related to ATC operations a well as the management of high-stress activities, the development and execution of complex plans and programs, and the instruction and training of air traffic control professionals.

EDUCATION   **M.B.A.,** California Coast University, Santa Ana, CA, 1992.
Bachelor of Professional Aeronautics degree, Embry-Riddle Aeronautical University, Daytona Beach, FL, 1988.

TRAINING   Excelled in extensive military training which included programs which emphasized the areas of Air Traffic Control communications switching systems, procedures standardization, and air space management.

CERTIFICATIONS Hold professional certifications in operational and functional areas which include:

> Air Traffic Control/Control Tower Operator
> Advanced Ground Instructor & Instrument Ground Instructor   Flight Instructor
> Airplane Multiengine Land Commercial Privileges   Aircraft Maintenance
> Airplane Single Engine Land   Rotorcraft/Helicopters
> Aerobatic Competency Evaluator   Restricted Radiotelephone Operator Permit

EXPERTISE   As an **expert in aviation safety,** served as a consultant for incidents which included:

> The crash of Algerian flight 395
> A mishap involving a Blackhawk helicopter which was "hot refueling"
> An incident when a C-47 lost engine killed 19 Bright Star Air Show crew members

- Offer a proven ability to identify the root cause of any ATC-related mishap or incident.
- Have testified in numerous courtroom situations and hearings on ATC matters; have earned a reputation as a powerful public speaker who is able to persuade others to adopt my reasoning and point of view.

EXPERIENCE   **AIRPORT MANAGER/OWNER AND FLIGHT INSTRUCTOR.** Colorado Airport Auxiliary, Denver, CO (1990-present). Have owned and operated several small facilities including numerous airstrips all over the west. Provided maintenance and hangar rentals and flight instruction.

SUPERVISORY AIR TRAFFIC CONTROLLER. U.S. Government, Washington, DC (1980-90). Widely recognized as the **subject matter expert in air traffic control operations,** directed the work of the nation's second largest Air Traffic Control (ATC) facility, which supported more than 300,000 flights a year.

- Personally trained and mentored more than 1,000 ATC professionals.
- Mentored, guided, trained, and supervised journeyman controllers while completing supporting documentation of their progress and performance.
- Applied communication and organizational skills working closely with personnel from the Federal Aviation Administration (FAA), the U.S. Air Force at nearby Pope AFB, and other organizations to coordinate the use of controlled air space.
- Provided a calm and controlled presence while supervising subordinates in emergency or hazardous situations which developed due to either controller or aviator error.

Highlights of earlier experience: Served in the U.S. Force as an Air Traffic Controller in locations throughout the world.

Mr. John Smith
Chief of Operations

By fax to: 910-483-6611

**AIR TRAFFIC
CONTROLLER**

Dear Mr. Smith:

With the enclosed resume, I would like to make you aware of the considerable aviation expertise and quality control experience I could put to work for you.

As you will see from my resume, I have been working as Air Traffic Controller in flight operations at Friendship Airport, one of the busiest airlift hubs. Through my background as a pilot, I have been able to make significant contributions in staff development and employee training because I have been able to help flight tower and other personnel better understand the concerns of aircrews. By applying my managerial skills, I have cut personnel costs by 35% without compromising our emphasis on safety and quality control. I have become skilled at numerous aspects of airport management.

In previous experience with the U.S. Air Force, I gained experience in quality assurance and inspections while acting as an Aircrew Loadmaster. In another job as an Aircraft Dispatcher with National Airport, I managed a $3.5 million budget subdivided into 204 areas. In addition to gaining expertise in managing a multimillion-dollar budget, I became skilled in managing multiple priorities while coordinating the utilization of human and physical resources in volatile conditions.

Throughout my work experience with the Air Force and at the airports, I have earned a reputation as a resourceful problem solver and skillful analyst who is capable of functioning with poise during emergencies. In every job I have held, I have become the individual to whom others have turned during crises and situations when many are in panic. I have learned to make decisions and solve problems in circumstances in which there is no room for error.

I would enjoy using my decision-making, problem-solving, and opportunity-finding skills in whatever capacity you feel you could best utilize them, and I hope you will contact me if you feel you have a suitable opportunity in mind. In the meantime, I send my best wishes for the holiday season.

Yours sincerely,

Larry Y. Smith

LARRY Y. SMITH

1110½ Hay Street, Fayetteville, NC 28305　•　preppub@aol.com　•　(910) 483-6611

OBJECTIVE　　To benefit an organization that can use an experienced executive who has achieved outstanding results through applying my strong problem-solving, decision-making, and management skills along with my expertise in aviation and air traffic control.

EDUCATION　　Completing **Airway Science degree**, Embry-Riddle Aeronautical University.
Earned **A.A.S. degree in Logistics Management**, Community College of the Air Force, 1993; and an **A.A.S. degree in Liberal Arts**, Virginia Central University, 1992.
Completed Pilot training and graduated **with honors** and in the top 10% of my class, 1995.
Extensive training related to airport management, safety, inspection management, quality assurance.

LICENSES　　Certified and experienced in air traffic control operations related to tower control, radar control, tower supervision, non-radar control, flight data progress strips.
Commercial Pilot License: Single/Multi-Engine Helicopter Land with Instrument rating.

TECHNICAL KNOWLEDGE　　Hold **Top Secret** security clearance
FAA AIS (Aviation Information Systems) Flight Data Computer
FAA Dial Labs – Flight Data Computer 986 flight-following computer
WSR 88D – Doppler Radar Set
ADWS – Automated Distribution Weather System
Service B – FAA Flight Following Computer

EXPERIENCE　　**AIR TRAFFIC CONTROLLER, FLIGHT OPERATIONS.** Friendship Airport, Philadelphia, PA (2000-present). At one of the busiest airlift hubs, have made significant contributions to efficiency and safety through my managerial skills as well as my experience as a pilot.
- Reduced personnel costs by 35% while resolving critical staffing issues.
- Supervise airfield management personnel; through my background as a pilot, have been able to increase the airfield management staff's understanding of aircrew concerns.
- Coordinate the responses to all flight emergencies, ground accidents, and contingency operations; plan and direct operations resource management activities.
- From 2000-present, have also served the Pennsylvania National Guard as an **Attack Flight Pilot** to provide national security for the United States.

AIRCRAFT DISPATCHER. National Airport, Washington, DC (1995-00). Planned and managed human resources and aviation assets for specific flights on flight schedules.
- Managed a $3.5 million budget.
- Transmitted enroute navigational aid and weather information.
- Controlled air traffic to ensure a safe, orderly, and expeditionary movement of aircraft along air routes and at airports.

C-130 AIRCREW LOADMASTER. U.S. Air Force, Clark AFB, NV (1992-95). Performed in-flight, pre-flight, and post-flight checks in a role similar to that of an Inspector; acted as the technical expert during ground and in-flight emergencies.

PERSONAL　　Offer outstanding analytical and problem-solving skills. Experience outside the aviation and teaching fields includes working for a year as an actor.

Exact Name of Person
Title or Position
Name of Company
Address (no., street)
Address (city, state, zip)

AIR TRAFFIC CONTROL
SUPERVISOR

Dear Exact Name of Person (or Dear Sir or Madam if answering a blind ad):

I would appreciate an opportunity to talk with you soon about how I could contribute to your organization through my versatile management skills and technical knowledge.

Management and leadership ability

My management and leadership skills were tested in numerous "hotseat" positions. After excelling in the rigorous U.S. Army Air Traffic Control School which has a failure rate of nearly 50%, I was selected for jobs which involved supervising people working on shifts at air traffic control facilities in the U.S. and overseas. While managing a multi-national work force in Panama, I became known for my skill as a supervisor in working with employees from different racial, ethnic, cultural, and economic backgrounds. "Attention to detail" is second nature to me, since I have been accustomed to working in environments in which there was "no room for error" because a careless mistake could cost human lives and multimillion-dollar assets. As a management philosophy, I believe in "leadership by example" and I am proud that I have helped many young soldiers turn their lives around and become hard-working go-getters.

Transportation industry knowledge

As you will see from my resume, I have become knowledgeable about how people and parcels get moved by aircraft in the safest and fastest way. In a "track record" of progression from radar controller to air traffic control supervisor, I was responsible daily for making "life-or-death" decisions related to the air transportation of people and products.

Telecommunications industry skills and knowledge

I offer extensive knowledge of telecommunications and computer equipment. I have become skilled in maintaining various types of communications equipment including interphone systems. I am knowledgeable of COMSEC equipment.

I would appreciate an opportunity to discuss your current and future needs and how I might serve them. Thank you in advance for your time.

Sincerely yours,

Reed Noble

REED NOBLE

1110½ Hay Street, Fayetteville, NC 28305   •   preppub@aol.com   •   (910) 483-6611

OBJECTIVE

To benefit an organization that can use a hard-working professional with extensive experience working in telecommunications and transportation environments along with highly refined skills in managing people, assets, maintenance services, inventory, and projects.

EXPERIENCE

AIR TRAFFIC QUALITY CONTROLLER/SHIFT SUPERVISOR. MacArthur Airfield, CA (2000-present). Worked in a highly computerized telecommunications environment in which there is "no room for error"; became known for my excellent judgement and decision-making skills.

- Coordinated the technical training of seven controllers which resulted in the facility's receiving an FAA rating in only six months.
- Routinely made decisions that resolved inflight and ground emergencies.

SHIFT SUPERVISOR/TRAINING SUPERVISOR. MacArthur Airfield, CA (1997-00). Implemented a training program that I designed in the job below that would enable newly arriving controllers to master a highly complex training curriculum in only six months; was promoted to the job above based on my outstanding performance in this job.

TRAINING SUPERVISOR. MacArthur Airfield, CA (1995-96). Designed a new training program involving state-of-the-art telecommunications and computer concepts, and then was promoted to the job above to implement that training program; administered exams to test the proficiency of air traffic controllers.

- Through my exceptional management skills related to controlling inventory and documentation, achieved a rare 100% score on a rigorous annual inspection.
- Acted as a consultant to shift supervisors, and assisted them in complying strictly with facility policies and procedures.

OPERATIONS CENTER SUPERVISOR. U.S. Army, Camp Christobal, Panama (1992-94). At this busy air traffic control center in Panama, supervised a multinational work force and was respected for my sensitivity as a supervisor to cultural and economic differences.

- Used sophisticated computerized telecommunications equipment to flight follow aircraft.

EQUIPMENT MAINTENANCE CHIEF. U.S. Army, Ft. Gordon, GA (1990-92). Managed a section responsible for maintaining a variety of telecommunications, computer, and air traffic control equipment in operational status around the clock.

RADAR CONTROLLER. U.S. Army, locations in Central America (1985-90). Worked long hours and learned to make prudent decisions under pressure while controlling inflight aircraft and providing precision approach radar guidance.

EDUCATION

Completed three years of college-level education and training sponsored by the U.S. Army.

- Excelled in Air Traffic Control School, a rigorous program with a 50% graduation rate.

SKILLS

Telecommunications knowledge: Knowledgeable of COMSEC and other telecommunications systems; have performed diagnostic checks on interphone systems.

PERSONAL

While in military service, I counseled many young people and helped them turn their lives around. Believe a strong example is the best teacher. Have a Secret security clearance.

Exact Name of Person
Title or Position
Name of Company
Address (no., street)
Address (city, state, zip)

**FLIGHT OPERATIONS
DIRECTOR**

Dear Exact Name of Person (or Dear Sir or Madam if answering a blind ad):

I would appreciate an opportunity to talk with you soon about how I could contribute to your organization through my talents as an administrator, instructor, and pilot who has excelled as a U.S. Air Force officer. You will see from my resume that I offer extensive experience in air operations and management as well as in developing and conducting flight and academic training programs.

In my current position as director of operations, I have been instrumental in establishing a unique organization which places three types of aircraft in one organization to allow them to work more productively together. I was handpicked for my current position which requires me to act in a highly classified environment as I manage activities and resources related to the war against terrorism.

Prior to my current assignment I was selected for an officer exchange program with the Chinese military forces. I spent approximately four years in China working on long-range five-year modernization plans for their weapons systems. During this period I was involved in planning procurement, testing, and budgeting activities for a $500 million war reserve munitions inventory.

Earlier experiences included coordinating and directing close air support for joint American-Korean flights throughout Korea, directing training activities, and instructing flight operations. I have logged in excess of 3,055 flight hours with 2,830 as pilot-in-command and 1,070 as an instructor. The recipient of three Meritorious Service Medals and an Air Force Commendation Medal, I have been officially evaluated as having "unsurpassed technical expertise" and as "a trailblazer" who "commands respect" for "his strong, positive leadership style."

I hope you will welcome my call soon to arrange a brief meeting at your convenience to discuss your current and future needs and how I might serve them. Thank you in advance for your time.

Sincerely yours,

Clark D. Turbine

Alternate last paragraph:
I hope you will call or write me soon to suggest a time convenient for us to meet and discuss your current and future needs and how I might serve them. Thank you in advance for your time.

CLARK D. TURBINE

1110½ Hay Street, Fayetteville, NC 28305   •   preppub@aol.com   •   (910) 483-6611

OBJECTIVE

To contribute to an organization that can use an innovative thinker who has excelled as a military officer through superior technical knowledge of aerospace operations, exceptional program development skills, and a knack for maximizing human, fiscal, and material assets.

EDUCATION & TRAINING

M.A., **Computer Resource Management**, Webster University; expected in 2003.
B.S. in Engineering Mechanics, The United States Air Force Academy, Colorado Springs, CO, 1983.

EXPERIENCE

DIRECTOR OF OPERATIONS. USAF, Washington, DC (2000-present). Was selected for a position in which I operate in a highly classified environment; oversee the management of activities ranging from life support systems, to fighter and airlift tactics, to weapons employment, to contingency planning, to simulator training for aircrew members.
- Created and developed the original framework for all aspects of the Air Force's first and only organization which allows A-10, F-16, and C-130 aircraft to work together in one organization.
- Working under the direction of the Joint Chiefs of Staff, manage 75 people in planning and executing all air operations for a rapid response contingency which has operated in Afghanistan in support of the war against terrorism.

CHIEF, TACTICAL WEAPONS OPERATIONS. USAF, China (1995-00). Handpicked as an exchange officer, developed air weapons modernization guidelines encompassing procurement, testing, and budget forecasting for the $500 million munitions inventory of the Chinese Air Force.
- Reduced five-year training program costs by $50 million with no loss of quality or effectiveness of operational capabilities.
- Directed the movement of $250 million in weapons during the war in the Middle East.

DIRECTOR OF CLOSE AIR SUPPORT COMBAT PLANS. USAF, Korea (1990-94). Provided "expert advice" while writing plans, making recommendations, and advising United Nations Command leadership about all American-Korean close air operations.
- Rewrote theater war plans integrating major U.S. force structure changes to maximize combat effectiveness.

CHIEF, WEAPONS AND TACTICS. USAF, England AFB, LA (1988-90). Controlled a $20 million annual training and weapons budget and directed the activities of 11 pilots and crew members involved in worldwide training and real-world missions.

INSTRUCTOR PILOT and **FLIGHT COMMANDER.** USAF, Korea (1985-88). Supervised eight pilots while involved in daily activities including developing training plans, managing flight requirements, and ensuring pilot proficiency as a flight examiner.
- Represented the Pacific Air Forces at international conferences.

Highlights of earlier experience: Excelled as an Instructor, Pilot, and Flight Commander.

AIRCRAFT EXPERTISE
- Hold an **FAA Commercial Pilot license,** airplane multi-engine land and instrument.
- Have 3,055 total flight hours with 2,830 as pilot-in-command and am familiar with the following aircraft: Fairchild Republic A-10A Thunderbolt II (OA-10A), Northrup T-38A/B Talon, Cessna T-37B, and Cessna T-41 Mescalero (C-172).

PERSONAL

Am familiar with Word, WordPerfect, PowerPoint, and various programming languages as well as specialized military software. **Top Secret/SCI** security clearance.

Exact Name of Person
Title or Position
Name of Company
Address (number and street)
Address (city, state, and zip)

FLIGHT OPERATIONS
MANAGER
&
SPACE
TECHNOLOGY
SPECIALIST

Dear Exact Name of Person (or Sir or Madam if answering a blind ad):

I would appreciate an opportunity to talk with you soon about how I could contribute to your organization through the application of my experience gained while serving in the U.S. Air Force with an emphasis on space technology management as well as research and development.

As you will see from my enclosed resume, I have served in the U.S. Air Force where I have earned a reputation as a professional who can be depended on for personal integrity, resourcefulness, and dedication to excellence in everything I attempt.

Presently in my final Air Force assignment prior to retirement, I am the Supervisor for Flight Support Operations at the Defense Support Program's European Ground Station. For this facility which provides immediate warning and space launch data to agencies and personnel throughout the world, I ensure adequate and trained staff members are scheduled for this 24-hour-a-day facility, maintain reports and training data, resolve human resources issues, and have become a resource point for questions concerning unit operations.

Earlier assignments detailed on my resume included developing policy and managing manpower and training programs for an 840-person enlisted space operations work force and working in the planning and conducting of standardization and evaluation team operations two years at Peterson AFB, CO. Prior experience was in missile warning operations, training evaluation, and technical electronics jobs where I earned a reputation as an articulate fast learner who can be counted on for keen analytical, problem-solving, and decision-making skills.

If you are looking for a mature professional with proven expertise in the applications of space technology with an emphasis on research and development as well as management, I hope you will call or write me soon to arrange a brief meeting to discuss your current and future needs and how I might serve them. Thank you in advance for your time.

Sincerely,

Earl Monty Nabisco

EARL MONTY NABISCO

1110½ Hay Street, Fayetteville, NC 28305   •   preppub@aol.com   •   (910) 483-6611

OBJECTIVE   To offer a broad base of expertise in the applications of space technology with emphasis on management and research and development gained while serving in the U.S. Air Force.

EXPERIENCE   **FLIGHT OPERATIONS MANAGER.** U.S. Air Force, Germany (2000-present). Oversee 44 people operating the space-based Defense Support Program's European Ground Station, a facility which provides immediate warning and space launch data to agencies and personnel throughout the world.
- Prepared monthly schedules in order to ensure adequate staffing at all times in a 24-hour-a-day operation vital to international security; monitored the operation's training program; solved staffing problems.
- Ensured high standards of crew proficiency and operational procedures so that potential missile warning and attack data was detected, analyzed, and reported to key users.

Earned advancement in this track record of accomplishments, U.S. Air Force, locations worldwide:
CHIEF OF MANPOWER UTILIZATION AND TRAINING. (1997-99). Developed and implemented policies and procedures for the management of an 840-person enlisted space operations work force while monitoring personnel utilization and job content issues.
- Coordinated with the Air Force's space command headquarters as liaison for all related training and subsequent personnel assignments.
- Was the author of the first-ever career field training plan for space operations.

RESOURCE DEVELOPMENT MANAGER. (1994-96). Served as the resident expert on manpower and personnel issues for space operations crew members with an emphasis on space surveillance, missile warning, satellite control, and spacelift missions.
- Revised procedures for scheduling 1,500 students for space operations training courses.
- Sanctioned the testing of the Core Automated Management Systems (CAMS) for space operations centers and developed the guidelines for worldwide applications.

EVALUATION TEAM SUPERVISOR. (1991-93). Assisted in planning, scheduling, and coordinating evaluation visits to space, warning, and surveillance units; prepared responses to review panels and higher headquarters; served on radar systems evaluation teams.
- Evaluated as an "exceptional" performer, was credited with revising the evaluator certification process used by 15 units throughout the world.
- Received the Air Force Association's "Best Space Operations Crew" for 1992.

MISSILE WARNING OPERATIONS CREW CHIEF. (1988-90). Provided direct assistance in a missile warning operations center vital to the defense of the North American continent; supervised five contractor personnel involved in satellite tracking and space object identification.
- Recognized by the Space Command's Inspector General for error-free and 100% professional response during real-world incidents and exercises.

SUPERVISOR FOR TRAINING EVALUATIONS. (1986-87). Managed a program of exercise evaluations and synthetic air defense exercises (SYNADEX) in order to determine the unit's capability to carry out peace and wartime operations.
- Trained and supervised evaluation team members; prepared reports; conducted debriefings; maintained records of problems.

EDUCATION   A.A.S. degree in Space Technology, Community College of the Air Force, 1998.

Exact Name of Person
Exact Title
Exact Name of Company
Address
City, State, Zip

**MATERIAL CONTROL
OPERATIONS
SUPERVISOR**

Dear Exact Name of Person (or Dear Sir or Madam if answering a blind ad):

With the enclosed resume, I would like to make you aware of my expertise in managing material, fiscal, and human resources while providing aviation operations with timely and effective supply and inventory control management support.

As you will see from my resume, I have held supervisory roles in support of aviation operations throughout the world. For instance, in my most recent position, I managed a $9 million budget while achieving a 99.58% utilization of funds for one recent fiscal year. While supervising 32 people, I received official evaluations which described me as the "consummate professional" and as a senior executive's "most trusted advisor on supply-related issues." I was credited with making improvements in increasing aircraft production rates and increased the number of test pilots.

In an earlier assignment as an Inventory Control Manager, I handled supply operations, to include planning for the transition to the newly designed facilities and reorganization of all supply operations and space. As the resident expert on aviation supply and material management, I controlled receiving, storing, issuing, and auditing of a $50 million inventory.

With excellent time management, planning, and organizational skills, I have recently completed degree requirements for a B.S. in Aviation Management. I am familiar with automated data processing systems used to maintain documents and records of operations from the procurement and requisitioning stages on through all aspects of storage, issuing, and control. I offer a strong base of experience in proving product support for both fixed- and rotary-wing aircraft which include C-130, P-3, F-14, FA-18, A-7, and S-3.

I hope you will call or write me soon to suggest a time convenient for us to meet and discuss your current and future needs and how I might serve them. Thank you in advance for your time.

Sincerely,

Allen E. Dumas

ALLEN E. DUMAS

1110½ Hay Street, Fayetteville, NC 28305 • preppub@aol.com • (910) 483-6611

OBJECTIVE

To offer a distinguished background of accomplishments and extensive knowledge and experience related to inventory control management to an organization that can benefit from my effectiveness in maximizing human, fiscal, and material resources.

EDUCATION & TRAINING

B.S. in **Aviation Management,** Rivier College, Nashua, NH, 2002.
Completed extensive training with an emphasis on aviation supply and maintenance material management, leadership development, program management, and financial operations. Other training included substance abuse counseling, shipboard firefighting, automated data processing operations and management, and Spanish language courses.

EXPERIENCE

MATERIAL CONTROL OPERATIONS SUPERVISOR. Raytheon Corporation, Spokane, WA (2000-present). Officially evaluated as the "consummate professional" and "most trusted advisor on all supply related issues," managed a $9 million budget while being credited with implementing improvements which improved aircraft production rates and increased the number of pilots in the testing program.
- Achieved a 99.58% utilization of funds for fiscal year 2002 while "aggressively" managing and expediting requisitions for a 45% reduction in outstanding requests.
- Cut aircraft parts "cannibalizing" 63% which increased availability 35 percent.
- Supervised 32 pilots in a special testing operation.
- Earned respect for my "positive and approachable demeanor" which translated to exceptional achievements in all levels of performance and inspected operational areas.

INVENTORY CONTROL MANAGER. Boeing Aircraft, Seattle, WA (1998-00). Recognized as the company's aviation supply and material management expert, supervised the receipt, storage, issue, location auditing, and inventory of material valued in excess of $50 million and which was located in ten separate warehouses.
- Provided support for a complex overhaul project in material management and control operations including reorganizing storerooms.

SUPPLY OPERATIONS SUPERVISOR. U.S. Navy, Naval Station, England (1990-97). Earned respect for my "astute management" while providing support for day-to-day operations and a wide range of special missions which received exceptional aircraft and administrative material support for a fleet air reconnaissance unit.
- Provided perfect accountability while issuing, controlling, and providing replenishment for a $4.5 million Weapons Replaceable Assembly pack up for a project in Crete.

Highlights of earlier U.S. Navy experience: Advanced in rank while building a reputation as a knowledgeable aviation supply, maintenance, and fiscal operations professional.

AIRCRAFT SKILLS

Offer extensive experience in providing product support for C-130, P-3, F-14, FA-18, A-7, and S-3 aircraft.

CLEARANCE

Top Secret security clearance with SBI

PERSONAL

Received several Joint Service and Navy/Marine Corps Achievement Medals in recognition of my accomplishments and expertise. Effective in dealing with culturally diverse teams.

Date

Exact Name of Person
Title or Position
Name of Company
Address (no., street)
Address (city, state, zip)

OPERATIONS CHIEF

Dear Exact Name of Person (or Dear Sir or Madam if answering a blind ad):

I would appreciate an opportunity to talk with you soon about how I could contribute to your organization through my expertise related to mobile satellite operations, telecommunications, and computer systems.

At the age of 35, I am considered one of the Air Force's most valuable military officers. After earning my bachelor's degree in Mathematics and my master's degree in Management, I have excelled in advanced technical training related to space systems, global communications, and space command and control.

Expertise in satellite systems and space operations

Most recently I have managed a large space operations crew force to include training and scheduling related to the operation of mobile satellite ground systems. In previous jobs at the Space Defense Operations Center (SPADOC), I directed the worldwide Space Surveillance Network in a center that tracks, detects, and catalogs all manmade space objects. Additionally, I developed and implemented plans for Space Defense Operations Center software, hardware, and other equipment upgrades. In 1998, I completed the Air Force's Undergraduate Space Training course and was the Class Leader during this three-month Ph.D. level program. A highly selective process was used to screen applicants for this program. This program was designed to prepare students for any position in the space industry.

Expertise in telecommunications and computer maintenance/logistics

You will see from my resume that I also offer expertise in the installation, management, and maintenance of telecommunications and computer systems. In one position, I was responsible for the management, administrative, and logistics support of 15 major communications-computer systems and telephone systems. In another job, I directed automated data processing related to global computer networks, local area networks (LANs), and electronic security computer systems. I have also managed the design, development, implementation, and maintenance of unique software used for command and control.

I hope you will call or write me soon to suggest a time convenient for us to meet and discuss your current and future needs and how I might serve them. Thank you in advance for you time.

Sincerely yours,

Corders Van Pelt

CORDERS VAN PELT

1110½ Hay Street, Fayetteville, NC 28305   •   preppub@aol.com   •   (910) 483-6611

OBJECTIVE

To contribute to an organization that can use an accomplished professional who offers experience in working with the world's most advanced mobile satellite technology and space systems while also offering experience in state-of-the-art telecommunications and computer systems installation, maintenance, and management.

EDUCATION

Masters of Arts degree in Management, Webster University, San Antonio, TX, 1998.
Bachelor of Science in Mathematics, Worcester State College, Worcester, MA, 1992.
As a military officer, completed advanced technical training in these and other areas:

Space Operations	
Mobile Satellite Systems Software Design	Fiber Optics
Space Command and Control	Software Analysis Techniques
Global Communications Network	Computer Security
Computer Networking	Data Query Techniques
Networking Protocols	Quality Improvement Process

Completed the Air Force's Undergraduate Space Training course which included subjects ranging from Space Sensor Operations, Satellite Command Center Operations, and Satellite Systems, as well as Space System Acquisition.

EXPERIENCE

OPERATIONS CHIEF. Department of Defense, Washington, DC (2002-present). Was handpicked to manage tactical operations for our nation's only survivable mobile Defense Support Program (DSP) satellite ground system which utilizes 123 vehicles and 144 personnel in order to communicate with missile warning and communication satellites.

- Manage crew force training and the scheduling of personnel in order to provide continuous 24-hour availability of mobile satellite ground systems.

DEPUTY BRANCH CHIEF, OPERATIONS. Space Defense Operations Center, Cheyenne AFB, CO (1998-01). Directed the worldwide Space Surveillance Network in a center that detects, tracks, and catalogs all man-made space objects; developed and implemented plans for Space Defense Operations Center (SPADOC) software, hardware, and ancillary equipment acquisitions and upgrades while resolving communication issues between the SPADOC and space system owner/operators.

- Learned the functions involved in managing a worldwide satellite tracking network.

CHIEF OF COMPUTER MAINTENANCE/LOGISTICS. Pope Air Force Base, NC (1990-97). Was responsible for management, administrative, and logistics support of over 15 major communications-computer systems and all secure telephone systems supporting the Electronic Security Command (ESC); supervised over 125 personnel in seven sections, 15 workcenters, and coordinated more than 30 vendor contractors.

- Was the DOD and national-level liaison on critical cryptologic programs.
- As the contractor/officer, played a key role in the Air Force's activation of a $13 million heavy earth satellite terminal (AN/GSC-52); avoided schedule delays through projects which installed backup power supply, diesel generators, and wire/cable runs.

CHIEF, SOFTWARE DEVELOPMENT FOR OPERATIONS SYSTEMS. Headquarters USAFE Information Systems, England (1987-90). Managed the design, development, implementation, and maintenance of unique software used for command and control; specialized in automated support while providing design specifications, flow charts, and computer programs.

CLEARANCE

Top Secret with SBI; have worked at SCI level

OPERATIONS MANAGERS & TRAINING PROFESSIONALS

Date

Exact Name of Person
Title or Position
Name of Company
Address (no., street)
Address (city, state, zip)

OPERATIONS LIAISON

Dear Exact Name of Person (or Dear Sir or Madam if answering a blind ad):

I would appreciate an opportunity to talk with you soon about how I could contribute to your organization through my expertise as a manager of human, fiscal, and material resources as well as my specialized experience in the aviation field and flight safety operations.

As an aviation industry leader, I have become recognized as a dynamic leader who continually uses creativity and insight to identify opportunities to reduce costs, improve profitability, and develop new programs and services.

Consistently evaluated as one of the Air Force's best fighter pilots and instructor pilots, I have extensive experience in the areas of safety program development and general operations management. I was handpicked for my present role as liaison with the Army to develop plans and oversee joint operations in worldwide locations based on my proven expertise and leadership skills. I thrive on challenge and work well under pressure and tight time constraints. I am known for my talents in developing workable programs which result in saving funds and increasing productivity and safety.

Through my know-how, exceptional written and verbal communications skills, and natural leadership abilities, I am confident that I could make valuable contributions to your organization.

I hope you will welcome my call soon to arrange a brief meeting at your convenience to discuss your current and future needs and how I might serve them. Thank you in advance for your time.

Sincerely yours,

Chester E. Glenn

Alternate last paragraph:
I hope you will call or write me soon to suggest a time convenient for us to meet and discuss your current and future needs and how I might serve them. Thank you in advance for your time.

CHESTER E. GLENN

1110½ Hay Street, Fayetteville, NC 28305   •   preppub@aol.com   •   (910) 483-6611

OBJECTIVE

To benefit an organization that can use an experienced administrator with versatile expertise related to aviation, safety program development, training administration, information systems management, and operations management.

COMPUTER KNOWLEDGE

Concentrated in computer information systems in graduate school and am well versed in using Word, Word for Windows, Windows, and PowerPoint.

EDUCATION & TRAINING

M.S., Management, The University of Arizona, Phoenix, AZ.
B.S., Aeronautical Flight Operations, University of Minnesota, Duluth, MN.
Excelled in 12 months of undergraduate pilot training; a 10-week graduate-level Flight Safety Officers Course; and programs in general management concepts and quality awareness.

EXPERIENCE

Advanced in aviation leadership roles with the U.S. Air Force:
OPERATIONS LIAISON. MacDill AFB, FL (2000-present). Handpicked for this critical job, represent the Air Force as an advisor to Army executives for planning joint activities in support of airborne operations.

- Managed and scheduled close air support for 13 geographically separated units from Louisiana to New York: remained constantly aware of each unit's requirements.

ADVISOR. MacDill AFB, FL (1997-99). Evaluated as an "exceptional and well-respected officer," served as an advisor on the utilization of air power in support of an 8,500-person force flying more than a dozen different aircraft throughout the world.

- Made pilot checklist changes which reduced wasted time and saved funds.
- Planned and conducted a recall project for 75 employees and 20 teams of close air planning specialists; evaluated their responsiveness and made improvements which reduced loading time 30% and eliminated duplication of equipment to be issued.
- Implemented a plan for safeguarding facilities and keeping family members informed when the organization was mobilized for no-notice worldwide assignments.

PLANS OFFICER. Germany (1996-97). Worked closely with counterparts from other services and nations while planning NATO missions.

- Developed three pilot checklists which were approved and adopted for use: demonstrated my flexibility while incorporating adjustments caused by political change.

OPERATIONS MANAGER and **FLIGHT COMMANDER**. Pope AFB, NC (1994-95). Applied my attention to detail and practical experience to handle daily operations including scheduling, coordinating with numerous agencies, and providing instruction and guidance to 13 instructor pilots and 26 student pilots.

- Ensured safety in a "flawless" program which twice won a prestigious award.

AVIATION SAFETY PROGRAM DIRECTOR. Williams AFB, AZ (1990-93). Managed the base's flight safety operations which included setting safety policy and goals, pilot safety training, investigating and analyzing incidents for trends, and developing preventive measures.

- Headed the safety program which was singled out from among seven bases to receive the General Lahm Trophy for best regional flight safety program.

Highlights of other experience: Was handpicked for high-visibility positions worldwide in the field of aviation safety.

Exact Name of Person
Exact Title
Exact Name of Company
Address
City, State, Zip

OPERATIONS MANAGER

Dear Exact Name of Person (or Dear Sir or Madam if answering a blind ad):

With the enclosed resume, I would like to make you aware of my interest in exploring executive positions within your organization which could make use of my aviation expertise as well as my strong problem-solving, organizational, and management skills.

As you will see from my resume, I have excelled in a track record of promotion within the Federal Aviation Administration. In my earliest jobs as a pilot, I was recognized for my initiative, judgment, knowledge, and leadership skills and was recommended for rapid advancement into supervisory and then into executive positions.

In one job, I was Chief of Branch Operations in charge of planning and directing strategic and operational airlift programs worldwide while managing airlift missions valued at $35 million. As an Operations Officer, I was praised as an "inspirational leader" while leading more than 430 aviators, maintenance personnel, and others involved in airlift missions supporting NATO and the Joint Chiefs of Staff. In a subsequent job as Chief of Safety at one of the nation's busiest airlift hubs, I directed mishap investigations while conceiving, developing, and implementing risk management, safety, and mishap prevention programs affecting thousands of people and multimillion-dollar aircraft.

As a pilot I have accumulated more than 3634 total flight hours with 1789 as Pilot-in-Command. I hold Airline Transport Pilot and Commercial Pilot Rotorcraft ratings.

With a reputation as a principled individual known for integrity, I always received the highest formal evaluations of my performance, and I was consistently described as a "model leader" with an exemplary work ethic and an enthusiastic management style. My problem-solving and decision-making skills have been refined while operating in environments in which there was "no room for error," and I have held one of our nation's highest security clearances (Top Secret SCI). I can provide outstanding personal and professional references.

If you can use a seasoned executive who has an outstanding reputation in the aviation industry, I hope you will contact me to suggest a time when we might meet to discuss your needs. I am single and can relocate worldwide according to your needs.

Sincerely,

James Woodard

JAMES WOODARD

1110½ Hay Street, Fayetteville, NC 28305   •   preppub@aol.com   •   (910) 483-6611

OBJECTIVE

To contribute to the pursuits of an organization needing a polished communicator and resourceful, strategic thinker offering vision, leadership, and team-building skills developed during a distinguished career as a military officer in international environments.

EDUCATION

Master of Business Administration, University of South Dakota.
Bachelor of Science in **Civil Engineering**, Virginia Military Institute.
Excelled in rigorous and extensive graduate-level professional development training for military officers including the Air War College, Air Command and Staff College, and Squadron Officer's School.

CLEARANCE

Presently hold **Top Secret (SCI)** security clearance.

EXPERIENCE 1992-present

Rose to the rank of GS-18 while serving with the Federal Aviation Administration:
OPERATIONS MANAGER. Los Angeles International Airport, Los Angeles, CA. Assisted in managing a $36.8 million budget and coordinating the activities of more than 1,000 people in five diverse organizations; ensured that all personnel were highly trained and integrated to accomplish wing mission. Instructor pilot for 240 officer aviators.

- Accomplished in-depth study of entire operations group's mission and processes; implemented changes to eliminate redundancy and reengineered internal systems to streamline resource allocation, vastly improving training quality and manpower efficiency.
- Institutionalized risk management throughout the operations group; principles utilized in every aspect of daily operations - enhanced safety.
- Led a runway extension project that will nearly double airlift capability; gained expertise in the Environmental Impact/Assessment Process and integrated civilian, environmental and military groups in "selling" the concept to the affected civilian communities.
- Superiors' evaluation: "Possesses superior leadership, management and organizational skills; productive leader who cultivates teamwork/winning attitude;" "Self-motivated; faces challenges rarely afforded his contemporaries;" and "Totally committed to excellence.

1987-92:

CHIEF OF SAFETY. Washington, DC. Conceived, developed, and implemented risk management, safety, and mishap prevention programs affecting 5,000 people, a fleet of 91 aircraft, and aircraft operations. Directly supervised 12 executives while overseeing safety programs in 32 diverse organizations. Instructor pilot.

- Ran a program rated "outstanding" by the nation's highest aviation authorities; oversaw 26,000 aircraft sorties handling 120,000 passengers and 3,600 cargo tons, and 65 major construction projects with no accidents.
- Oversaw research of bird/aircraft strike data that resulted in elimination of costly, ineffective risk control measures for Air Mobility Command C-130 aircraft.
- Proposed risk management strategies for flight and maintenance operations were incorporated into major command operating policy.
- Refined ability to "sell" and implement weapons, ground, and flight safety programs on macro scale; justified on a cost-benefits basis without tangible returns to users; result: no duty-related accidents.

Highlights of other experience: Accumulated more than 3600 total flight hours as a Pilot in Command. Acted as a troubleshooter to airports worldwide experiencing security and safety problems. Testified in numerous legal proceedings regarding my analysis of accidents. Was involved in numerous projects supporting NATO and the Joint Chiefs of Staff.

City of Miami Personnel Department
3333 Palm Street
Miami, FL 33445

**OPERATIONS
MANAGER**

Dear Sir or Madam:

With the enclosed resume, I would like to begin the process of making formal application for the job of Airport Director for the City of Miami.

As you will see from the enclosed resume, I have excelled in jobs that included air traffic controller, airport manager, aviation training superintendent, and inspector of airport operations nationwide.

I have reviewed your vacancy announcement carefully, and I possess all the knowledge and abilities you seek. I have achieved my present position because of my administrative skills and problem-solving ability as well as my expert knowledge of every aspect of airport operations.

You would find me in person to be a congenial individual who is skilled at working with people at all levels, from ground support equipment personnel to decision makers at the highest government levels. I offer excellent personal and professional references, and I could easily pass the most rigorous background investigation.

I hope you will call or write me soon to suggest a time when we could meet to discuss your requirements and goals as well as my strong qualifications for the job you have advertised. Thank you in advance for your time.

Sincerely yours,

Horace A. Fallerton

HORACE A. FALLERTON

1110½ Hay Street, Fayetteville, NC 28305   •   preppub@aol.com   •   (910) 483-6611

OBJECTIVE   To contribute to an organization that can use an experienced airport director who offers experience in administering all airport services and activities including aircraft operations, building and field maintenance, and the training of personnel in air traffic control.

EDUCATION   **Bachelor of Professional Aeronautics in Air Traffic Control/Airport Management**, Embry-Riddle Aeronautical University, Daytona Beach, FL, 1993.
Associates in Applied Science in Air Traffic Control, University of Washington, Seattle, WA, 1990.
Completed coursework towards an MBA degree, University of Miami, Coral Gables, FL, 2001-present.

PROFESSIONAL TRAINING   Completed the most advanced courses for Airport Directors and Air Traffic Controllers related to Total Quality Management, air ground operations, budgeting, personnel selection and training, national and international rules and regulations, airport construction and management, and other areas.

EXPERIENCE   **AVIATION OPERATIONS MANAGER.** Grimley Airport, Miami, FL (2001-present). Manage 60 people, including air traffic controllers, radio/vehicle maintenance specialists, supply technicians, and administrative support personnel, who are involved in activities at this busy airport.
- Have maintained a perfect safety record while supervising the setting up "from scratch" and management of an average of three air strips; supervise surveying of sites, identification of maintenance required, establishment of communication, and provision of air traffic control services.

AVIATION OPERATIONS SUPERINTENDENT. Arleigh Airfield, Kenosha, WI (1997-00). Managed 35 people and a budget of $500,000 while coordinating programs and services for a small airfield.
- Coordinated commercial contracts for maintenance, equipment, and parts.
- Supervised the management and control of 12 functional areas.

AIRFIELD & AVIATION OPERATIONS INSPECTOR. Federal Aviation Administration (FAA), Washington, DC (1992-96). Authored and maintained functional area inspections guides and checklists while planning and implementing projects designed to test the performance of every task involved in airport management.
- Surveyed airfield locations nationwide, and inspected air traffic control procedures, airfield operations, radio and NAVAID maintenance, life support, and vehicle maintenance functions; briefed and wrote inspection reports for top executives.

AVIATION TRAINING SUPERINTENDENT & AIR TRAFFIC CONTROLLER. Federal Aviation Administration, Scott AFB, IL (1988-91). Was specially selected for this job because of my aviation expertise as well as my administrative skills and strategic planning ability; formulated training goals.
- Managed the formal training school programs designed to train air traffic controllers.

INSTRUCTOR. Wright's School of Aviation, Tacoma, WA (1985-88). Earned a reputation as a gifted public speaker and talented course planner while teaching a variety of subjects at this training school for aviators; trained personnel.

PERSONAL   Excellent personal and professional references on request. Visionary thinker.

Exact Name of Person
Exact Title
Exact Name of Company
Address
City, State, Zip

LOADMASTER

Dear Exact Name of Person (or Dear Sir or Madam if answering a blind ad):

With this letter and the enclosed resume, I would like to express my interest in receiving consideration for employment opportunities within your organization. I am interested in discussing your need for an experienced Loadmaster. Although I am held in the highest regard in my current position, I am relocating with my wife to your area, and I am exploring opportunities with regional airports.

In my current position as a Loadmaster and Operations Manager for the Dayton Airport, I provide strong leadership for staffing, training, and planning with the goal of ensuring error-free services for passengers and cargo. Shipments vary from a single box to multiple loads which require special loading to guarantee the proper placement according to precise weight-and-balance computations. In the aftermath of the terrorist attack of September 11, 2001, I played a key role in initiating numerous policies and procedures which have improved security and passenger safety.

I am proud of my reputation as a professional who is dedicated to safety and total quality management objectives. I have been selected for ever-increasing levels of managerial responsibilities because of my special skills related to managing resources for maximum productivity as well as my ability to develop and implement training designed to produce the most highly skilled employees.

Through my experience and training, I have become widely recognized as a technical expert who sets high personal standards while leading others to maximum application of their own skills. My versatile accomplishments have included developing computer programs for tracking and scheduling personnel, as well as providing technical training for personnel.

If you can use a versatile and detail-oriented professional with special knowledge of aircraft support operations such as load planning and scheduling, I hope you will call me soon for a brief discussion of how I could contribute to your organization.

Sincerely,

Albert Finch

ALBERT FINCH

1110½ Hay Street, Fayetteville, NC 28305   ·   preppub@aol.com   ·   (910) 483-6611

OBJECTIVE

To contribute through a track record of exceptional performance as a results-oriented resource manager who excels in developing and implementing training activities while ensuring the details of complex scheduling, inspecting, and planning of aircraft loading operations.

EDUCATION & TRAINING

Associate's degree, Aircrew Operations, Community College of the Air Force, 2001. Excelled in extensive training which emphasized aircraft load-planning and inspection procedures, leadership, and instructional techniques; completed Volunteer Firefighter Course.

AREAS OF EXPERTISE

Clearance: entrusted with a **Top Secret** security clearance.
Computers: working knowledge of Microsoft Windows, Word, and Excel.
Flight hours: logged in excess of 6,300 hours as an aircrew professional and am certified as an Instructor Loadmaster for the C-130 Hercules aircraft.

EXPERIENCE

LOADMASTER & OPERATIONS MANAGER. Dayton Airport, Dayton, OH (2002-present). Am excelling in a position with three major areas of emphasis: acting as point of contact to ensure flights are adequately staffed with qualified personnel; ensuring the up-to-date training status of 28 people; and carrying out pre-, in-, and post-flight support activities.
* Oversee personnel loading all types of cargo, from single boxes to heavy equipment and personally prepare all weight-and-balance paperwork to ensure safe flight.

TECHNICAL INSTRUCTOR. Loadmaster School, Dallas, TX (2000-01). Recognized as an expert on technical issues, taught classes on the loading of aircraft and the calculations necessary to ensure safety of both the plane and its crew and passengers.

LOADING SUPERVISOR. Midway Airport, Chicago, IL (1999-00). Earned praise for my "meticulous attention to detail" while supervising and training several seven-person crews on loading, such as performing weight-and-balance computations, load planning, and inspections.

Highlights of military experience as a Loadmaster:
SUPERVISORY AIRCRAFT LOADMASTER. US Air Force, Japan (1996-99). Advanced to assist senior supervisors and personally oversee management and scheduling of up to 12 people; ensured quality control and conducted safety inspections of heavy equipment platforms and container delivery system bundles.
* Singled out to handle details of numerous multinational exercises and operations, provided support for such groups as Navy SEALS and Australian Special Air Services.

LOADMASTER SCHEDULER. McChord AFB, WA (1991-96). Coordinated/monitored schedules for more than 50 loadmasters while advising senior management officials on personnel issues or problems which would impact on performance.
* Developed a comprehensive computer tracking program of loadmaster status.

Highlights of other experience (1984-91): Advanced as a loadmaster and security specialist.

PERSONAL

Volunteered as a firefighter and worked with the Big Brothers Program and Special Olympics. Earned honors including five Air Force Commendation Medals and two AF Achievement Medals. Excellent references on request.

Exact Name of Person
Exact Title
Exact Name of Company
Address
City, State, Zip

LOADMASTER   Dear Exact Name of Person (or Dear Sir or Madam if answering a blind ad):

With this letter and the enclosed resume, I would like to express my interest in receiving consideration for employment opportunities within your organization.

As you will see from my resume, I have become known as an exceptional performer in my position as Aircraft Loadmaster at American Airlines. I am proud of my reputation as a professional who is dedicated to safety and total quality management objectives. In earlier positions while serving in the U.S. Air Force, I was selected for ever-increasing levels of managerial responsibilities because of my special skills related to managing resources for maximum productivity as well as my ability to develop and implement training designed to produce the most highly skilled employees.

As a Loadmaster Instructor, I provided strong leadership for staffing, training, and planning with the goal of ensuring that personnel provide error-free services for passengers and cargo. Shipments vary from a single box to multiple containers which require special loading to guarantee the proper placement according to precise weight-and-balance computations.

If you can use a versatile and detail-oriented professional with special knowledge of aircraft support operations such as load planning and scheduling, I hope you will call me soon for a brief discussion of how I could contribute to your organization. I can provide excellent professional and personal references at the appropriate time.

Sincerely,

Oscar E. Homer

OSCAR E. HOMER

1110½ Hay Street, Fayetteville, NC 28305 • preppub@aol.com • (910) 483-6611

OBJECTIVE	To offer specialized experience in cargo handling operations to an organization that can use my expertise in planning, arranging, and overseeing the safe placement of cargo and passengers.
SPECIAL SKILLS	Through experience and training, have developed thorough knowledge in such areas as: *customs representative for aircrews:* am knowledgeable of the proper procedures and ensuring compliance with all applicable customs regulations *cargo scheduler:* prepare schedules weeks in advance to eliminate conflicts *supervising people and motivating* them to complete the job quickly and safely

- Have logged 1,500 flight hours in fixed wing aircraft with 200 hours as an instructor.
- Was certified by the U.S. Air Force as an *Aircraft Load Planner.*
- Hold a Top Secret security clearance with SBI (Special Background Investigation).
- Offer special knowledge as an *Aircraft Loadmaster* for the Lockheed Martin C-141B.

EXPERIENCE	**AIRCRAFT LOADMASTER.** American Airlines, Los Angeles, CA (2001-present). Supervise on- and off-loading of cargo and up to 200 passengers onto aircraft with an emphasis on safety while ensuring cargo is balanced and properly placed in the aircraft.

- Became knowledgeable of a broad, diverse number of regulations, laws, and guidelines in order to ensure compliance with customs, agricultural, and immigration requirements.
- Learned applicable emergency exit procedures for in-flight and ground contingencies.
- Prepare detailed loading plans to include reviewing weight and balance records and determining the center of gravity for the aircraft so that safe limits were not exceeded.
- Prevented major damage to an aircraft by quickly assessing the situation after a cargo winch failed: safely completed downloading using alternate techniques.
- Assisted 50 passengers to safety when a #3 hydraulic accumulator valve ruptured in a cargo compartment.

Previous military experience as a Loadmaster:
LOADMASTER INSTRUCTOR. USAF, Scott AFB, IL(1996-2000). Selected in October 1996 on the basis of my self-motivation and ability to lead and motivate others, provided hands-on training for unqualified personnel and make certain they are thoroughly and properly trained.

- Advanced to this vital role ahead of my peers and became one of the youngest people to fill this position in the unit's history.

AIRDROP LOADMASTER. England (1995-96). Gained additional skills which earned me qualification to rig aircraft for proper dropping of personnel and cargo. Oversaw paratroopers as they prepared and exited the aircraft in order to guarantee their safety.

SCHEDULER. Pope AFB, NC and locations worldwide (1988-94). Was handpicked for numerous positions which involved scheduling and supervising up to 30 loadmasters each month in order to verify their qualifications and job knowledge. Used computers to maintain records and was cited for my superb management of details.

- Was singled out for my contributions during efforts to restore democracy in third world countries; safely airlifted millions of pounds of critical cargo.

EDUCATION & TRAINING	Am completing an A.A.S. degree from the Community College of the Air Force. Graduated at the top of the class in every phase of formal loadmaster training.
PERSONAL	Generously donate my time in my community. Excellent references.

OPERATIONS MANAGERS & TRAINING PROFESSIONALS

Date

Exact Name of Person
Title or Position
Name of Company
Address (no., street)
Address (city, state, zip)

Dear Exact Name of Person (or Dear Sir or Madam if answering a blind ad):

I would appreciate an opportunity to talk with you soon about how I could contribute to your organization through my managerial and supervisory experience as well as my proven ability to "sell" my knowledge to others through effective communication.

As you will see from my resume, I am presently serving my country in the U.S. Air Force. Throughout my career I have been involved in instructing employees in the highly specialized field of aircraft load planning. I feel that my success in this area has been due to my determination to constantly seek new and better ways to get things done. I consistently increased productivity in every organization where I worked through my ability to schedule for maximum utilization of available space.

I am a self-motivated hard worker with a reputation for superior planning skills and attention to detail. During the war in the Middle East I was handpicked for a critical role in setting up and running training and "refresher" courses for specialists in load planning. My organization kept 16 aircraft properly loaded and flying on schedule throughout the period of conflict. During the recent war on terrorism, I played a key role in directing load planning operations in Afghanistan.

I hope you will welcome my call soon to arrange a brief meeting at your convenience to discuss your current and future needs and how I might serve them. Thank you in advance for your time.

Sincerely yours,

Garth J. Rivers

Alternate last paragraph:
I hope you will call or write soon to suggest a time convenient for us to meet and discuss your current and future needs and how I might serve them. Thank you in advance for your time.

GARTH J. RIVERS

1110½ Hay Street, Fayetteville, NC 28305 • preppub@aol.com • (910) 483-6611

OBJECTIVE

I want to apply my management experience and sales "know-how" to an organization that can use an adaptable and energetic professional skilled in maximizing human and material resources through superior abilities as a planner, communicator, and instructor.

EXPERIENCE

OPERATIONS SCHEDULER and **CHIEF INSTRUCTOR**. U.S. Air Force, Pope AFB and Afghanistan (2000-present). Was specially selected in 2002 to serve as Supervising Loadmaster during special classified activities in Afghanistan which were related to the war on terrorism; have routinely handled a variety of operational functions ranging from training, to scheduling, to technical aspects of planning aircraft loads, keeping safety and security restrictions in mind.
- Instructed programs in the technical aspects of loading, securing, and operating aircraft aerial delivery systems.
- Prioritized work loads and assigned personnel in order to accomplish work in the most economical and timely fashion.
- Coordinated with other government agencies to ensure high-quality training for both air crews and ground support personnel.

TRAINING PROGRAM COORDINATOR/CHIEF INSTRUCTOR. USAF, Oman (1996-00). Handpicked on the basis of my proven expertise in load planning and providing instruction, established training for inexperienced personnel which prepared them for performing under combat conditions to provide support for allied personnel during the war in the Middle East. Accomplished the upgrading of four new personnel in minimum time.
- Worked under extreme pressure while planning flights on very short notice and kept 16 aircraft on schedule throughout the period of combat.
- Provided security for cargo, mail, and personnel by performing preflight and post flight inspections of air crew personnel.

CARGO HANDLING OPERATIONS SUPERVISOR. USAF, Clark AFB, NV (1993-95). Coordinated various aspects of aircraft loading and unloading operations including the use of material handling equipment, preparation and inspection of air delivery cargo, and ensuring all steps were completed in checklists of proper procedures.
- Increased productivity through improvements to standard procedures for transporting material handling equipment to and from operational areas.

INSPECTOR and **SENIOR CARGO HANDLING SUPERVISOR**. USAF, Germany (1991-93). Selected to attend several advanced training programs on the basis of my performance, contributed my expertise while inspecting aerial delivery loads, training new employees, and supervising loading and unloading operations at one of the military's largest and busiest overseas passenger and cargo terminals.
- Earned certification in hazardous cargo handling, air drop inspection, C-130 aircraft inspection procedures, and effective instruction techniques.

Highlights of other USAF experience: Gained experience related to providing formal classroom instruction, repairing avionics, and moving cargo and personnel safely and rapidly.

EDUCATION

Associate's degree in Aerospace Management, Community College of the Air Force, 1992.

PERSONAL

Have a reputation for constantly seeking improvement and always giving my best — no matter what the job. Hold a Top Secret security clearance. Will relocate.

Mr. Jack W. Smith
Lockheed, Inc.
PO Box 44444
Dallas, TX, 44330

**PRODUCT TEST
DIRECTOR**

Dear Mr. Smith:

I would appreciate an opportunity to talk with you soon about how I could contribute to your organization through my expertise in planning and conducting Special Operations training, my extensive experience in Mideast affairs and culture, and my versatile technical knowledge and competence.

Please be assured that I am available for relocation worldwide immediately, and I will provide outstanding personal and professional references upon your request. I am particularly interested in the job as Product Test Director with the Lockheed organization.

As you will see from my resume, while serving my country I have worked at the highest levels of government while involved in product testing of aviation products. I speak Arabic, Egyptian, German, Spanish, and French, and I hold a Top Secret security clearance with SBI. I offer expert knowledge of military contracting procedures, diving and scuba operations, navigation and demolitions, as well as marine and optical and airborne/parachute equipment.

With a reputation as an outstanding communicator, I have excelled as a Special Forces instructor and I have written Special Operations policies and procedures related to a wide variety of areas. I am skilled at all aspects of planning training and authoring training doctrine. You would find me to be a resourceful manager and problem-solver who is known as a thoroughly honest, adaptable, and versatile professional.

I hope you will contact me soon to suggest a time when we might meet in person to discuss your needs and goals and how I might serve them. Thank you in advance for your time.

Yours sincerely,

Micah V. Pure

MICAH V. PURE

1110½ Hay Street, Fayetteville, NC 28305   •   preppub@aol.com   •   (910) 483-6611

OBJECTIVE

To benefit an organization that can use a resourceful manager and problem-solver who offers expertise in testing and fielding new equipment, designing and implementing new systems, and managing the change of physical assets and operating procedures.

EXPERIENCE

PRODUCT TEST DIRECTOR. U.S. Army, Washington, DC (2001-present). Am considered the technical expert on matters related to airborne and parachute operation; also assist in assuring the technical proficiency of underwater and waterborne operations.

- Wrote a regulation for Army personnel on airborne operations that defines standard operating procedures used worldwide.
- Authored policies for Special Operations for all branches of the service.
- Developed a Jumpmaster Guide for the Army's Special Operations.
- Have earned a reputation as an exceptional technical writer: produced major changes to airborne operations and parachute operations regulations.

STUDENT, EXECUTIVE DEVELOPMENT PROGRAM. U.S. Army Sergeants Major Academy, Ft. Bliss, TX (2001). Graduated in the top 10% of the class from the highest-level military school for enlisted officers; this graduate-level school is designed to refine the management abilities of the Army's "best and brightest" mid-level managers.

GENERAL MANAGER. U.S. Army Special Forces, Ft. Campbell, KY (1998-00). In this Sergeant Major position, supervised a 110-person Special Forces company, and directed the involvement of this company in the war in the Middle East.

OPERATIONS MANAGER. U.S. Army Special Forces, Ft. Campbell, KY (1994-97). Directed the often-classified activities of a Special Forces "A" team during special projects in Jordan, Egypt, and Saudi Arabia.

INSTRUCTOR SUPERVISOR. U.S. Army Special Warfare Center, Ft. Bragg, NC (1990-93). Designed major changes in the program of instruction related to construction, civil actions, and demolitions while excelling as an instructor of Special Forces engineering.

- Taught more than 1,000 people during three years.

Other U.S. Army experience: Was singled out for rapid promotion while distinguishing myself academically and professionally: was named "Soldier of the Year" for the 3rd Armored Division, 1997, and was "Distinguished Graduate" of the NCO Course, 1991.

**SPECIAL
SKILLS
&
KNOWLEDGE**

<u>Languages</u>: Speak Arabic, Egyptian, German, Spanish, and French
<u>Clearance</u>: Top Secret security clearance with SBI
<u>Computers</u>: Use software including Word and PowerPoint
<u>Military contracting</u>: Expert knowledge of how Department of Defense buys equipment
<u>Piloting</u>: FAA certified Private Pilot, single-engine land
<u>Navigation and demolitions</u>: Am a demolitions instructor; proficient with navigation aids

EDUCATION

Completed four years of college-level training in management, electrical engineering, technical military subjects, business, and other areas; Del Mar College and Lamar University.

PERSONAL

Am known as a thoroughly honest, resourceful, adaptable, and versatile professional. Believe in leadership by example and am proud of the young people I have mentored.

Exact Name of Person
Exact Title
Exact Name of Company
Address
City, State, Zip

QUALITY CONTROL
INSPECTOR

Dear Exact Name of Person (or Dear Sir or Madam if answering a blind ad):

With the enclosed resume, I would like to make you aware of my interest in exploring employment opportunities within your organization.

In my most recent position at Atlanta Airport in Georgia, I was singled out as playing a major role in earning the airport's reputation for maintenance excellence and efficiency. As Training Manager, I supervised training for 25 maintenance managers and oversaw up to 40 people involved in performing aircraft maintenance.

In a previous assignment at Delta Airlines in California, I was rapidly promoted to Assistant Shop Chief in charge of fourteen maintenance personnel while handling numerous other responsibilities. As hazardous waste monitor, I provided oversight for the safe handling and disposition of chemicals and other materials.

As you will see from my resume, I offer knowledge and experience in numerous areas. Originally trained as an Aircraft Mechanic, I was subsequently trained in hazardous waste management, quality assurance, safety, and automated inventory control. I was selected for leadership and management training and, upon graduation from Airman Leadership School, I received the award given to the graduate who was "most outstanding in academic testing, performance evaluations, and demonstrated leadership as determined by student and faculty votes."

I am proficient in using automated systems for inventory ordering and control, and I have become skilled at obtaining hard-to-locate parts.

I hope you will contact me to suggest a time when we might meet in person to discuss your needs. I can provide excellent references.

Sincerely,

Larry French

LARRY FRENCH

1110½ Hay Street, Fayetteville, NC 28305 • preppub@aol.com • (910) 483-6611

OBJECTIVE   To benefit an organization that can use a versatile background which includes extensive technical training, personnel training and supervision, operations management, and inventory control.

EDUCATION   **College:** Two years of college courses, Claremont Community College, Claremont, CA, 1994-95.
Technical: Completed Aircraft Maintenance and Repair Course, Wichita Falls, TX, 1993.
- Subsequently completed Hazardous Waste Management Training which covered fire and safety procedures, handling and transportation, record keeping, and contingency planning.
- Extensive training in The Quality Concept, including process evaluation and improvement.
- Received more than twelve Certificates of Training from schools covering subjects including the F-15E Engine Run Qualification Course and aircraft maintenance training.

Leadership: Completed Airman Leadership School, Cannon AFB, NM, 1991.
- Received the John L. Levitow Award presented to the individual in the graduating class who is *"most outstanding in academic testing, performance evaluations, and demonstrated leadership as determined by student and faculty votes."*

Computers: Utilize database and customized automated inventory systems; Excel; Word.

EXPERIENCE   **QUALITY CONTROL INSPECTOR & CREW CHIEF.** Atlanta Airport, Atlanta, GA (2000-present). Played a key role in producing this airport's reputation for maintenance excellence as well as its efficiency.
- Through my management ability and relentless attention to detail, played a key role in achieving outstanding results on several rigorous departmental inspections.
- As Training Manager, supervised training for 25 maintenance managers.
- Supervised up to 40 people involved in aircraft maintenance; trained aircraft technicians in technical troubleshooting as well as in safety and quality control.
- Became known for resourcefulness in locating hard-to-obtain parts and equipment.
- Passed all quality control inspections with "flying colors."

SAFETY COORDINATOR & ASSISTANT SHOP CHIEF. Delta Airlines, Claremont, CA (1997-00). Began as an Aircraft Mechanic and was promoted to Assistant Shop Chief; supervised 14 people and was in charge of ordering, receiving, and controlling a multimillion-dollar inventory of equipment and supplies which supported a fleet of airplanes.
- Was Training Manager for the shop, supervising the scheduling of training.
- Supervised 14 mechanics.
- Acted as hazardous waste monitor and oversaw the safe handling and disposition of grease chemicals, cleaning fluids, byproducts and other materials.
- Provided oversight for hazardous waste storage and disposition; maintained excellent records according to strict OSHA and EPA standards.

MAINTENANCE TECHNICIAN. Lockheed-Martin, Riverside, CA (1995-97). Was personally singled out by management for my expert management of the CORE automated maintenance system, a database of every maintenance activity performed within the department.
- Supervised 20 aircraft mechanics as well as 6 other technicians.
- Utilized an automated maintenance system to control a multimillion-dollar inventory.

Military experience: Served in the U.S. Air Force; advanced to Quality Control Inspector.

PERSONAL   Excellent personal and professional references on request. Highly motivated and reliable.

OPERATIONS MANAGERS & TRAINING PROFESSIONALS

SCOTT M. ALLEN

1110½ Hay Street, Fayetteville, NC 28305

preppub@aol.com　　•　　(910) 483-6611

OBJECTIVE

To offer a reputation as a mechanically adept professional known for the ability to quickly and easily master new procedures, concepts, and equipment.

QUALITY CONTROL TECHNICAL INSPECTOR

EXPERIENCE

QUALITY CONTROL SHOP SUPERVISOR and **HELICOPTER TECHNICAL INSPECTOR.** U.S. Army, Afghanistan. (2002-present). Handpicked for the vital role of Quality Control (QC) Shop Supervisor, performed technical and shop inspections as well as monitoring QC maintenance programs for 24 OH-58D(I) Kiowa Warrior helicopters.
- Supervise six Technical Inspectors; reorganized the QC Shop.
- Initiated a Corrosion Control Program for 24 aircraft, and conducted technical training programs related to maintenance, supply, and safety techniques.
- Maintained operational readiness rates above 80% despite rugged conditions, including high altitude, which interfered with proper functioning of the helicopters.

HELICOPTER REPAIR TECHNICIAN. U.S. Army, Ft. Campbell, KY (1995-00). Supervised and evaluated the performance of eight subordinates while overseeing maintenance activities and service scheduling on eight helicopters valued in excess of $32 million; gained expertise in maintaining the following helicopters:

OH58D(I) Kiowa Warrior	OH-58C
UH-60E Blackhawk	AH-64C Apache

- Cited by technical inspectors and test pilots as "one of the best repairmen ever seen."
- Maintained and accounted for in excess of $32 million worth of assets.
- Specially selected as Communications NCO responsible for the initial set-up of the aviation company's Tactical Operations Center, became highly proficient in the use of UHF, VHF, and SINCGAR radios; maintained perfect accountability of $155,000 worth of secure communications equipment.
- Provided technical support for the Army's only qualified attack helicopter unit.

EDUCATION & TRAINING

A.A. degree in General Studies from Central Texas College, 1997.
Completed executive development courses in management and supervision.
Excelled in the following technical training programs sponsored by the U.S. Army:
BNCOC: Learned skills of advanced leadership and perfected my technical inspection procedures for Army Aviation while maintaining a 94% average and excelling in positions as a platoon sergeant and squad leader; received written praise for my "exception leadership skills" and "unparalleled motivational abilities and contribution to group work."
Army Combat Lifesaver Course: Completed training in first aid and medical procedures including initiating an intravenous infusion; this knowledge permitted me to save a soldier's life who had lost consciousness due to

dehydration.

OH-58D Helicopter Repairer Course: Assisted instructors in teaching maintenance procedures for the Kiowa Warrior aircraft.

PLDC: Refined my leadership, supervisory, and management skills.

OH-58A/C Helicopter Repair: Acquired basic skills in helicopter repair.

CERTIFICATION   **FAA Airframe and Power Plant** mechanic's rating, License #838383838.

SPECIAL
SKILLS
Perform maintenance and inspections on both airframe and power plant systems of three different types of Army aircraft with specific expertise as follows:

Performed maintenance on the following aircraft: AH-64C, OH-58 A/C, OH-58D(I), and UH-60E

- *Experienced in performing airframe procedures which include:*
  sheet metal fabrication and repair; composite repair
  non-destructive testing and evaluation
- *Troubleshooting, servicing, and maintenance of:*
  pneudraulics, rotor systems, transmissions, power trains, electrical systems, landing gear, aircraft instruments, and environmental control systems
- *Power plant expertise includes:*
  engine removal, disassembly, inspection, and re-installation
  removal and replacement of mounts
  engine alignments and vibration analysis
  combustion and compressor section disassembly and inspection
  inlet guide vane inspection and repair
  scheduled services on various types of engines
  replacement of ignition exciter boxes, wire harnesses, and temperature probes
  adjustment, removal, and replacement of fuel controls, liner actuators, droop compensators, HMUs, and ECUs
  performance of engine borescope and hot-end inspections
  troubleshooting, servicing, and maintenance of engine utility systems
- *Inspection expertise includes experience with the following:*
  UH60E Blackhawk Helicopter
  Engine T-700-GE-700 turbine and Allison T703-AD-700 turbine
  Garett Turbine CPs6-50(H) (AGPU)
  Auxiliary Gas Turbine Engine on Blackhawk T-62T-40-1
  TSS-L-712 turbine and GE T700-701 turbine
  Engine Vibration Balance kit
  Rotary Vibration Analysis by Scientific America
  High Pressure Nitrogen servicing on air oil struts, Apache and Blackhawk helicopters

HONORS
Earned several medals and awards, including but not limited to the following, in recognition of my "meritorious achievements and expertise":

Army Achievement Medal for *making a direct impact on my unit's success during the war against terrorism in Afghanistan,* 2001

Army Achievement Medal for *outstanding service during an external evaluation: cited for "exemplary performance of duty which helped set a new and higher standard,"* 1994

CLEARANCE   Entrusted with a Secret security clearance.

COMPUTERS   Program in BASIC, Pascal, and FORTRAN; use Microsoft Excel, Windows, and PowerPoint

LANGUAGE   Fluent in Spanish; have a U.S. Army interpreter's rating.

PERSONAL   Non-smoker. Excellent physical condition. 27 years old. Native of California.

Exact Name of Person
Title or Position
Name of Company
Address (no., street)
Address (city, state, zip)

QUALITY CONTROL
INSPECTOR

Dear Exact Name of Person (or Dear Sir or Madam if answering a blind ad):

I would appreciate an opportunity to talk with you soon about how I could contribute to your organization through my excellent technical electronics skills, expertise in trouble-shooting and fault isolation, and supervisory abilities.

You will see from my resume that I offer a strong background of accomplishments. With eight years of experience with synthetic aperture systems and five with infrared and laser targeting, I am current with state-of-the-art electronics.

I enjoy a challenge and feel that I could make important contributions in new system development projects through the combination of my "hands-on" technical skills and quality control experience. My working knowledge extends to microwave test and diagnostic equipment as well as the standard electronics test equipment and I have good soldering skills.

My communication skills, both verbal and written, have been described as "precise and informational." I have contributed my knowledge while rewriting technical orders and procedures and have written operational instructions and maintenance awareness bulletins which have been accepted and adopted for use worldwide.

I hope you will welcome my call soon to arrange a brief meeting at your convenience to discuss your current and future needs and how I might serve them. Thank you in advance for your time.

Sincerely yours,

Martin W. Zikorsky

Alternate last paragraph:
I hope you will call or write me soon to suggest a time convenient for us to meet and discuss your current and future needs and how I might serve them. Thank you in advance for your time.

MARTIN W. ZIKORSKY

1110½ Hay Street, Fayetteville, NC 28305   •   preppub@aol.com   •   (910) 483-6611

OBJECTIVE

To apply my excellent technical electronics skills and troubleshooting abilities for an organization that can use my experience in maintenance, production, and quality control.

TECHNICAL EXPERTISE

- Troubleshoot and repair to the component level, radar and targeting sensors on the Low Altitude Navigation and Targeting Infrared for Night (LANTIRN) system manufactured by Martin Marietta Electronic Systems, the Advanced Synthetic Aperture Radar System (ASARS2) by Hughes Aircraft, and the CAPRE radar system by Goodyear Aerospace.
- Operate test equipment including: Hewlett Packard 54111D digitizing oscilloscope, 438A average power meter, and 70000 spectrum analyzers; Tektronix 1240 logic analyzer; Racal Dana universal counter; Fluke multimeters; Wavetek 8501 peak power meter.
- Program the DEC PDP 11/44 computer in FORTRAN, Assembler, and Basic languages.
- Can troubleshoot the DEC Microvax II to the circuit card level.
- Offer technical writing experience which has included rewriting technical orders and procedures and writing maintenance operating instructions and maintenance awareness bulletins.

EDUCATION

A.A.S., Avionics, Community College of the Air Force, 1988.

TRAINING

Excelled in more than 800 hours of technical and leadership training including:
    LANTIRN advanced maintenance — 190 hours
    ASARS2 advanced maintenance — 172 hours
    leadership and human relations — 160 hours
    advanced management and leadership — 240 hours

EXPERIENCE

QUALITY CONTROL INSPECTOR. General Dynamics, Los Angeles, CA (2000-present). Evaluated as an "exceptional" performer and "outstanding technician," was selected for the critical job of inspecting avionics maintenance personnel and recommended corrective actions.
- Played a "vital role" on an F-100 jet engine inspection which resulted in the development of findings which significantly reduced engine downtime and aircraft abort rates.
- Developed a more effective system of reporting defective parts.
- Prevented LANTIRN pod access panel damage by correcting faulty procedures.
- Wrote an electrical safety guidelines bulletin for maintenance personnel.

PRODUCTION SUPERVISOR. General Dynamics, Los Angeles, CA (1998-00). Was consistently sought out for my "technical expertise" and "exceptionally effective leadership" while involved in prioritizing work flow and directing/controlling repairs in support of the LANTIRN systems for F-15 and F-16 aircraft.
- Brought about a 20% production increase and a "complete turnaround" in morale.
- Developed a method for recovering a coolant which resulted in first-year savings of $32,800 and eliminated environmental hazards.

Highlights of U.S. Air Force career: Served as a **PRODUCTION SUPERVISOR** (1995-97) in maintenance operations; **SUPERVISORY RADAR SYSTEMS SPECIALIST** (1992-94), and **AVIONICS TECHNICIAN** (1988-94).

PERSONAL

Earned numerous awards and medals including three commendation medals and the Southwest Asia Service Medal for service in support of the war in the Middle East.

Date

Exact Name of Person
Exact Title
Exact Name of Company
Address
City, State, Zip

**QUALITY CONTROL
INSPECTOR**

Dear Exact Name of Person (or Dear Sir or Madam if answering a blind ad):

With the enclosed resume I would like to introduce you to a highly motivated and technically proficient professional who offers versatile experience in jobs requiring a high level of attention to detail and the ability to work independently while also overseeing team efforts.

My greatest strengths are my initiative, ability to handle pressure and deadlines, and capacity for dedicating my efforts to solve problems and exceed management expectations. Selected to receive extensive and advanced training, I have earned respect for my expertise in aircraft quality control and Non-Destructive Inspection (NDI) procedures. Having advanced to supervise five subordinates, I oversee support for A-10 and C-130 aircraft while employing the latest high-tech analytical methods to detect problems so they can be corrected and aircraft quickly returned to service.

My Air Force experience helped me develop strong skills in supply operations as well as in utilizing automated systems to maintain records and documentation. While working in these areas of operations, I have been credited with making significant contributions which reduced the time needed to procure critical parts as well as the downtime of aircraft because of delays in obtaining parts.

If you can use an adaptable self starter who will not give up until a problem is solved and a workable solution in place, please call or write me soon to suggest a time when we might have a brief discussion of how I could contribute to your organization. I will provide excellent professional and personal references at the appropriate time.

Sincerely,

Frances Simmons

FRANCES SIMMONS

1110½ Hay Street, Fayetteville, NC 28305   •   preppub@aol.com   •   (910) 483-6611

OBJECTIVE

To offer excellent technical skills and knowledge to an organization that can use a self-motivated professional with a high level of initiative and drive along with dedication to producing excellent results during critical aircraft quality control and inspection activities.

EDUCATION & TRAINING

Pursuing a Bachelor's degree, Minot State University, Minot, ND; 3.6 GPA.

Excelled in U.S. Air Force leadership school as well as in technical schools and extensive on-the-job training for specialists in Non-Destructive Inspection (NDI) aircraft maintenance.

TECHNICAL EXPERTISE

Equipment: Operate/troubleshoot technical equipment which includes: FAS 2C spectromer; Spectrom, Spectro Jr., and Lorad x-ray units; magnetic particle machines; penetrant lines, USN 50 ultrasound machines; and 19 E II, Hocking, and Nortec 2000 machines.

Computers: Operate a wide variety of computer programs used for record keeping and documentation of quality control and supply operations.

Aircraft: Work on B-1B, C-130, A-10, KC-135, C-141 and C-17 aircraft and TF-34 engines; perform oil analysis on F-15 and F-16 engines.

EXPERIENCE

Have earned a reputation as a skilled professional with an eye for detail and dedication to ensuring safety and quality of multimillion-dollar aircraft, USAF:

SUPERVISORY QUALITY CONTROL INSPECTOR. Luke AFB, AZ (2001-present). Credited with performing at a level "head and shoulders above" my peers, have saved the Air Force in excess of $3.5 million by applying technical expertise leading to early detection of cracks which can then be repaired and aircraft quickly returned to service.

- Support A-10 and C-130 aircraft while supervising as many as five people.
- Run the Joint Oil Analysis Program (JOAP) lab: processed more than 500 samples with no flight cancellations due to oil-related metal wear and problems.
- Interpret and evaluate indications of defects in aircraft, support equipment, components, and pressurized systems using a wide range of industrial radiography, ultrasonic, eddy current magnetic particle, and fluorescent dye penetrant methods.
- Utilize the Process Control Automated Management System (PCAMS) to document each stage of the procedures; establish and monitor radiation areas; am a certified Hazardous Material Handler.
- Completed a project inspecting C-130 satellite communications antenna airframe mounts ahead of schedule which allowed a large-scale joint services exercise to proceed on time.

NDI APPRENTICE. Beale AFB, CA (1997-01). Evaluated as an "exceptional performer," performed the full range of penetrant, magnetic, ultrasound, eddy current, and x-ray inspections of B-1B and C-130 aircraft and aerospace ground equipment.

- Developed and implemented procedures which improved supply requisitioning and accounting records maintenance 60%; reduced inventory maintenance 30% by creating a new hazardous material ordering and tracking system for 22 critical items.

SUPPLY TECHNICIAN. McGuire AFB, CA (1993-96). Awarded an Achievement Medal and evaluated as a diligent and detail-oriented professional who made significant contributions, solved supply problems, monitored repair parts processing documentation and records while inputting changes, deletions, and additions to maintenance records.

- Revitalized an Awaiting Parts (AWP) programs and cut both the number of sidelined aircraft and period of time required to get the parts in half.

PERSONAL

Secret security clearance. Am a hard worker who gets results. Excellent references.

Date

Exact Name of Person
Exact Title
Exact Name of Company
Address
City, State, Zip

**RESEARCH &
DEVELOPMENT
COORDINATOR**

Dear Exact Name of Person (or Dear Sir or Madam if answering a blind ad):

I am in the process of relocating to your area and would like to express my interest in exploring employment opportunities with your organization. As you will see, I have served my country with distinction in the U.S. Air Force and advanced rapidly in rank ahead of my peers. Although I was strongly encouraged to remain in military service and assured of continued rapid advancement, I decided to leave the military and enter the civilian work force.

While earning rapid promotion, I was selected for some of the U.S. Air Force's most advanced technical training programs and leadership development courses, which helped me acquire versatile knowledge in a wide range of areas. As a Project Manager, I traveled worldwide in order to apply my technical expertise and management abilities, and I made significant contributions to numerous vital projects and activities. I helped a team during the planning and implemented of a project which saved thousands of dollars during a 90-day project by recovering and renovating special mission equipment. On another occasion, I contributed ideas which averted multimillion-dollar costs on boat engines. I routinely worked with military and civilian professionals of the U.S. as well as foreign governments and frequently trained and cross-trained other employees. I have earned respect as an articulate and persuasive communicator.

In a special project for the U.S. State Department, I conducted airfield surveys in a hazardous environment which expedited the return of U.S. military members' remains. I excelled at walking into new environments where it was my job to quickly assume responsibility for solving problems and producing quality results.

I hold one of the nation's highest security clearances: Top Secret SCI. With an aptitude for easily mastering new bodies of knowledge, I have earned certifications as an air traffic controller, diver and diving supervisor, military freefall parachutist and jumpmaster, and weapons expert.

I hope you will contact me soon to suggest a time we might meet to discuss how my unlimited personal initiative and ability to quickly become a valuable part of a team, would allow me to contribute to your organization. I can provide excellent professional and personal references. Thank you in advance for your consideration.

Sincerely,

Fred N. Lerner

FRED N. LERNER

1110½ Hay Street, Fayetteville, NC 28305   •   preppub@aol.com   •   (910) 483-6611

OBJECTIVE

To contribute to team efforts as a versatile young professional with strong leadership and management skills who possesses proven communication and team-building abilities and a broad base of technical knowledge used in problem-solving and project management.

EDUCATION & TRAINING

Pursuing Associate's Degree, Community College of the Air Force.
Excelled in U.S. Air Force training programs related to leadership and technical subjects.

EXPERIENCE

Advanced to the rank of Staff Sergeant ahead of peers while building a reputation as a self-motivated professional with unlimited personal initiative in the U.S. Air Force:
RESEARCH & DEVELOPMENT COORDINATOR. The Pentagon, Washington, DC (2000-present). Specially selected for a job in research and development, am making contributions to the development of new, improved equipment for the U.S. military.

PROJECT MANAGER. Scott AFB, IL (1996-2000). Developed, tested, and integrated equipment/procedures into daily operations; adapted to various challenges worldwide while applying management ability and technical knowledge. Participated in search-and-rescue operations. Worked under pressure to establish/control zones for air landing or air dropping personnel and equipment into hostile territory; utilized communications for navigating, developing ground-to-air/point-to-point communications, and obtaining weather information.
Highlights of selected achievements:
- **Formulated and implemented a plan** for saving thousands of dollars and produced significant bottom-line savings recovering lost equipment during a 90-day project.
- **Contributed ideas** praised for their "seamless" integration into new communications packages.
- **Stepped in and solved a long-standing problem** – developed measures which averted multimillion-dollar costs on boat engines by switching to a less expensive but more dependable product.
- Despite being junior in rank to 90% of participants in a first-of-its-kind training project, **provided planning leadership** which resulted in an "Outstanding" rating.

AIR TRAFFIC CONTROLLER. Luke AFB, AZ (1992-96). Handled activities including air traffic control services, measuring and reporting on weather conditions, gathering and reporting intelligence data, and neutralizing unexploded ordnance to provide a safe landing zone for parachutists in often-hostile areas throughout the world.
Highlights of selected achievements:
- **Displayed exceptional initiative** by inventorying, labeling, packing, and centralizing vital supply packages and establishing a method to improve the rate of distribution and deployment.
- Provided valuable input that impacted on the development of improvements to aircraft design while acting as a test parachutist.
- Honored for **"distinguished performance" as the primary communications link between Army and Air Force** during a large-scale airfield assault exercise.
- **Assisted the U.S. State Department as a Special Projects Officer:** conducted surveys in a hazardous environment which expedited the return of U.S. military members' remains.

PERSONAL

Numerous military honors included the Joint Service and Air Force Commendation Medals, AF Achievement and Outstanding Unit and the National Defense Service Medals.

Exact Name of Person
Exact Title
Exact Name of Company
Address
City, State, Zip

SAFETY OFFICER

Dear Exact Name of Person (or Dear Sir or Madam if answering a blind ad):

With the enclosed resume, I would like to make you aware of my interest in the position as Safety Engineer, Job Code DZZHP4647.

As you will see from my enclosed resume, I have excelled in a track record of accomplishment as an Aviation Safety Officer with the U.S. Army. Because of my safety expertise, I have earned promotion to the rank of Chief Warrant Officer 4 and have been recommended for promotion to CW5. I have decided, however, that I would like to leave the U.S. Army and embark upon a career in aviation safety with a civilian organization.

I began my career in aviation safety as an Aviator and then performed with distinction in jobs as an Aircraft Maintenance Technician, Maintenance Test Pilot, and—more recently—Aviation Safety Officer. In my current position as Aviation Safety Officer in Afghanistan, I coordinate work safety, aviation product safety, accident prevention, as well as compliance with federal regulations. I have developed accident-prevention safety programs related to aviation maintenance, hazardous material storage and handling, as well as radiation commodity storage and handling. In my previous position as Aviation Safety Officer, I reduced ground accidents by 50% while organizing pre-accident plans, writing safety standard operating procedures, and implementing environmental clean-up operations. In a previous position, I created a new radiation protection program for nondestructive X-ray equipment which became a model for the parent organization. I also transformed a hangar described as a "hazardous material disaster" into a facility exhibiting a high degree of environmental awareness.

Considered one of the nation's leading aviation safety authorities, I have served as an official U.S. Army Accident Investigation Board member. I have worked with aviation officials all over the world as well as with the officials of major companies including Sikorsky, Boeing, GE, and Lockheed Martin.

You will notice from my resume that, in addition to my extensive training and certifications, I hold two master's degrees: one in Aviation/Aerospace Safety and the other in Airline Operations. I am held in the highest regard in the international aviation community and can provide outstanding references at the appropriate time.

Sincerely,

Brian B. Denning

BRIAN B. DENNING

1110½ Hay Street, Fayetteville, NC 28305   •   preppub@aol.com   •   (910) 483-6611

OBJECTIVE

To contribute to an organization that can use a highly skilled aviation safety professional who offers experience in providing analysis and recommendations related to aircraft damage prevention strategies, developing safety programs, conducting investigations of mishaps, analyzing trends, and preparing economic and financial reports.

EDUCATION

Master of Aeronautical Science in Aviation/Aerospace Safety, Embry-Riddle University, Daytona Beach, FL, 2002; **Master of Aeronautical Science in Airline Operations,** Embry-Riddle University, 2002.
B.S. in Biology, minor in Chemistry, Regent College, Syracuse, NY, 1982.

TRAINING

Aviation Safety Officer Course	Technical Transportation of Hazardous Material
Radiological Safety Training	Aviation Accident Prevention Management
Maintenance Manager	Test Pilot Apache
Attack Helicopter Apache Pilot	Aviation Senior Officer
Maintenance Manager/Test Pilot	Attack Helicopter AH-1 Cobra Pilot
Helicopter Flight Training	

EXPERIENCE

Have excelled in a track record of promotion to Chief Warrant Officer 4 (CW4) while becoming one of the foremost safety experts, U.S. Army; recommended for promotion to CW5:
AVIATION SAFETY OFFICER. Afghanistan (2002-present). Manage ground and aviation safety for 650 individuals and 240 aircraft; coordinate programs related to worker safety, aviation product safety, accident prevention, as well as compliance with local, state, and federal regulations.

- Developed numerous accident-prevention safety programs including programs related to aviation maintenance, hazardous material storage and handling, as well as radiation commodity storage and handling.
- Provided expert testimony and safety engineering case management in aviation accident and mishap investigation; I am skilled at accident reconstruction and analysis to determine cause and suggest solutions.

QUALITY CONTROL LEADER & AVIATION SAFETY OFFICER. Washington, DC (1995-01). For two separate organizations with hundreds of employees, managed the safety program, hazardous materials program, radiation safety program, and quality assurance.

- On my own initiative, created and implemented a new radiation protection program for nondestructive X-ray equipment which became a model for the parent organization.
- Through my hazardous materials knowledge, transformed a hangar described as a "hazardous material disaster" into a facility exhibiting environmental awareness.

Highlights of other U.S. Army experience: Excelled in these "building block" jobs while acquiring knowledge and skills essential to becoming an aviation safety expert.
MAINTENANCE TEST PILOT. Europe.. Maintained five AH-64 attack helicopters while performing as a test pilot and maintenance test pilot.
AH-64 AIRCRAFT MAINTENANCE TECHNICIAN. Refined my expertise in working with weight and balance documents as well as maintenance manuals and publications while also performing as **Night Vision System Pilot-in-Command.**

CERTIFICATIONS & LICENSES

FAA Airline Transport Pilot (BH 206)
Commercial/Instrument Pilot & Certified Flight Instructor, multiengine airplane & helicopter.
Airplane and Powerplant mechanic, license number 123586430

OPERATIONS MANAGERS & TRAINING PROFESSIONALS

Date

Exact Name of Person
Exact Title
Exact Name of Company
Address
City, State, Zip

Dear Exact Name of Person (or Dear Sir or Madam if answering a blind ad):

I would appreciate the opportunity to talk with you soon about how I could contribute to your organization through my experience in the aviation field.

As you will see from my resume, I have completed approximately seven-and-a-half years in operations resource management. Most recently assigned as an Airspace Scheduling Manager at Kennedy Airport in New York, I was consistently singled out for my initiative, drive, and attention to detail. In this job I worked on a routine basis with numerous governmental agencies while coordinating airspace requirements and maximizing the utilization of the facilities available at Kennedy.

In earlier positions as a Flight Records Technician and Flight Operations Technician, I applied the same qualities and high standards and received recognition for operational efficiency and performance.

Highly computer literate, I am proficient with Windows, Excel, and Word. In every position I have held, I have been credited with applying analytical skills, initiative, and a results-oriented approach to find methods of getting the work done faster and with greater efficiency. My accomplishments have included creating new Air Movement Table procedures which saved thousands of man-hours annually, correcting deficiencies in a database which allowed accuracy to improve to 95%, and managing a communications security program which received "excellent" ratings.

I hope you will welcome my call soon when I try to arrange a brief meeting to discuss your goals and how my background might serve your needs. I can provide outstanding references at the appropriate time.

Sincerely,

Adam Hensley

ADAM HENSLEY

1110½ Hay Street, Fayetteville, NC 28305　　•　　preppub@aol.com　　•　　(910) 483-6611

OBJECTIVE

To contribute to an organization that can use a versatile professional offering outstanding managerial skills and in-depth knowledge of dispatching and scheduling, production operations, automated system applications and operations, and resource management.

EDUCATION

Completed two years of college course work, Aviation Technology, Northwest Technical College, Bemidji, MN; pursuing completion of degree in my spare time.

Completed training which included Quality Awareness and Quality Leadership courses as well as leadership school and a six-week program in technical forms processing.

CLEARANCE

Top Secret security clearance with SBI

TECHNICAL KNOWLEDGE

Highly computer literate, am proficient with Windows, Excel, and Word.

Offer additional skills with FM, VHF, and UHF radios and procedures including dispatching and flight scheduling.

EXPERIENCE

SCHEDULING MANAGER. Kennedy Airport, New York, NY (2001-present). Cited for my analytical skills and initiative, excelled in handling the details of scheduling flights and ensuring safe and effective use of airspace.

- Produced drafts and final copies of Air Movement Tables (AMTs).
- Became extremely knowledgeable of a complex variety of regulations, procedures, rules, and operations orders including Jeppesen Airway Manuals.
- Resolved issues with air traffic controllers and the FAA to ensure adequate staffing and resource availability.
- Created new AMT procedures which saved thousands of man-hours annually.

FLIGHT RECORDS TECHNICIAN. O'Hare Airport, Chicago, IL (1998-01). Evaluated as a fast learner with a positive and professional manner, controlled flight and pay records for 1,600 people to including inputting data into an automated system.

- Collected, audited, and monitored data on flying time, medical recommendations, physiological training, and aviation service information on flight crews.
- Audited computer listings and corrected deficiencies in the database; as a result, database accuracy improved to 95%.

FLIGHT OPERATIONS TECHNICIAN. Delta Airlines, Atlanta, GA (1992-97). Scheduled flight operations for more than hundreds of pilots and aircraft weekly to include collecting and auditing data both manually and using an automated system.

- Prepared written flight authorizations and flying schedules; compared allocated flight hours with maintenance requirements.
- Played an important role in revising a ground training program which resulted in a 30% reduction in scheduling conflicts and enhanced the effectiveness of training ground service equipment (GSE) operators.
- Managed a communications security program which received "excellent" ratings and was described by a senior manager as "the best it's been in recent memory."

PERSONAL

As the son of a pilot and A&P Mechanic, grew up in an aviation background. Earned honors including the Southwest Asia Service, an AF Achievement, and two Commendation Medals. Enhance my knowledge through extensive reading of aviation magazines. Secret clearance.

Date

Exact Name of Person
Title or Position
Name of Company
Address (no., street)
Address (city, state, zip)

SUPPORT OPERATIONS DIRECTOR

Dear Exact Name of Person (or Dear Sir or Madam if answering a blind ad):

Can you use a proven professional who is dedicated to promoting profitability, controlling and reducing costs, and motivating employees to work as teams enjoying reduced turnover and increased job satisfaction?

During the last seven years I have excelled and built a "track record" of rapid advancement with Giant Air Transportation, Inc. and at 30 became the company's youngest vice president. This position, as you will see by my resume, included controlling a multimillion-dollar annual budget in a division with more than $3.5 million annually in new revenue. I was involved in international cargo operations and managed the negotiations which gave the airline the authority to operate in Canada.

I have consistently contributed to successful operations through my abilities related to training and motivating employees, budgeting/planning/scheduling/controlling costs for highest profitability, and applying analytical and problem-solving skills to reduce loss and improve operating procedures. While at Giant Air, I played a major role in leading the company in its growth from 70 to 700 employees.

I returned to college full time early in 1996 and in December 1996, received my B.S. degree in Aviation Security Administration, graduating with a 3.6 GPA. I am certain that I offer a combination of knowledge and experience which would impact favorably on your organization's "bottom line."

I hope you will welcome my call soon to arrange a brief meeting at your convenience to discuss your current and future needs and how I might serve them. Thank you in advance for your time.

Sincerely yours,

Mason W. Tinder

Alternate last paragraph:
I hope you will call or write soon to suggest a time convenient for us to meet and discuss your current and future needs and how I might serve them. Thank you in advance for your time.

MASON W. TINDER

1110½ Hay Street, Fayetteville, NC 28305　　•　　preppub@aol.com　　•　　(910) 483-6611

OBJECTIVE　　To benefit an organization that can use a proven professional offering superior abilities in cost reduction and control, multi-unit budgeting and management, and training employees for high productivity and satisfaction.

EDUCATION　　**B.S., Aviation Security Administration**, Montana State University, Billings, MT, Dec 1996; graduated with a 3.6 GPA.

EXPERIENCE　　*Earned rapid advancement in this "track record" of promotion within this publicly traded carrier, Giant Air Transportation, Inc.:*
DIRECTOR OF SUPPORT OPERATIONS. Chicago, IL (2001-present). Took charge of a 30-employee operations center: hire/train/supervise dispatchers and schedulers, analyze and interpret data on flight and crew legalities, and ensure compliance with FAA regulations.
- Initiated new policies which resulted in fuel cost reductions, more efficient crew scheduling, and higher productivity.
- Represented the corporation in several successful court cases arising from employee claims under EEOC regulations.

VICE PRESIDENT FOR CARGO CONTRACTING. Chicago, IL (2000-01). Became the company's youngest vice president at 30; controlled multimillion-dollar budget, negotiation and bidding for both domestic and international routes, aircraft procurement, and maintenance/flight/scheduling crews.
- Personally generated new contracts that produced $3.5 million in revenue.
- Handled all negotiations which led to Canadian operating authority.
- Coordinated operations at 18 cities in 11 states.

DIRECTOR OF OPERATIONS. Chicago, IL (1998-00). Conducted negotiations for leases and construction contracts at 23 airports in seven states; coordinated with FAA officials to ensure compliance with security regulations; hired and trained security personnel.
- Played the key role in setting up seven new facilities.
- Applied analytical and budgetary skills in innovating cost reductions.

TRAINING MANAGER. Chicago, IL (1996-97). Created manuals and teaching aids used in training all new personnel; personally interviewed and hired over 150 employees; inspected facilities.
- Decreased employee turnover by 40%; reduced training costs.
- Challenged FAA rulings: won judgements which resulted in reduced fines.
- Opened seven new customer service facilities and supervised as many as 20 employees in each of nine offices.

GENERAL MANAGER. Billings, MT (1993-95). Supervised 15 people while overseeing functional areas including marketing, training, budget, and facilities management.
- Provided successful customer service which resulted in doubling revenue.

HIGHLIGHTS OF OTHER EXPERIENCE:
- Recovered approximately $500,000 in lost and stolen property as manager of an 11-person resort security force.
- Gained manufacturing inspection/quality control skills with General Dynamics.

Exact Name of Person
Exact Title
Exact Name of Company
Address
City, State, Zip

TRAINING PROGRAM MANAGER

Dear Exact Name of Person (or Dear Sir or Madam if answering a blind ad):

With the enclosed resume, I would like to initiate the process of exploring employment opportunities within your organization and make you aware of my background as a manager.

I was recently handpicked for a position with the Department of Defense's Flight Training School, and I am playing a key role in refining the skills of pilots involved in the global war against terrorism. In previous positions, I excelled in a track record of accomplishment in the U.S. Air Force while rising to the rank of Major. After completing pilot school in both helicopters and fixed wing aircraft, I was selected for positions which involved training others, managing projects, and testing new concepts and assets.

With a reputation as an innovator and self-starter, I am proud that I have contributed significantly to every organization for which I have worked. On my own initiative, I have developed new training programs, refined existing ones, authored or revised existing training materials, and streamlined internal procedures. Although I have been recognized for outstanding writing and oral communication skills, I have also been commended for my ability to work well with others. I am a leader whom others like to follow as well as a loyal team player who motivates by example.

Throughout my aviation career, I have become accustomed to working in environments in which there is "no room for error." In the high-speed aviation environment in which I have worked, critical thinking skills and an ability to make the best decision quickly were vital. I have been called "a stickler for detail" and "the best at maximizing resources." In one job I implemented a new quality assurance program which resulted in an unprecedented safety level along with zero accidents.

If you can use a skilled manager whose common sense, problem-solving ability, and resourcefulness have been tested in both peacetime and combat situations, I hope you will contact me to suggest a time when we might meet. I have received numerous awards and honors while in the Air Force including being named the top Crew Chief in the Air Force worldwide as well as the top Tactics Officer in the Air Force worldwide. My greatest satisfaction, however, came from strengthening organizations strategically and operationally and helping individuals improve their skills. I can provide outstanding references at the appropriate time.

Yours sincerely,

Lynne Nimocks

LYNNE NIMOCKS

1110½ Hay Street, Fayetteville, NC 28305   •   preppub@aol.com   •   (910) 483-6611

OBJECTIVE

I want to contribute to an organization that can use a strong leader and resourceful problem solver who has received numerous honors recognizing my ability to lead, train, motivate, and manage others in environments in which there is "no room for error."

EDUCATION & TRAINING

Master's degree in Aviation Management, Embry-Riddle Aeronautical University, Las Vegas, NV, 1999.

Bachelor's degree in Aeronautical Science, Embry-Riddle Aeronautical University, Daytona, Beach, FL, 1995.

Pilot training, helicopters and fixed wing aircraft; management training for military officers as well as the Aircraft Mishap Investigator Course designed to refine fact-finding and problem-solving skills.

TECHNICAL SKILLS

Clearance: Top Secret security clearance with SBI

Computers: Highly proficient in utilizing the Microsoft Suite and other programs.

Licenses & flight hours: FAA Airline Transport Pilot rating (multi-engine land); FAA commercial instrument helicopter rating. Total flight time exceeds 4100 hours.

EXPERIENCE

PROGRAM MANAGER. Department of Defense Flight Training School, Ocala, FL (2002-present). Have been described in writing as an "outstanding leader" and "superb instructor" while managing a multimillion-dollar flying/training program for pilots.

- On my own initiative, streamlined internal efficiency and introduced new training tools.

OPERATIONS OFFICER. U.S. Air Force, classified location (1998-02). Was handpicked for this position in an organization which was selectively staffed by top military leaders; operated and maintained a fleet of aircraft involved in test and rescue activities.

- Supervised 8 pilots, 10 middle managers, and 80 junior employees while controlling $200 million in assets and a $150,000 operational budget.
- Recognized as an expert in developing multi-unit training, built a joint helicopter/fire department training program, and also shaped a new program for pilots and engineers in combat rescue units.
- Described in writing as "a stickler for detail" and "the best at maximizing resources," was praised for implementing a new quality assurance program which resulted in an unprecedented safety level along with zero accidents during my tenure.
- In a formal performance evaluation, was described as "my best operations officer and an outstanding leader managing unique challenges in a dynamic unit."
- Maintained a 24-hour search and rescue force; was involved in saving numerous lives.

BRANCH CHIEF. U.S. Air Force, classified location (1990-97). Was handpicked for this job directing the operations of a fleet of multimillion-dollar aircraft involved in test, support, and search-and-rescue activities.

- Upgraded pilot skills; rewrote a master test bank; initiated an evaluation tracking system which guaranteed strict quality control of aircrew proficiency.

Other U.S. Air Force experience (various locations worldwide): Served as **OPERATIONS OFFICER & PILOT, CHIEF OF TACTICS, AIRCRAFT COMMANDER,** and **HELICOPTER COPILOT.**

HONORS

Have received numerous awards including being named **USAF Crew Chief of the Year** and **USAF Tactics Officer of the Year.** Outstanding references on request.

Exact Name of Person
Exact Title
Exact Name of Company
Address
City, State, Zip

TRAINING PROGRAM MANAGER

Dear Exact Name of Person (or Dear Sir or Madam if answering a blind ad):

With the enclosed resume, I would like to make you aware of my strong interest in receiving consideration for a position as an aircrew scheduler with your airline.

As you will see from my resume, I offer an extensive background in flight and ground scheduling and have held the position of superintendent of aircrew scheduling while employed by the Federal Aviation Administration.

While serving in demanding jobs with rapidly shifting priorities and constantly changing schedules, I have earned two associate's degrees from the Community College of the Northeast, including an A.A. in Aircrew Operations.

Excelling as a technical instructor ensuring training standardization and the quality of training received by refueling specialists and boom operators, I have earned a reputation as the "go-to person" for guidance and instruction. In a previous job as an instructor and boom operator, I consistently guided my students to 100% pass rates and produced well-trained and knowledgeable professionals.

In my position as Supervisor of Aircrew Scheduling, I supervised five people who worked with a team of nine managers in a scheduling center where I oversaw and coordinated compilation of weekly schedules and monthly operations plans for nine units. I was credited with the knowledge which allowed affiliated centers to become automated and their functions consolidated into one centralized control center. During this period I was credited with developing a vital personnel tracking center, a ground training computer process, and the modernization of the center's automated data processing equipment which replaced outdated systems.

If you can use an experienced scheduler and supervisor who is known for his high levels of drive, initiative, and energy, I hope you will welcome my call soon when I try to arrange a brief meeting to discuss your airline's goals and how my background might serve your needs. I can provide outstanding references at the appropriate time.

Sincerely,

Brian Dihabuti

BRIAN DIHABUTI

1110½ Hay Street, Fayetteville, NC 28305   •   preppub@aol.com   •   (910) 483-6611

OBJECTIVE

To offer a strong aviation background to an organization that can benefit from my versatile experience which has emphasized handling the details of aircrew scheduling as well as the application of excellent technical electronics, inventory control, and planning skills.

EDUCATION

Earned Associate's degrees in **Aircrew Operations,** 1998, and **Aviation Technology,** 2000, Community College of the Northeast, Columbine, ND.

EXPERIENCE

Gained a base of experience in ground and flight scheduling while excelling as a technical instructor and operations superintendent, Federal Aviation Administration:
TRAINING PROGRAM EVALUATOR. Malmstrom AFB, MT (2001-present). Officially cited as an "exceptional performer" and one "who leads the way," ensure the standardization of training and flight crew performance while documenting training, identifying trends, and personally instructing technical subjects for KC-135 aircraft crews.

- Provide instruction on refueling systems, cargo loading, and passenger handling procedures on these $52 million aircraft; evaluate boom operators during worldwide refueling and airlift missions.
- Became the unit's first instructor to be certified in special operations during a $695 million avionics upgrade program transferring some duties previously held by navigators to boom operators; oversaw training and certification of 15 operators in the new duties.

INSTRUCTOR and **KC-135 REFUELING BOOM OPERATOR.** Beale Aviation Training Center, Causey, CA (1998-01). Frequently sought out to provide guidance and instruction to peers and subordinates, planned and carried out initial flight and ground training using "hands-on" simulators for realistic training.

- Developed and presented comprehensive courses on crew scheduling and coordination as well as aircraft systems, cargo loading, and passenger handling.
- Consistently achieved 100% pass rates while producing knowledgeable students.
- Played a major role in the center's recognition with a flying safety award, and was instrumental in an overall "excellent" rating during a quality awareness inspection.
- Created a computer process used to track mobility ground training which increased program effectiveness significantly to a 98% effectiveness rating.
- Coordinated flight crew scheduling by consolidating activities of eight stateside flying organizations and five others deployed to international locations into one location.
- Removed outdated equipment and modernized the organization's ADP systems.

SUPERVISOR OF AIRCREW SCHEDULING. Washington, DC (1993-97). Officially described as an "exceptional performer" whose initiative improved productivity and efficiency, supervised five specialists working with nine managers in a scheduling center.

- Oversaw and coordinated the compilation of weekly flying and ground training schedules and monthly operations plans for nine units.
- Assisted in the design of custom computer systems utilized in automating operations.
- Identified and solved a scheduling problem which saved ten man-hours a month by clarifying and defining procedures so personnel did not perform double duty.
- Was recognized as an "Outstanding Performer" for my initiative in developing a personnel tracking system vital to the smooth operation of a 24-hour-a-day office.

PERSONAL

Entrusted with a Top Secret/SBI security clearance. Offer aircraft expertise with the HH-53ES and all 135 series (707). Excellent safety record. Outstanding references on request.

AIRFRAME MECHANIC

Dear Sir or Madam:

I would appreciate an opportunity to talk with you soon about how I could contribute to your organization through my proven expertise in aircraft maintenance, production control, and personnel supervision.

As you will see from my resume, I have skills and abilities that could make me a valuable part of your team. A licensed Airframe and Powerplant Mechanic, I am highly skilled in the maintenance of CH-47 Chinook, AH-64 Apache, UH-60 Blackhawk, OH-58 Kiowa Scout, and UH-1H Huey helicopters.

You would find me to be a hard-working and reliable professional who prides myself on doing any job to the best of my ability. I can provide excellent personal and professional references, and I am known for my intense commitment to the highest standards of safety and quality assurance.

I hope you will call or write me soon to suggest a time convenient for us to meet and discuss your current and future needs and how I might serve them. Thank you in advance for your time.

Sincerely,

Adam A. Evensong

ADAM A. EVENSONG

1110½ Hay Street, Fayetteville, NC 28305 • preppub@aol.com • (910) 483-6611

OBJECTIVE
To benefit an organization that can use a safety-conscious airframe and power plant mechanic who offers hands-on experience in maintenance, production control, and personnel supervision, as well as excellent motivational, planning, and time-management skills.

AIRCRAFT EXPERTISE
Can repair, troubleshoot, maintain, disassemble, and assemble a wide range of helicopters and other aircraft, including CH-47 Chinooks, UH-60 Blackhawks, OH-58 Kiowa Scouts, AH-64 Apaches, and UH-1H Hueys; am proficient in troubleshooting, repairing, and replacing power trains, power plants, hydraulics, flight controls, and general airframe components on various helicopters.

EXPERIENCE
AIRFRAME MECHANIC. Sikorsky Aircraft Corp., Los Angeles, CA (2001-present). Refined general mechanic and airframe skills while working on a team disassembling, reassembling, cleaning, repairing, and troubleshooting AH-64 Apache, UH-60 Blackhawk, CH-47 Chinook, and OH-58 Kiowa Scout helicopters.
- Promoted to modifications team, installing new structural systems and modifying old systems to current specifications.
- Earned praise for utilizing technical expertise and excellent time-management skills to reduce modification time.
- Performed extensive Fiberglas and rotor blade repairs on CH-47 Chinooks.
- Trained new personnel in helicopter maintenance, supply procedures, and safety rules.
- Used operational tests to certify the airworthiness of repaired aircraft.
- Planned work so that all repairs and maintenance were completed with accuracy and either on or before schedule.

AIRCRAFT STRUCTURAL REPAIRER. Sikorsky Aircraft, Los Angeles, CA, Los Angeles, CA (1996-00). Refined technical expertise while performing rotor blade erosion modifications on the CH-47 Chinook helicopter.
- Commended for quick and accurate completion of modifications.
- Discovered ability to rapidly adapt to adverse climate and conditions while still achieving performance goals.

HELICOPTER STRUCTURAL REPAIR MANAGER. Sikorsky Aircraft, Los Angeles, CA (1996-00). Wore many hats while acting as shop leader, quality assurance specialist, and mechanic for a CH-47 Chinook repair shop.
- Trained, supervised, evaluated, and directed two mechanics.
- Controlled all departmental inventory management and parts ordering.
- Quickly earned a reputation as a valuable team leader with the ability to ensure safe working conditions under the pressure of tight deadlines and long hours.
- Recognized by top-level management for attention to detail and excellent decision-making.

EDUCATION
Completed a wide range of technical training and continuing education courses, including leadership, management, effective teaching, and aircraft structural repair.

LICENSE
Airframe and Power Plant License

PERSONAL
Am an enthusiastic, hard-working professional who believes in always giving 100%. Work well independently or as a contributing member of a team.

Exact Name of Person
Title or Position
Name of Company
Address (number and street)
Address (city, state, and ZIP)

AVIONICS & AIRFRAME TECHNICIAN

Dear Exact Name of Person (or Sir or Madam if answering a blind ad):

I would appreciate an opportunity to talk with you soon about how I could contribute to your organization through my technical electronics and mechanical skills as well as through my personal qualities of reliability, dependability, and dedication to excellence.

As you will see from my enclosed resume, I received my FAA Power Plant License in 1997. I had the unique opportunity to attend Aviation High School in Chicago, IL. This school is the only high school in the country with this technical program which allows its graduates to receive their license upon graduation. I also completed 68 credit hours in Aerospace Maintenance at the College of Aeronautics in Chicago. Upon entering the Air Force, I was advanced in rank because of this prior education and selected for six months of technical training in basic electronics and communications/navigation technology.

My Air Force experience has allowed me to refine my technical and mechanical skills working mainly on the C-130E aircraft radios, radars, and navigation equipment while also gaining new skills in electronics. I feel that this blend of training, education, and experience has allowed me to advance ahead of my peers and become known as a skilled and talented young professional.

I hope you will welcome my call soon to arrange a brief meeting to discuss your current and future needs and how I might serve them. Thank you in advance for your time.

Sincerely,

Winston K. Turner

Alternate last paragraph:
I hope you will call or write me soon to suggest a time convenient for us to meet and discuss your current and future needs and how I might serve them. Thank you in advance for your time.

WINSTON K. TURNER

1110½ Hay Street, Fayetteville, NC 28305 • preppub@aol.com • (910) 483-6611

OBJECTIVE   To offer electrical and mechanical skills to an organization in need of an experienced aircraft power plant mechanic with a reputation as a hard-working, dedicated young professional.

LICENSE/ AIRCRAFT EXPERTISE

FAA Power Plant License, 1997
Maintained Lockheed C-130E aircraft and am also qualified to work on C-141, C-5, and A-10 aircraft.

EDUCATION & TRAINING

Graduated from Aviation High School, Chicago, IL, 1996.
Completed 68 credits in Aerospace Maintenance, College of Aeronautics, Chicago, IL.
* Completed the diploma program at the only high school in the country which teaches this technical program leading to the FAA Power Plant License.
Excelled in six months of Air Force technical training programs in basic electronics and communications/navigation technology, Fort Gordon AFB, GA, 2000.

EXPERIENCE

AVIONICS AND AIRFRAME TECHNICIAN. USAF, Classified locations worldwide (1997-present). Became qualified as communications and navigation equipment technician responsible for maintaining critical C-130E radios, radars, and navigation equipment valued in the millions of dollars.
* Learned electronics skills and was entrusted to work in airframe maintenance.
* Maintained inventories of special and common tools.
* Debriefed air crews to gain information about any discrepancies or problems.
* Refined my leadership qualities and learned the importance of taking care of even the smallest details and of not giving up on a job until it is complete.
* Was promoted ahead of my peers based on my advanced technical knowledge from attending the College of Aeronautics.
* Earned a Maintenance Badge in recognition of my completion of advanced "5 level" training.
* Applied my organizational abilities while providing support for air crews during the war against terrorism in Afghanistan.

TECHNICAL KNOWLEDGE

Through training and experience, have become familiar with operational activities, special tools and equipment, and procedures including the following:
communications security (COMSEC) — observing proper precautions to prevent security violations in verbal and written communication including safeguarding classified material familiarity with *occupational safety, health, and environmental hazards*
inspecting maintenance activities and using automated data collection systems
avionic systems maintenance — using common hardware, corrosion control procedures, and repairing/fabricating coaxial cables
using *powered aerospace ground equipment* including light carts, power carts, heaters, air conditioners, and air compressors
using *test equipment* including power meters, data bus analyzers
troubleshooting, checking, and repairing communication systems such as:

ARC-186 very high frequency radio	KY 58/75 secure voice equipment
AN/URC-4 emergency locator transmitters	cockpit voice recorder
UHF direction finders	Identity Friend or Foe transponders

PERSONAL   Speak, read, and write Spanish fluently. Enjoy using my technical and mechanical skills in activities including working with computers and as an auto mechanic. Secret clearance.

Exact Name of Person
Exact Title
Exact Name of Company
Address
City, State, Zip

**AVIATION & RADAR
SYSTEMS SPECIALIST**

Dear Exact Name of Person (or Dear Sir or Madam if answering a blind ad):

I would appreciate an opportunity to talk with you soon about how I could contribute to your organization through my troubleshooting and technical electronics skills as well as through my motivational and supervisory abilities. I am responding to your advertisement in "Avionics Weekly" for avionics professionals who are willing to relocate worldwide for challenging assignments related to the war on terrorism.

You will see from my enclosed resume that I completed requirements for an A.A.S. degree in Avionics Systems Technology from the Community College of the Air Force. After serving my country in the Air Force as a Radar Systems Technician, I was recruited by the Lockheed organization for employment as a Radar and Automated Systems Technician.

I offer a background in troubleshooting and functional testing of analog and digital circuits to the system, subassembly, and component level. I am confident that the expertise and knowledge I have acquired will allow me to easily adapt to any situation where personal integrity and dedication to quality are valued.

If you can use a positive, results-oriented professional, I hope you will from you soon to arrange a time when we might meet to discuss your needs. I can assure you in advance that I have an excellent reputation and would quickly become a valuable asset to your company.

Sincerely,

Charles V. Horner

CHARLES V. HORNER

1110½ Hay Street, Fayetteville, NC 28305 • preppub@aol.com • (910) 483-6611

OBJECTIVE

To offer excellent technical electronics skills, with an emphasis on telecommunications, avionics, and radar systems, as well as a reputation as an adaptable quick learner to an organization that can benefit from my supervisory and planning abilities.

EDUCATION & TRAINING

A.A.S., *Avionics Systems Technology*, Community College of the Air Force, 1999. Completed advanced technical training in digital techniques, radar systems, aircraft communications systems, navigation, and hazardous materials handling.

TECHNICAL EXPERTISE

Use and interpret: layout drawings, schematics, and diagrams to solve problems while maintaining aircraft electronics, radar, communication, and navigation systems and associated support equipment.

Operate, program, install, maintain, troubleshoot, and repair: AN/APQ-120 and AN/APQ-109 Weapons Control Radar Systems, UHF radio ARC-164, VHF AM and FM radio, ARC-186, secure speech KY-58 system, Intercommunication System AIC-18, Identify Friend or Foe (IFF), APX-101 System, Tactical Air Navigation ARN-18, and Instrument Landing System ARN-108.

Aircraft expertise: McDonald Douglas F-4, Fairchild Republic A-10, and Lockheed AC-130.

EXPERIENCE

SUPERVISORY AVIONICS CRAFTSMAN. McDonald Douglas, Seattle, WA (2000-present). Supervised four communications and navigation specialists and 10 avionics and guidance control specialists.
- Repaired electrical systems, removing faulty wiring systems, installing or replacing wiring harnesses, electrical connectors, antennas, transmission lines, and cables.
- Exercised safety precautions while working with or around electronic or radioactive equipment and high-frequency radiation hazards.

AVIONICS TECHNICIAN. McDonald Douglas, Riverside, CA (1997-99). Applied expert knowledge while performing scheduled and unscheduled maintenance, troubleshooting, repairs, and modifications to the communication, navigation, and radar systems of F-4 aircraft.
- Reduced man-hour requirements and streamlined procedures during the testing and modification of missile tuning systems.
- Earned praise for my effectiveness as a leader of 30 people in six job specialties.

RADAR AND AUTOMATED SYSTEMS TECHNICIAN. Lockheed Corp., Orlando, FL (1996). Developed a reputation as a knowledgeable and skilled technician while assisting in organizational and intermediate maintenance to include fault isolation, performance analysis, and system performance monitoring.
- Contributed expertise in situations which included saving $26,000 by repairing an improperly wired potentiometer and supervising the complete rebuild of a pitot static boom assembly which aided in Lockheed's efforts to develop a software solution.

RADAR SYSTEMS TECHNICIAN. USAF, Germany (1992-96). Became recognized as a professional who could be counted on to solve problems and show the technical expertise needed to ensure quality of maintenance and modifications to F-4G systems.
- Completed a repair to a highly complex matrix assembly of test sets which eliminated long shipping delays while waiting for replacements from a depot.

PERSONAL

Secret security clearance. Outstanding references on request.

Exact Name of Person
Title or Position
Name of Company
Address (number and street)
Address (city, state, and ZIP)

AVIONICS TECHNICIAN   Dear Exact Name of Person (or Sir or Madam if answering a blind ad):

I would appreciate an opportunity to talk with you soon about how I could contribute to your organization through my technical electronics expertise, education in computer technology, and proven managerial abilities.

As you will see from my enclosed resume, I possess strong technical skills and the ability to quickly learn and absorb new information and technological advances. Currently pursuing a B.S. degree in Computer Information Systems at Colgate University in Hamilton, NY, I previously received an A.S. degree in Aircraft Systems Maintenance Technology from the Community College of the Air Force.

I have consistently been singled out for praise for my versatility areas including direct avionics maintenance, hazardous material control, support equipment maintenance and repair, as well as in the training and supervision of employees. I have always been described as a professional who can be counted on to find innovative ways to increase productivity, ensure safety in the work place, and troubleshoot complex problems quickly so that aircraft downtime is kept to a minimum.

Through experience and education, I have become familiar with computer operating systems and software including Windows as well as Microsoft Office. I enjoy using my technical skills to repair computers, VCRs, and TVs and completely built my own computer from scratch.

I hope you will welcome my call soon to arrange a brief meeting to discuss your current and future needs and how I might serve them. Thank you in advance for your time.

Sincerely,

Leonardo N. Vincent

Alternate last paragraph:
I hope you will call or write me soon to suggest a time convenient for us to meet and discuss your current and future needs and how I might serve them. Thank you in advance for your time.

LEONARDO N. VINCENT

1110½ Hay Street, Fayetteville, NC 28305 • preppub@aol.com • (910) 483-6611

OBJECTIVE

To contribute to an organization that can use my technical electronics expertise along with my proven skills in supervising employees and managing the operation of technical support facilities through my ability to prioritize, plan, and organize activities.

EDUCATION

Pursuing a **B.S.** degree in **Computer Information Systems**, Colgate University, Hamilton, NY.

Earned an **A.S.** degree in **Aircraft Systems Maintenance Technology**, Community College of the Air Force, 1996.

TRAINING

Completed extensive Air Force training programs emphasizing the development and refinements of both technical and supervisory skills

EXPERIENCE

AVIONICS TECHNICIAN. Department of Defense, Hamilton, NY (1998-present). Have displayed my versatility while working in several distinctly different aspects of aircraft support services including direct avionics maintenance, hazardous material control, support equipment maintenance and repair, and training and personnel supervision.

- Was placed in charge of the program which maintained, repaired, tested, and inspected an inventory of night-vision goggles (NVG) used by pilots and flight crew members: conducted regular training sessions in all aspects of use and maintenance.
- Widely regarded as an expert in NVG repair, co-authored modifications to the technical manual used throughout the world.
- Was singled out to manage a hazardous waste collection point and ensure that storage and transport were properly handled.
- In official evaluations, was described as having superior technical knowledge; was selected to oversee the special electronics branch which repaired, maintained, and tested high-tech surveillance equipment used in Afghanistan and other locations as vital tools in the war against terrorism.
- Monitored a training program which produced specialists who were fully qualified to install and maintain equipment used to modify aircraft for Special Operations Low Level (SOLL) missions; achieved a 99% reliability rate in SOLL missions.
- Was consistently singled out for my expertise in troubleshooting and making repairs to electro-environmental systems which saved downtime and helped my units achieve high performance levels.

Highlights of earlier USAF experience: **locations worldwide.**

Built a reputation as a hard-working and knowledgeable technician and supervisor who could be counted on to find ways to make the work area safe and more productive by finding ways to improve procedures.

- While stationed in Kuwait, constructed a new mobility tool kit and modified existing tool kits so that they included tools unique to F-16 aircraft maintenance.
- Was credited with being a key player in my unit, earning a prestigious award as the top electrical shop in the parent organization..
- During a period while assigned as a technical supervisor, was cited for my ability to solve highly complex problems under stressful conditions and for my skill in troubleshooting and making repairs quickly.

PERSONAL

Enjoy working with computers and built my own PC from scratch. Repair computers, VCRs, and TVs. Am heavily involved in helping young people through coaching youth basketball.

Date

Exact Name of Person
Title or Position
Name of Company
Address (no., street)
Address (city, state, zip)

**COMMUNICATIONS &
NAVIGATION
TECHNICIAN**

Dear Exact Name of Person (or Dear Sir or Madam if answering a blind ad):

I would appreciate an opportunity to talk with you about how I could contribute to your organization through my outstanding technical skills related to troubleshooting, reading schematics, and electronics maintenance, installation, and repair.

Offering abilities in the specialized field of avionics and aircraft electrical systems, my background includes Aviation/Navigation Technician experience, specializing in navigation and communication systems. I have also completed training in electronics. This program covers 2,000 hours of instruction and actual work experience.

In my current position with United Airlines, I am excelling as a Communications/ Navigation Specialist. This position involves activities ranging from removing and overhauling, reinstalling, aligning and adjusting, and modifying avionics and electrical wiring systems on company aircraft. Although I am held in the highest regard by my employer and can provide outstanding references at the appropriate time, I am selectively exploring opportunities with other airlines.

I hope you will welcome my call soon to arrange a brief meeting at your convenience to discuss your current and future needs and how I might serve them. Thank you in advance for your time.

Sincerely yours,

Troy H. Leader

Alternate last paragraph:
I hope you will call or write me soon to suggest a time convenient for us to meet and discuss your current and future needs and how I might serve them. Thank you in advance for your time.

TROY H. LEADER

1110½ Hay Street, Fayetteville, NC 28305　　•　　preppub@aol.com　　•　　(910) 483-6611

OBJECTIVE

To benefit an organization through my experience in aviation systems and maintenance, my ability to supervise people and equipment, and my exceptional skills in troubleshooting and repairing airframe and electronics systems to the component level.

EXPERIENCE

COMMUNICATION/NAVIGATION TECHNICIAN. United Airlines, Denver, CO (2000-present). Excel as swing shift supervisor overseeing communications and navigation systems.

- Helped fuel shop personnel isolate a faulty signal processor on the air-to-air refueling system of an important aircraft.
- Maintained a low avionics repeat rate of 1.4 percent for fiscal year 2001.
- Assist guidance control specialists and electronic personnel in a wide range of priority tasks.
- Perform a variety of administrative duties, including production inspections and training new personnel.
- Cross-trained to provide support to crew chiefs in removing, installing, repairing, troubleshooting, and servicing various aircraft components and systems.

Highlights of previous U.S.A.F. experience:
COMMUNICATION/NAVIGATION SPECIALIST. U.S. Air Force, Travis AFB, CA (1996-2000). Repaired, adjusted, and installed a wide range of aviation guidance and operational systems. Used test equipment to conduct checks and adjustments of components for optimum performance.

- Enabled the 76 AMU Mode IV program pass rate to exceed the expected standard.

COMMUNICATION AND NAVIGATION SPECIALIST. U.S. Air Force, Offutt AFB, NE (1993-96). Directed flight line maintenance, including airframe and electrical flight control repairs. Promoted ahead of peers due to a supervisory ability and a flawless quality assurance record.

- Performed additional duties as crew chief of several different aircraft.
- Qualified on the intricate Variable Omnirange and Instrument Landing Systems.
- Trained new personnel on the operations and repairs of 10 aircraft mockups.
- Commended for improving motivation and morale of coworkers.

SECURITY GUARD. Maximum Security, Inc., Trenton, NJ (1989-92). Headed security team responsible for the safekeeping of six buildings.

AIRCRAFT EXPERTISE

Maintained systems and components on aircraft, including F-4E/G, AXU-14 Data Link Pod mockup, and 76 AMU Mode IV.

EDUCATION & TRAINING

Completed an extensive number of electronic/aviation-related courses including over 2,000 hours of hands-on electronic classes.

TECHNICAL EXPERTISE

Through training and experience, gained extensive knowledge of systems and equipment including: avionics systems, communications/electrical/construction systems, various test equipment, and countermeasures equipment.

AWARDS

Merited several service awards, including those for achievement and outstanding unit, as well as being named Airman of the Month. Outstanding references on request.

Date

Exact Name of Person
Title or Position
Name of Company
Address (no., street)
Address (city, state, zip)

CREW CHIEF
&
A&P
MECHANIC

Dear Exact Name of Person (or Dear Sir or Madam if answering a blind ad):

I would appreciate an opportunity to talk with you soon about how I could contribute to your organization through my expertise as an aircraft mechanic and experience as a crew chief.

As you will see from my resume, I hold the FAA Airframe & Powerplant Mechanic License, and I am considered an expert in troubleshooting and repairing aircraft systems and engines.

On numerous occasions I have creatively applied my knowledge and technical skills to save downtime and money. For example, during a borescope inspection of a Pratt & Whitney F100 engine, I discovered a massive burn-through of a combuster liner that, if undetected, would have caused a major fire. On another occasion while working with a colleague, I conceived of a way to change a component of a GE110 engine without removing the engine from the aircraft, and that procedure reduced the number of people needed for the task from five to two while saving 40 manhours of work.

While employed by one of the world's largest defense contractors, I was promoted ahead of my peers to F-16 Crew Chief, and I usually wore other "hats" as well such as Flight Chief, Crew Chief Expediter, and Line Chief. Known for my dedication to quality standards while emphasizing safety, I can provide excellent personal and professional references, and I will cheerfully travel and relocate worldwide as your needs require.

I hope you will call or write me soon to suggest a time convenient for us to meet and discuss your current and future needs and how I might serve them. Thank you in advance for your time.

Sincerely yours,

Richard Pleasure

Alternate last paragraph:
I hope you will welcome my call soon to arrange a brief meeting at your convenience to discuss your current and future needs and how I might serve them. Thank you in advance for your time.

RICHARD PLEASURE

1110½ Hay Street, Fayetteville, NC 28305 • preppub@aol.com • (910) 483-6611

OBJECTIVE   To offer my skills as an aircraft mechanic and my experience as a crew chief to a company that can use a skilled troubleshooter who offers a proven ability to work gracefully under pressure while correcting stubborn problems affecting aerospace powerplant systems.

LICENSE   FAA Airframe and Powerplant Mechanic, #555-12-XX

AIRCRAFT
EXPERTISE
- Expert in troubleshooting and repairing F-16 aircraft systems — A,B,C,D models
- Familiar with Pratt & Whitney engines including F100 PW 200
- Experienced with General Electric engines including F110-GE100 and F110-GE129
- Offer ability to operate jet engine trim box, F-16 test cell

EXPERIENCE   **CREW CHIEF.** Fleming Aviation Services, London, England (2000-present). For a defense contractor providing maintenance and quality assurance support to NATO forces involved in the war against terrorism, supervise other technicians while also performing as Crew Chief Expediter, Flight Chief, and Line Chief.
- Inspected, installed, repaired, maintained, troubleshot, serviced, and modified tactical aircraft system components including airframe and powerplant.
- Interpreted and provided advice on maintenance procedures and policy.
- Analyzed layouts, blueprints, and technical orders to diagnose problems.
- Conducted preflight and postflight inspections.
- Removed, installed, repaired, troubleshot, and serviced components/systems such as hydraulic systems, electrical systems, oxygen systems (gaseous and liquid), powerplant, environmental systems, and ventilation and heating systems and others.
- Analyzed and made recommendations regarding such features as parts, clearances. fuel leaks, cracks. tolerances, corrosion, tire wear, skin damage, and overall aircraft performance.

Highlights of accomplishments:
- Was involved in 48 engine changes in a 60-day period.
- With a co-worker, conceived of a way to change a component of a GE110 engine without removing the engine from the aircraft; this reduced the number of people needed for this task from five to two and saved 40 man-hours of work.
- During a borescope inspection of a Pratt & Whitney F100 engine, discovered a massive burnthrough of a combuster liner that, if undetected, would have caused a major fire.

F-16 CREW CHIEF. Fleming Aviation Services, Germany and the Middle East (1988-99). Performed most of the tasks above while learning to expertly operate F-16 engines.
- Earned a respected medal for my contributions to the war in the Middle East.

F-16 CREW CHIEF. Fleming Aviation Services, Korea (1986-88). Earned an unusually rapid promotion to Crew Chief as an E-3, and became known for my emphasis on teamwork and "safety first, last, and always."
- Achieved a 100% pass rate on all quality assurance inspections.

EDUCATION   Excelled in more than two years of technical training related to aircraft maintenance, F129 engine operation, F110 engine operation, and other technical areas; also excelled in management and leadership development courses for maintenance managers and crew chiefs.

PERSONAL   Will cheerfully travel and relocate worldwide as needed. Can provide outstanding personal and professional references upon request.

Date

Exact Name of Person
Exact Title
Exact Name of Company
Address
City, State, Zip

CREW CHIEF
&
A&P
MECHANIC

Dear Exact Name of Person (or Dear Sir or Madam if answering a blind ad):

I would appreciate an opportunity to talk with you soon about how I could contribute to your organization through my experience and training in the areas of aircraft maintenance and technical inspection gained while working for the Federal Aviation Administration.

As you will see from my enclosed resume, I have my FAA Airframe and Power Plant License and earned excellent scores in military training programs which evaluated technical skills and knowledge as well as written and verbal communication, leadership, and analytical abilities.

Recently promoted to the position of Technical Inspector after building a reputation as a knowledgeable and productive Crew Chief, I oversee technicians maintaining eight multimillion-dollar OH-58D(I) Advanced Scout helicopters. I have been singled out to receive several awards in recognition of my technical expertise, ability to train and motivate others, and familiarity with support activities such as record keeping and documentation of maintenance activities, hazardous material handling and disposal, workplace safety, and weights and balances.

I am a hard-working, dedicated professional who offers a broad range of knowledge and skills related to aircraft maintenance. I am confident that I can make valuable contributions to your organization through my mechanical skills as well as my leadership abilities.

I hope you will contact me to suggest a time when we might meet to discuss your needs. I can assure you in advance that I could rapidly become an asset to your organization.

Sincerely,

Christopher Jenkins

CHRISTOPHER JENKINS

1110½ Hay Street, Fayetteville, NC 28305   •   preppub@aol.com   •   (910) 483-6611

OBJECTIVE   To offer skills in aircraft maintenance, technical inspection, and documentation support to an organization that can use a self-motivated young professional with a background of success in training, safety, hazardous material handling, and resource management.

LICENSE   FAA Airframe and Power Plant License.

TECHNICAL KNOWLEDGE   Have maintained the OH-58D (I) Advanced Scout helicopter.
Through experience and training, offer knowledge of operating areas including, but not limited to, the following:

conducting technical inspections	installing a variety of components
maintaining aircraft	keeping forms and records
determining aircraft weights/balances	handling/disposing of hazardous materials

EDUCATION & TRAINING   Completed six months of general studies at St. Pauls Technical College, MN.
Excelled as a student in military programs which included the Aviation Logistics School's OH-58D (I) helicopter repair supervisor, helicopter repairer, professional leadership development, and technical inspector training courses.

EXPERIENCE   *While working for the Federal Aviation Administration, am earning a reputation as a knowledgeable professional and effective supervisor:*
TECHNICAL INSPECTOR. Ft. Polk, LA (2002-present). Was chosen to act in a critical support role as the manager of maintenance activities and supervisor for technicians maintaining multimillion-dollar helicopters at military bases all over the east coast.
- Process and maintain historical records, weight and balance forms, and all related maintenance files. Ensure that records of components added to or removed from aircraft are accurately entered in appropriate historical records in a timely manner.
- On my own initiative, made valuable contributions to aviation safety during the war on terrorism in Afghanistan.

CREW CHIEF. Washington, DC (1999-02). Promoted to supervise and train three aircraft technicians maintaining and servicing four OH-58D(I) aircraft, ensured that engine changes, component changes, and inspections were done thoroughly and in a timely manner.
- Controlled an $18 million inventory of aircraft and associated equipment.
- Refined my ability to motivate and lead employees to reach goals and work together as a team and as a result, produced personnel who performed extremely well on promotion boards, in professional development and technical schools, and during skill testing.
- Chosen to oversee personnel retention and NBC (nuclear, biological, and chemical) programs, received commendable ratings on the NBC element of operations during a major inspection of operational readiness for a unit supporting quick response world-wide missions carried out by the 82nd Airborne Division.
- Achieved an operational readiness rate 15% above Department of the Army standards during one joint services task force assignment during which the unit completed more than 400 accident- and incident-free flight hours.

CREW CHIEF. The Middle East (1995-98). Supervised and carried out maintenance on a six-helicopter fleet to include performing hourly and periodic inspections and controlling the handling and disposal of hazardous materials such as engine and transmission oil.

PERSONAL   Secret security clearance. Am known for emphasizing safety in the workplace.

Date

Exact Name of Person
Exact Title
Exact Name of Company
Address
City, State, Zip

CREW CHIEF   Dear Exact Name of Person (or Dear Sir or Madam if answering a blind ad):

With the enclosed resume, I would like to make you aware of my background as an articulate young professional with exceptional technical and supervisory skills as well as experience in staff development and training, maintenance management, and aircraft maintenance.

As you will see, I offer approximately four years as a C-130E Crew Chief with composite tool kit (CTK) experience. While at Lockheed Corp., Seattle, WA, I have been recognized as a skilled professional and selected to participate in numerous special projects. I am used to working under tight deadlines, high levels of pressure, and rapidly changing circumstances.

If you can use an experienced aircraft mechanic, crew chief, and troubleshooter, I hope you will contact me to suggest a time when we might meet to discuss your needs. I can assure you in advance that I could rapidly become an asset to your organization.

Sincerely,

Anthoney Hopkins

ANTHONEY HOPKINS

1110½ Hay Street, Fayetteville, NC 28305 · preppub@aol.com · (910) 483-6611

OBJECTIVE
To benefit an organization that can use an articulate young professional with exceptional technical and supervisory skills who offers a background in staff development and training, maintenance management, and aircraft repair and maintenance.

EDUCATION & TRAINING
Excelled in numerous training programs and courses which have included the C-130 Aerospace Maintenance Journeyman Program as well as the following:
Airlift Aerospace Maintenance Apprentice
CAMS Operator/Maintenance Data Collection
C-130 Phase III Maintenance Qualification
C-130 Cargo Rail System Technician

AIRCRAFT EXPERTISE
Offer knowledge and experience with the Lockheed C-130E including logging approximately 130 hours as a flying crew chief.
Operate: fire extinguishers, measuring tools, multimeters, torque wrenches, maintenance stands, aircraft engine stands and dollies, aircraft jacks, liquid oxygen servicing equipment, air compressors, ground heaters and blowers, generator sets, lighting equipment, gas turbine compressors, MB-4 tow vehicles, liquid nitrogen servicing equipment, gaseous nitrogen servicing equipment, and radio/interplane communications systems
Perform: aircraft inspections, corrosion identification, inspections of engine air intake and exhaust, pre-use inspections, and refuel/defuel operations
Operate and inspect: aircraft oxygen systems and fire/overheat warning systems, flight control systems, fuel systems, electrical systems, and hydraulic systems
Other services and training: hot brakes, high-intensity sound, lubricants/solvents/ cleaning agents, use and disposal of hazardous chemicals, parts ordering and inventory control, records maintenance, airframe construction (remove, install, and inspect components), and towing procedures

EXPERIENCE
Refined skills and knowledge of C-130 , Lockheed Corp., Seattle, WA :
C-130E CREW CHIEF and **COMPOSITE TOOL KIT TECHNICIAN (CTK).** Locations worldwide (2001-present). Earned recognition of my skills and leadership while working the flight line as a crew chief, learning to maintain the cargo dual-rail system, monitoring vehicle operations, and supporting approximately 40 crew members.
- Handled a variety of day-to-day actions including issuing tool boxes, test equipment, and bench stock items while controlling an inventory of maintenance equipment.
- In the dual rails shop, maintained the system and all aircraft support equipment such as fire extinguishers, oxygen bottles, and floor conveyers.

C-130E CREW CHIEF. Europe (1995-01). Began earning recognition as a skilled technician and dedicated professional while performing aircraft maintenance and servicing and inspections.
- Was selected for additional duties and training as a flying crew chief.
- Was entrusted with a Secret security clearance.

Highlights of earlier civilian experience: **PRODUCTION SUPERVISOR.** Burger King, Hillsboro, MO (1992-95). Learned the importance of teamwork and customer service while supervising ten people, running cash registers, cooking, and closing the restaurant while excelling in this full-time job as a high school student-athlete.

PERSONAL
Graduated from David Walters High School; was the "Most Improved Runner."

Date

Exact Name of Person
Title or Position
Name of Company
Address (no., street)
Address (city, state, zip)

CREW CHIEF
&
TECHNICAL
WEAPONS
SPECIALIST

Dear Exact Name of Person (or Dear Sir or Madam if answering a blind ad):

I would appreciate an opportunity to talk with you soon about how I could contribute to your organization through applying my well-developed mechanical skills as well as my experience related to hazardous materials handling.

You will see when you look at my resume that I offer a reputation as a quick learner with a talent for easily gaining and applying my knowledge for outstanding results. I have been successful in the highly specialized field of handling and maintaining nuclear and non-nuclear aircraft weapons systems. I feel that the qualities that helped me advance in the military are easily transferable to any field of work requiring mechanical and technical aptitude combined with a willingness to work hard and long to achieve goals and quality.

I am very proud to have been chosen as one of the "Outstanding Young Men of America" and was nominated and selected on the basis of my professional achievement and leadership skills.

You would find me to be an honest and determined individual who can handle pressure, deadlines, and stress while always maintaining a professional attitude. I am a team player with the ability to work well with others to reach team goals and in leadership and supervisory positions.

I hope you will welcome my call soon to arrange a brief meeting at your convenience to discuss your current and future needs and how I might serve them. Thank you in advance for your time.

Sincerely yours,

Keith B. Arrow

Alternate last paragraph:
I hope you will call or write me soon to suggest a time convenient for us to meet and discuss your current and future needs and how I might serve them. Thank you in advance for your time.

KEITH B. ARROW

1110½ Hay Street, Fayetteville, NC 28305   •   preppub@aol.com   •   (910) 483-6611

OBJECTIVE

To offer my versatile technical knowledge and troubleshooting skill to an organization that can use a hard-working young professional who can perform expertly under pressure and deadlines and who offers well-developed training, motivational, and leadership abilities.

EXPERIENCE

Earned rapid advancement ahead of my peers to "no-room-for-error" management positions in the complex technical weapons field, Department of Defense:
MAINTENANCE CREW CHIEF/SUPERVISOR. London, England (2001-present). Directed the activities of a three-person team involved in installing and removing specialized and regular equipment and systems on aircraft so that other teams could perform maintenance, repairs, or inspections.

- Was named Maintenance Supervisor of the Quarter in 2002 because of the managerial skills I have exhibited in this 450-person squadron; have enjoyed training and developing the managerial skills of the junior enlisted personnel I supervise.
- Supervised preflight, thruflight, and postflight inspections of weapons systems.
- Delivered a high quality of maintenance which allowed the aircraft to achieve near-perfect 99.5% and 99.8% weapons release rates during a recent six-month period.
- Was selected to attend a troubleshooting course and then selected for advancement to serve as crew chief during a functional reorganization.
- Earned praise for expertise in isolating faults and making repairs in minimum time which allowed aircraft to meet their flight schedules with no delay.
- Evaluated as an exceptional performer, was named Supervisor of the Month, May 2001.

AIRCRAFT MAINTENANCE INSPECTOR. Offutt AFB, NE (1999-01). While inspecting the work performed by up to 20 employees, was cited for superior technical knowledge and for my managerial commitment to "total quality control at all times" in activities including installing/removing equipment so that maintenance and repair could be done.

- Was credited with being the key player in seeing that assigned work was completed during a period of critical manpower shortages.
- Significantly contributed to an excellent rating received in a major inspection by a quality evaluation team from the regional headquarters.
- Was selected to help with a project which resulted in the smooth transfer of 14 aircraft from Europe to the U.S.
- Was selected for advancement ahead of my peers to a supervisory level based on my talents, accomplishments, and leadership abilities.

SPECIAL WEAPONS LOADING TEAM LEADER. Locations throughout the Pacific (1996-99). Consistently earned praise for my technical expertise and leadership abilities while gaining valuable experience in the training and certification of personnel in handling nuclear and non-nuclear weapons systems.

- Earned favorable comments from evaluators during two error-free training exercises.
- Contributed long hours to successfully transform five-person loading teams to four-person teams during a functional reorganization.
- Was selected as an "Outstanding Young Man of America for 1998" in recognition of "outstanding professional achievement and superior leadership."

**TRAINING &
SPECIAL
SKILLS**

Through experience and training, offer special abilities and knowledge in these areas:
Performing major and minor wire repairs to digital, analog, and video systems.
Operating automated management systems, aircraft computers, and PCs.
Driving vehicles: 5-ton semi-trailers, pickup trucks, 5-ton and 15-ton forklifts.

Date

Exact Name of Person
Exact Title
Exact Name of Company
Address
City, State, Zip

Dear Exact Name of Person (or Dear Sir or Madam if answering a blind ad):

ELECTRICAL SHOP FOREMAN

I would appreciate an opportunity to talk with you soon about how I could contribute to your organization through my experience in aviation maintenance management which includes supervising and training personnel, controlling budgets, and managing inventory control, warehouse, and automated support activities.

As you will see from my enclosed resume, I have managed and personally performed repairs and maintenance on a variety of aircraft including UH-60 Blackhawk, CH-47 Chinook, OH-58 Kiowa, AH-64 Apache, and UH-1 Huey helicopters. I have logged more than 350 hours of flight time in rotary aircraft as an electrical shop foreman and mechanic.

Currently working as an Avionics Electrical Shop Foreman in Ft. Gordon, GA, I was recently awarded my fifth Army Achievement Medal. Throughout my military career I have been singled out for leadership and supervisory roles ahead of my peers. I have overseen support actions for fleets of up to 41 aircraft, supervised teams with as many as 12 technicians and mechanics, and controlled multimillion-dollar budgets and expenditures.

If you can use a dedicated young professional who has consistently been singled out for drive and initiative, sound judgment, and technical expertise, I hope you will contact me to suggest a time when we might meet to discuss your needs. I can assure you in advance that I could rapidly become an asset to your organization, and I can provide excellent references.

Sincerely,

Miguel LaSandra

MIGUEL LASANDRA

1110½ Hay Street, Fayetteville, NC 28305   •   preppub@aol.com   •   (910) 483-6611

OBJECTIVE

To offer experience related to the field of aviation maintenance management to an organization that can use a dedicated and hard-working young professional with a versatile background which includes problem-solving, budgeting, and inventory control.

EDUCATION & TRAINING

Studied Human Resource Management at Technical Career Institutes, NY.

Excelled in military training programs which included courses in aircraft electrical systems, professional leadership development, automated inventory control (ULLS), warehouse inventory control, hazardous materials handling, and the Defense Reutilization and Marketing System as well as emergency lifesaving and airborne training.

TECHNICAL EXPERTISE

Aircraft: Have logged 350 hours of flight time in rotary aircraft; offer experience in managing and performing maintenance on rotary aircraft.
* Am also skilled in performing maintenance on fixed-wing aircraft.

Computers: Have become familiar with automated systems used to manage aviation maintenance activities such as the Windows operating system.

EXPERIENCE

Advanced ahead of my peers to critical leadership and managerial roles, U.S. Army:
ELECTRICAL SHOP FOREMAN. Ft. Gordon, GA (2001-present). Supervise a team of up to eight avionics technicians and mechanics involved in repairing and maintaining all wiring and radios on a fleet of 41 Blackhawk helicopters; order all bench stock.
* Known for my skills as a troubleshooter, am called on to locate and solve the most difficult problems while specializing in fixing electrical malfunctions.
* Awarded my fifth Army Achievement Medal in June 2002, was cited for my focused attitude and significant contributions as an Avionics Technician for a joint task force.

ELECTRICAL SHOP FOREMAN. Ft. Polk, LA (2000). Supervised a work force of from eight to 12 people with varied job specialties which included providing electrical, engine, and technical supply support for an aviation battalion.
* Managed the electrical repair and maintenance actions which supported a fleet of 16 CH-47 Chinook helicopters; ordered bench stock.
* Received an Army Achievement Medal in recognition of my "experience, judgment, and professionalism" which allowed the company to exceed goals and maintain high levels of equipment readiness and availability.

AUTOMATED LOGISTICS SPECIALIST. Ft. Lewis, WA (1995-99). After excelling as an Automated Logistics Specialist from 1995-96 at the motor pool level, was promoted to support an 800-person organization with computer tracking of vehicle maintenance and parts availability information.
* Was selected ahead of more experienced personnel for this critical "hot seat" position.
* Accepted orders for non-expendable items (such as hand tools) from the supply supervisors at five companies and purchased items ranging in price from $5 to $15,000.
* Named as Budget Manager, tracked purchases for each of the five supported companies and made expense allocations to each.
* Was honored with Army Achievement Medals for my positive attitude, initiative, and commitment to excellence while preparing for major external evaluation in 1999, 1998, and 1997 during which the organization received high ratings in all operational areas.
* Managed $3 million in expenditures; used SAMS software for warehouse management.

PERSONAL

Was entrusted with a Top Secret security clearance. Excellent references on request.

**ELECTRICAL SYSTEMS
SUPERVISOR**

Dear Sir or Madam:

I would appreciate an opportunity to talk with you soon about how I could contribute to your organization through my versatile background of accomplishments as an electrical technician and supervisor with experience in supply, warehousing, and distribution.

As you will see from my enclosed resume, I offer a long history of success in the area of aircraft electrical and hydraulics systems repair and maintenance while working as a civilian supporting military aircraft worldwide. In my current position as supervisor for 19 highly skilled employees, I have received numerous citations and commendations recognizing my ability to guide and lead my personnel to consistently exceed expected performance standards.

Throughout my years with the Federal Aviation Administration, I have been known for my ability to find ways to increase productivity and reduce costs. Several of my suggestions were adopted and resulted in immediate savings including one modification to existing helicopter systems which saved more than $500,00 in its first year of use.

In every job I have held I have been selected for advancement and recognized as a very resourceful and decisive professional with an eye for detail, organizational skills, and a leadership style which has proven very effective.

I hope you will call or write me soon to suggest a time convenient for us to meet and discuss your current and future needs and how I might serve them. Thank you in advance for your time.

Sincerely yours,

Archibald W. Kingfish

ARCHIBALD W. KINGFISH

1110½ Hay Street, Fayetteville, NC 28305　　•　　preppub@aol.com　　•　　(910) 483-6611

OBJECTIVE
　　　　To offer outstanding mechanical skills as well as supervisory and leadership abilities to an organization that can use a mature, experienced professional known for having a keen eye for detail, a decisive manner, and the ability to manage multiple tasks simultaneously.

EXPERIENCE
　　　　Earned a reputation as a versatile and adaptable professional who could be counted on to exceed performance standards, Federal Aviation Administration, Washington, DC:
　　　　SUPERVISOR, AIRCRAFT ELECTRICAL SYSTEMS REPAIR TEAM. (2001-present). Was singled out for numerous commendations and citations in recognition of my suggestions which resulted in saving time and money as well as my expertise as a leader while supervising 19 employees and ensuring that aircraft repairs were completed on time and correctly.
- Played a key role in the development of repair procedures which resulted in saving more than $500,000 on two aircraft transmissions and allowed the aircraft to return to service three to four months ahead of schedule.
- Contributed my expertise during a project in which engineers developed new procedures for repairing components and by designing test equipment which not only saved time and promoted safety but also resulted in a $1 million cost savings.

　　　　AIRCRAFT ELECTRICIAN. (1990-00). Was consistently cited for my resourcefulness, initiative, and dependability while excelling in repairing aircraft electrical, hydraulic, and pneumatic systems; performed magnetic particle and liquid penetrant inspections; repaired power train and drive system components.
- Made a suggestion which resulted in a first-year savings of more than $500,000 after modifications were made to fuel quantity indicating systems on the OH-58 aircraft.
- Received a cash award for designing a device which reduced safety hazards.

TRAINING
　　　　Attended training courses, programs, and seminars related to these and other areas:

Combination Welding	Oil Burner Servicing
Microcomputer Programming	Photography
Total Quality Management (TQM)	Reciprocating Engines
Human Relations and the Customer	Labor Relations
Maintenance Familiarization Course	Safety Procedures
UH-60A Maintenance and Electrician's Courses	Technical Drawing
Prevention of Sexual Harassment for Supervisors	Aircraft Propellers
Magnetic Particle/Liquid Penetrant Levels II and I	Hydraulics
AH-64 Main Landing Gear Mount Inspection Training	Common Hardware
Helicopter High Performance Hoist Operation and Maintenance	
Hazardous Waste/Material Management (Environmental Coordinators' Course)	

CERTIFICATIONS Certified at Level II NDI, Magnetic Particle and Liquid Penetrant.

AIRCRAFT EXPERTISE
　　　　Adapted to the unique characteristics of a wide variety of aircraft including:

Fixed-wing:	C-54	U-1	U-6	U-21
YC-7A	X-26A	T-1A	T-2	T-38A
TF-8A	F-4	A-4	A-6	A-7
P-3	OV-1	F-27	T-28	OV-10
T-33	T-41	T-42	PT-31A	C-8
Rotary-wing:	OH-13	UH-34	CH-46	CH-470
UH-1	AH -15	AH-64	UH-60	

Exact Name of Person
Exact Title
Exact Name of Company
Address
City, State, Zip

**ELECTRICAL SYSTEMS
REPAIRMAN**

Dear Exact Name of Person (or Dear Sir or Madam if answering a blind ad):

With the enclosed resume, I would like to make you aware of my considerable technical electronics and electrical skills as well as my experience in managing the repair of armament and electrical systems.

As you will see from my resume, I have served my country with distinction since 1993, when I joined the U.S. Army. While being promoted ahead of my peers and receiving several medals for distinguished technical knowledge and management skills, I have earned a reputation as a skilled troubleshooter and problem-solver.

In my most recent assignments I excelled in managing up to seven individuals involved in maintaining aircraft/missile systems, including electrical systems. I have become accustomed to working in environments in which there was "no room for error" because a mistake by me or one of my associates could cost the loss of human lives and assets. On the formal written citation for one medal which I received, I was praised for my "superb work ethic and troubleshooting ability," and I was also described in writing as "the key to the maintenance effort" during a major project involving 24 helicopters.

With a belief that strong training programs produce highly skilled technicians, I have on my own initiative developed training programs which improved the skill levels of electricians and armament fire control specialists. I have been praised in formal performance evaluations for "unswaying commitment to improving the skills of subordinates," and I have been described in writing as "one of the most trusted and respected electrical troubleshooters."

If you can use a creative young professional who responds to challenges and pressure with hard work and dedication, I hope you will contact me to suggest a time when we might meet to discuss your needs. I can assure you that I could quickly become an asset to your organization and can provide outstanding references at the appropriate time.

Sincerely,

William J. French

WILLIAM J. FRENCH

1110½ Hay Street, Fayetteville, NC 28305 • preppub@aol.com • (910) 483-6611

OBJECTIVE   To offer excellent technical electronics skills, with an emphasis on armament and electrical systems repair to an organization that can use an adaptable quick learner with extensive diagnostic, troubleshooting, and problem-solving experience.

EDUCATION   Completed nearly a year of college coursework, University of Massachusetts, Lowell, MA.
& TRAINING   Extensive U.S. Army training in electricity and armaments repair.

TECHNICAL   *Use and interpret:* layout drawings, schematics, and diagrams to solve problems while
EXPERTISE   maintaining aircraft electronics, radar, communication, and navigation systems and associated support equipment.
                 Aircraft expertise: AH-64.
                 Awards & Medals: Won two prestigious medals recognizing my exceptional technical skills, hard work, positive attitude, and resourcefulness.
   * On the citation, was praised for "superb work ethic and troubleshooting ability" which enabled all unit aircraft to complete six table gunnery and harmonize gun systems.
   * On the formal write-up for one medal, was described as "the key" to the maintenance effort during the war in Afghanistan, resulting in 18 Apache crews qualified and 48 Hellfires shot with a minimum of aircraft downtime.

EXPERIENCE   *Built a reputation as a knowledgeable technical expert, U.S. Army (1993-present):*
                 SUPERVISOR & AH64-A ARMAMENT FIRE CONTROL REPAIRER. U.S. Army, Afghanistan (2002-present). As a Squad Leader in an Aviation Intermediate Maintenance Company, supervise six employees as well as shop equipment valued at $100,000.
   * Led six team projects which completed more than 50 work orders which were interrupting mission capability. Was selected as Assistant Maintenance Supervisor over four other mid-managers based on my vast technical abilities.
   * Emphasize training and retraining and am noted for my "unswaying commitment to improving the skills of subordinates;" cross-trained ten armament technicians in electrical component repair, and implemented a new advanced skill-level training program.
   * Supervise and perform aviation unit, intermediate, and depot maintenance on the AH-64 electrical and instrument systems and the electrical, electronic, mechanical, and pneudraulics systems associated with the AH-64 armament/missile and fire control systems.
   * Have become noted for my skill in diagnosing and repairing malfunctions in the AH-64 armament as well as electrical, instrument, and fire control systems and components according to technical devices and instruments.
   * Perform operational checks, ammunition loading/unloading, and weapons systems configuration changes for all AH-64 fire control systems.
   * Test/troubleshoot and repair test sets and diagnostic equipment.

                 AH-64A ARMAMENT FIRE CONTROL REPAIRER. U.S. Army, locations in the Middle East and Korea. (1993-02). Performed essentially the same duties as those described above while managing a squad of seven employees in an attack helicopter battalion capable of worldwide relocation at any time.
   * Was accountable for $4.5 million in tools and ground support equipment.
   * Was described in writing as "one of the unit's most trusted and respected electrical troubleshooters" and praised for "excellent squad supervision and problem-solving techniques which helped the unit achieve an exceptional readiness rating."

PERSONAL   Highly motivated professional with an intense dedication to safety. Excellent references.

Date

Exact Name of Person
Title or Position
Name of Company
Address (no., street)
Address (city, state, zip)

FLIGHT LINE
MECHANIC

Dear Exact Name of Person (or Dear Sir or Madam if answering a blind ad):

I would appreciate an opportunity to talk with you soon about how I could contribute to your organization through my experience in the areas of aircraft maintenance and inspections as well as through my outstanding communication and supervisory abilities.

While serving my country in the U.S. Air Force, I advanced to positions of responsibility ahead of my peers and earned a reputation as an aggressive professional who demands perfection from myself before expecting it from others. My ability to perform under pressure while consistently exceeding standards was recognized throughout my military career.

As you will see from my resume I recently received the **FAA Airframe and Power Plant License**. I have supervised up to ten specialists as an inspector and crew chief. In my most recent job as Supervisory Flight Line Mechanic, I continued my record of extremely high equipment availability and quality control evaluation rates.

I feel that my proven technical and supervisory abilities as well as my "courteous and cheerful personality" combine to make me a mature professional of potential value to your organization.

I hope you will welcome my call soon to arrange a brief meeting at your convenience to discuss your current and future needs and how I might serve them. Thank you in advance for your time.

Sincerely yours,

Andrew J. Owl

Alternate last paragraph:
I hope you will call or write soon to suggest a time convenient for us to meet and discuss your current and future needs and how I might serve them. Thank you in advance for your time.

ANDREW J. OWL

1110½ Hay Street, Fayetteville, NC 28305   •   preppub@aol.com   •   (910) 483-6611

OBJECTIVE

To apply my skills related to aircraft maintenance and inspection to an organization in need of a technically proficient professional who offers outstanding abilities in communicating with and supervising others.

LICENSE & AIRCRAFT EXPERTISE

FAA Airframe and Power Plant License.
Through training and experience, am qualified to operate all ground equipment, engine test equipment, and towing vehicles.
Offer experience with the following aircraft:

McDonnell Douglas F-4E   General Dynamics F-16A/B/C/D   Fairchild A-10A

EXPERIENCE

SUPERVISORY FLIGHT LINE MECHANIC. U.S. Air Force, Washington, D.C. (2002-present). Was promoted to direct the efforts of four mechanics as the "Dedicated Crew Chief" charged with overseeing all scheduled/unscheduled maintenance, accompanying aircraft through inspections, providing advice on repairs, and performing preventive maintenance and functional checks.

- Made important contributions to the unit's recognition as "2002 Fighter Squadron of the Year." Earned praise for "maintenance knowledge and dedication" which resulted in a 100% quality assurance rate and a 94.2% "mission capable" rate.

F-16 AIRCRAFT MECHANIC. U.S.A.F., The Middle East (1999-01). Served as the focal point for all maintenance and inspection support of an $18 million aircraft as well as completing and reviewing documents.

- Was chosen to apply my expertise as a technician and inspector on the "battle damage repair team." Achieved a 97% availability rate significantly above the 85% standard.

F-16 CREW CHIEF. U.S.A.F., Travis AFB, CA (1996-98). Supervised two specialists maintaining and servicing a $16 million aircraft and also performed towing, inspections, launch and recovery operations as well as controlling parts ordering and documentation.

- Performed "flawlessly" as evidenced by five separate "no-fault" ratings.
- Led a team on a special assignment to repair engine malfunctions which resulted in a downed F-16 being repaired and completing its schedule.
- Was officially described as an "unselfish and dynamic leader."

SUPERVISORY AIRCRAFT INSPECTOR. U.S.A.F., England (1993-95). Earned rapid promotion from crew member to oversee ten specialists involved in inspecting A-10A structures and systems including: flight control, landing gear, electrical, hydraulics, and power plant systems.

- Established an Air Force record of 105 planes airborne at the same time during a readiness evaluation due to expertise of inspection procedures.
- Completed a relocation project with no loss of effectiveness due to my ability to prioritize work and inspire dedication in employees.

INSPECTION TEAM SPECIALIST. U.S.A.F., Hurlburt Field, FL (1991-92). Became familiar with procedures for inspecting aircraft structures and systems and gained experience as a supervisor. Achieved six "zero defect" quality assurance evaluations.

EDUCATION

Completed two years of computer science course work at multiple academic institutions.

PERSONAL

Hold Top Secret security clearance. Excellent references on request.

MAINTENANCE PROFESSIONALS
Date

Exact Name of Person
Title or Position
Name of Company
Address (no., street)
Address (city, state, zip)

**FUEL SYSTEMS
MECHANIC**

Dear Exact Name of Person (or Dear Sir or Madam if answering a blind ad):

I would appreciate an opportunity to talk with you soon about how I could contribute to your organization through my experience in the area of aircraft maintenance. My specialized knowledge relates to aircraft fuel systems, the supervision of teams of mechanics, and ensuring total quality control procedures are observed.

As you will see from my resume, I have served my country in the U.S. Air Force, and I have been selected for special assignments and projects in the United Kingdom as well as in Afghanistan and in Saudi Arabia during the war in the Middle East. I have recently made contributions to aviation safety and aviation operations during the war against terrorism while stationed in Afghanistan. On numerous occasions I have received several letters of recognition and earned praise for my professionalism, technical skills, and leadership abilities.

I offer a history of outstanding performance in positions where I was able to stream-line procedures and find ways to increase productivity. A firm believer in the Total Quality Maintenance Concept, I have completed thousands of aircraft discrepancy repairs with no defects noted.

Known for my "participatory" style of leadership, I enjoy the challenge of learning and passing my knowledge to others. I feel that it is important to take advantage of every opportunity to attend training programs and classes and follow this formal learning with self study. Only in this way will I be able to maximize my own potential and continue to grow personally and professionally.

I hope you will welcome my call soon to arrange a brief meeting at your convenience to discuss your current and future needs and how I might serve them. Thank you in advance for your time.

Sincerely yours,

Howard R. Waite

HOWARD R. WAITE

1110½ Hay Street, Fayetteville, NC 28305   •   preppub@aol.com   •   (910) 483-6611

OBJECTIVE

To apply my technical knowledge and experience related to aircraft maintenance to an organization that can use a creative team player who offers outstanding leadership skills, special knowledge of aircraft fuel systems, and a strong belief in total quality control.

CLEARANCE

Was entrusted with a Top Secret security clearance.

EXPERIENCE

SUPERVISORY AIRCRAFT FUEL SYSTEMS MECHANIC. U.S. Air Force, Afghanistan (2001-present). Earned consistent advancement through increasing supervisory levels to this position as the leader of a 10-person team of specialists involved in repairing and replacing aircraft fuel systems and subsystems.

- Emphasized the importance of the Total Quality Maintenance Concept and have completed thousands of aircraft discrepancies with no defects.
- Found ways of streamlining maintenance procedures which led to an impressive 43% increase in productivity.
- Established new methods for maintaining up-to-date and current technical information which helped the unit attain 100% quality maintenance.
- Was awarded an achievement medal for my part in removing hazardous materials, containing a fuel spill, and removing a crashed aircraft from a ditch on a runway.
- Developed job knowledge and skills which led to my selection for a role in training new personnel and supervising mechanics in a vital activity at this major air force facility.
- Acquired extensive experience in troubleshooting, analyzing problems, and finding solutions through my creativity and knowledge.

*Contributed to the success of special projects and temporary assignments which included working in Saudi Arabia and in the United Kingdom as a **Fuel Cell Mechanic**:*
Saudi Arabia. Received awards including the Kuwait Liberation Medal and a Certificate of Recognition for my hard work and efforts during the war in the Middle East.

- Displayed my adaptability and technical knowledge while participating in aircraft launchings, recovery, and repairs.
- Earned praise for my contributions to team efforts which ensured allied personnel were able to complete their assignments and free the people of Kuwait from Iraqi oppression.

The United Kingdom. Was selected to participate in several two-month projects aimed at assisting maintenance and training in Royal Air Force (RAF) units.

TRAINING

Received special training in areas which included the Air Force's technical order system, aircraft battle damage repair, records management orientation, and quality awareness. Received Department of Defense special training in counterterrorism.

TECHNICAL AIRCRAFT EXPERTISE

- Am trained to analyze, pinpoint, and troubleshoot aircraft component systems as well to supervise the repair process from inprocessing to the ready-for service stage.
- Received technical training in inspection, Total Quality Maintenance Control, and replacement.
- Am familiar with aircraft including the following:
  Lockheed C-130 and C-141 (C-135)   McDonnell-Douglas F-16 (A-10)   Boeing 747

PERSONAL

Have a reputation as a very "open-minded" and adaptable professional. Am a creative thinker who enjoys "brainstorming" and team efforts to find solutions.

Date

Exact Name of Person
Title or Position
Name of Company
Address (no., street)
Address (city, state, zip)

GROUND SUPPORT
EQUIPMENT
MECHANIC

Dear Exact Name of Person (or Dear Sir or Madam if answering a blind ad):

I would appreciate an opportunity to talk with you soon about how I could contribute to your organization through my experience in airfield operations including loading, repair parts supply support, and refueling with special emphasis on ground support equipment maintenance, repair, and inspection.

You will see from my enclosed resume that I have earned a reputation as a skilled technician and mechanic. My ability to rapidly absorb new information and pass my knowledge on to others earned me the praise of my superiors and caused them to select me for special projects. In my current position I not only accounted for a 2,300-line-item inventory of ground support equipment but also participated in training others in inspection techniques, contributed my troubleshooting and repair skills, and became the work station's safety specialist.

You would find me to be a congenial person who offers a high degree of self motivation and dedication to excellence. I am a natural leader who inspires others to join me in order to accomplish our group's peak levels of performance.

I hope you will welcome my call soon to arrange a brief meeting at your convenience to discuss your current and future needs and how I might serve them. Thank you in advance for your time.

Sincerely yours,

Terry A. Kinston

Alternate last paragraph:
I hope you will call or write me soon to suggest a time convenient for us to meet and discuss your current and future needs and how I might serve them. Thank you in advance for your time.

TERRY A. KINSTON

1110½ Hay Street, Fayetteville, NC 28305   •   preppub@aol.com   •   (910) 483-6611

OBJECTIVE

To offer a background which includes a strong base of experience in aviation ground support equipment repair to an organization that can use a talented, dedicated professional with a reputation for personal qualities of dedication and reliability.

SPECIAL KNOWLEDGE & SKILLS

Through training and experience, have become skilled in repairing, maintaining, and testing aircraft ground support equipment including:

tow tractors: TA-75A, B, and C; JG-40 and 75; TA-35	fire fighting unit: P-16
liquid oxygen carts: TMU-27 and TMU-70	oxygen cart: O2
hydraulic units: A/M27T-5, A/M27T-7, and AHT-63	forklifts: 4, 6, 20,000-lb.
mobile electric power plants: NC-8A, NC-2, NC-10 and MMG1A	
gas turbine compressors: GTC-85, NC-PP105, and AM47A-4	

Repair and adjust fuel controls, flow dividers, oil and fuel pumps, generators, motors, relays, voltage regulators, thermostats, and air valves.

Am licensed on the ground support equipment listed above as well as being qualified in the areas of Hydraulic Contamination and Tire and Wheel.

Maintained aircraft including the following:

F-18A   A-6E   EA-6B   C-2   S-3   C-141   C-5   E-2

EXPERIENCE

*Built a reputation as a talented technician/mechanic with leadership and supervisory abilities while advancing as a **GROUND SUPPORT EQUIPMENT (GSE) MECHANIC**, United Airlines:*

EQUIPMENT CONTROL SPECIALIST and **SUPERVISOR.** Dulles Airport, NY, NY (2000-present). In addition to regular responsibilities as a supervisor and mechanic, was selected to oversee a support activity in which 2,300 items of equipment for 22 customer units were properly issued, received, and accounted for.
- Developed well-trained personnel who were thoroughly knowledgeable of pre- and post-operational inspection techniques.
- Implemented a system which made scanning repair/maintenance status boards (VIDS-MAF) easier to read at a glance and streamlined maintenance tracking activities.
- Was singled out for the critical position of work center safety petty officer.
- Applied expert troubleshooting skills which allowed for flightline repairs and eliminated aircraft downtime for repair.

EQUIPMENT REPAIR SPECIALIST. LaGuardia Airport, New York, NY (1999-00). Applied my expertise to perform repairs on gas turbine compressors and preventive maintenance on all categories of ground support equipment.
- On my own initiative, spent 360 hours to create a state-of-the-art training facility which saved $40,000 by eliminating the need for outside labor.

PREVENTIVE MAINTENANCE AND REPAIR SPECIALIST. Atlanta International Airport, Atlanta, GA (1993-98). In addition to repair and maintenance on all classes of ground support equipment, gained experience in operating a 6,000-lb. forklift during a period of functional reorganization and change as activities were closed and the facility deactivated.
- Handpicked as one of two people to participate in a special project, learned the proper techniques for loading a C-2 aircraft and performed maintenance on 30 items of equipment.

PERSONAL

Offer well-developed mechanical and technical skills. Have a strong interest in continuing to grow and develop new abilities related to aviation. Logged 20 flight hours in a C-2.

PETER NIMROCK

1110½ Hay Street, Fayetteville, NC 28305

preppub@aol.com · (910) 483-6611

OBJECTIVE

To benefit an organization that can use a versatile professional with expertise related to hazardous materials program management, maintenance management, and troubleshooting and problem solving.

CLEARANCE

Hold Top Secret security clearance, SSNI

EXPERIENCE

HAZARDOUS MATERIALS PROGRAM MANAGER. Department of Defense, Washington, DC (2001-present). Supervised 30 people in meeting support requirements for 33 C-130E aircraft in a combat airlift squadron which provides worldwide support for the war against terrorism. Was responsible for $900 million in support equipment, and managed a 1,200 line-item bench stock and more than 180 composite tool kits (CTK).

- Managed and controlled 22 complete sets of technical orders over $10 million in test equipment, tools, radios, computers, and vehicles.
- Oversaw the Hazardous Materials (HAZMAT) Program, and on a formal performance evaluation was commended for "completely overhauling the unit's HAZMAT program, making it the best of any squadron in the wing."
- In revamping the HAZMAT Program, also revamped the maintenance Hazardous Communications program into one which exceeded stringent safety and environmental standards, and was commended for "aggressively managing the HAZMAT Program for waste accountability and control."
- Earned an Outstanding rating on the 2001 Environmental Compliance/Assessment Management Program.
- Instituted many changes in the Composite Tools Kit (CTK) area which greatly enhanced productivity; identified and procured $200,000 in badly needed tools for flightline operations.
- Installed a new bar code inventory system to track tool usage which resulted in better accountability and reduced the incidence of lost tools by 50%.
- Was evaluated in writing as a "top performer whose positive attitude motivates his troops and energizes his superiors."

PRODUCTION SUPERINTENDENT. Department of Defense, Classified locations worldwide (1999-00). Extensively involved in Quality Assurance (QA), managed a 40-person work center; provided trained, qualified maintenance technicians for isochronal inspections.

- Managed 45 aircraft maintenance personnel and 10 separate maintenance specialties during ongoing isochronal aircraft inspections as well as an average of four aircraft isochronal inspections monthly.
- Supervised all quality production, safety, security, and foreign object damage prevention requirements in the KC-135 maintenance dock.
- Orchestrated 33 isochronal (ISO) inspections with a quality evaluation rating of 99.7% and zero ISO backlogs.
- Instilled a "safety first and quality assurance first" attitude in all

employees which resulted in 99% customer satisfaction; led the organization to win the Commander's Organizational Quality Award.

- Conducted hazardous waste training for shop personnel on proper storage of hazardous material; received zero significant findings from the 2000 Environmental Compliance Assessment Management Program (ECAMP).

INSPECTION DOCK CHIEF. Department of Defense, Belgium (1997-99). Managed and supervised maintenance performed during the phase inspections on 18 E-3A aircraft and associated equipment valued at $3.9 billion. Coordinated work scheduled for 35 people from 11 NATO nations in 17 different occupational specialties.

- Controlled, maintained, and repaired shop equipment valued at $1.3 million.
- On my own initiative, developed a new work flow for the corrosion-control and aircraft-painting portions of the phase inspection.
- Emphasized safety and identified the safety hazards associated with the aircraft dry polish; my diligence resulted in the elimination of an unsafe material.
- Following an air abort of an aircraft, took decisive actions during recovery which resulted in replacement of aborted aircraft within 30 minutes.
- Utilized my technical knowledge and resourcefulness to benefit NATO on numerous occasions: on one occasion, discovered and corrected a fleet-wide discrepancy on nose landing gear lubrication fitting. On another occasion, built an inspection timetable which consolidated the phase and corrosion prevention programs.

MAINTENANCE MANAGER. Department of Defense, Korea (1996-97). Managed a multi-million-dollar flying-hour budget while directing and managing all maintenance performed on aircraft producing an average of 12 sorties and 80 flying hours per month.

- Distinguished myself in all aspects of troubleshooting and quality assurance; once identified the problem causing an intermittent nose-steering problem and saved NATO the cost of contracting a depot team to repair the problem.

Other Department of Defense experience:
AIRCRAFT MAINTENANCE TECHNICIAN. Supervised and accomplished depot-level maintenance inspections and modifications of aircraft systems and components on C/KC-135, B-1B, and B-52 aircraft. Developed a training program for personnel.
SHIFT SUPERVISOR. Supervised test measurement and diagnostic equipment, tool room operations, and shop personnel involved in aircraft maintenance.
Excelled in jobs as a Recovery Team Member, Aircraft Maintenance Specialist, Assistant Crew Chief, Unit Bench Stock Monitor, Non-Powered AGAE Mechanic, and Aircraft Mechanic. Was responsible for total maintenance on the $140 million E-3A Sentry aircraft.

HONORS/AWARDS Received 28 different awards for distinguished performance.

EDUCATION Completed Hazardous Waste Operation and Emergency Response (HAZWOPER) Certification Course.
Licensed Aircraft and Powerplant (A&P) Mechanic. FAA Airframe and Powerplant Certified.
Completed training programs related to aircraft maintenance, care and use of test equipment, quality assurance, hazardous waste and environmental awareness, corrosion control and fire prevention, chemical warfare, OSHA and EPA standards, aircraft battle damage repair, leadership and management.
Skilled in using test equipment and diagnostic measurement tools.

SKILLS Certified Crane operator (15-ton wheel hydraulic); Certified De-icer Truck Basket/Vehicle operator; Certified forklift operator, gas and diesel; Certified Tow vehicle (MB-2, MB-4).

Date

Exact Name of Person
Title or Position
Name of Company
Address (number and street)
Address (city, state, and zip)

HELICOPTER
MECHANIC CHIEF

Dear Exact Name of Person (or Sir or Madam if answering a blind ad):

I would appreciate an opportunity to talk with you soon about how I could contribute to your organization through my extensive experience in military aviation operations worldwide while developing a reputation as a highly skilled troubleshooter and mechanic with excellent supervisory abilities.

With approximately four years of experience with the UH-60 Blackhawk utility helicopter and another 3-1/2 years with the AH-1 Cobra, I am recognized as a dedicated professional. Working toward my FAA Airframe and Power Plant License, I am licensed to operate heavy machinery used to remove aircraft blades and engines. I have logged 600 flight hours as a Crew Chief in multi-engine, rotary-wing aircraft and 100 hours as an Instructor.

In my current assignment as a UH-60 Dedicated Crew Chief, I was singled out by the brigade commander as his Crew Chief and chosen for special UN peacekeeping missions in Macedonia and Bosnia-Herzegovina.

I would be a valuable asset to any government contractor who can use a knowledgeable troubleshooter and aircraft mechanic who has lived and worked in international settings and is familiar with the unique needs of the military aviation community.

I hope you will welcome my call soon to arrange a brief meeting to discuss your current and future needs and how I might serve them. Thank you in advance for your time.

Sincerely,

Moss A. Spruce

Alternate last paragraph:
I hope you will call or write me soon to suggest a time convenient for us to meet and discuss your current and future needs and how I might serve them. Thank you in advance for your time.

MOSS A. SPRUCE

1110½ Hay Street, Fayetteville, NC 28305   ·   preppub@aol.com   ·   (910) 483-6611

OBJECTIVE   To offer my extensive experience and skills related to aircraft maintenance to an organization that can use a detail-oriented professional who learns quickly, excels in supervisory roles, and is knowledgeable of the unique requirements of military aviation operations.

AIRCRAFT EXPERTISE & TRAINING   Offer approximately eight years of experience as a helicopter mechanic on the UH-60 Blackhawk and AH-1 Cobra with additional exposure to the UH-1 helicopter.
Am licensed to operate heavy machinery used in the removal of aircraft blades and engines.
Currently am studying for the FAA Airframe and Power Plant License.
Have logged 600 hours of flight time in multi-engine, rotary-wing aircraft as a Crew Chief and 100 hours as an Instructor.
Excelled in more than 1,000 hours of advanced individual training programs including AH-1 and UH-60 helicopter maintenance as well as leadership development.

EXPERIENCE   *Have advanced ahead of my peers to supervisory roles while refining my troubleshooting, mechanical, and technical skills in the U.S. Army aviation community:*
UH-60 CREW CHIEF. England (2001-present). Train and supervise the performance of eight mechanics providing maintenance support for four UH-60 Blackhawk helicopters and associated equipment with a total value in excess of $40 million.
- Recognized as the unit's most knowledgeable and skilled troubleshooter and mechanic, was handpicked by the brigade commander as Crew Chief for his personal aircraft.
- Was singled out as Flight Instructor/Evaluator to train and ensure the quality of performance for incoming, less experienced flight crew members.
- Completed temporary assignments in Bosnia-Herzegovina and Macedonia as a supervisor of aircraft maintenance support activities: earned an Army Achievement Medal for maintaining my aircraft at 95% operational readiness, a full 20% above standard, under hostile conditions while maximizing limited parts and equipment inventories.
- Maintained forms and records necessary to ensure a complete and accurate trail of all maintenance associated with each aircraft.
- Became qualified in the operation of the ULLS-A system.

AVIATION MAINTENANCE AND INVENTORY CONTROL SPECIALIST. Germany (1998-00). Controlled more than $4 million worth of ground support equipment and managed the tool room for an aviation company.
- Totally reorganized tool room procedures so that 100% accountability was maintained.

UH-60 HELICOPTER MECHANIC. Korea (1995-97). Performed aircraft maintenance and ground support activities as a crew member in the only medical airlift unit in Korea.
- Was instrumental in implementing the first-ever live hoist training in the unit.

SENIOR AH-1 MAINTENANCE SUPERVISOR and **TRAINING SPECIALIST.** Ft. Gordon, GA (1993-94). Conducted on-the-job training for 110 mechanics and ground crew specialists while overseeing extensive maintenance on multimillion-dollar aircraft systems including conducting 12 AH-1 helicopter maintenance phases.

CLEARANCE   Hold a Secret security clearance, updated in April 2001.

PERSONAL   Am productive as a supervisor as well as while working in close cooperation with others as part of a team. Learn quickly and offer strong mechanical aptitude.

Date

Exact Name of Person
Title or Position
Name of Company
Address (no., street)
Address (city, state, zip)

**HELICOPTER REPAIR
SUPERVISOR**

Dear Exact Name of Person (or Dear Sir or Madam if answering a blind ad):

I would appreciate an opportunity to talk with you soon about how I could contribute to your organization through my proven expertise in aircraft maintenance, production control, personnel supervision, and project management.

As you will see from my resume, I have gained valuable technical expertise and managerial abilities during my service in the U.S. Army, becoming highly skilled in the operation, repair, and maintenance of CH-47 Chinook, AH-64 Apache, UH-60 Blackhawk, OH-58 Kiowa Scout, and UH-1H Huey helicopters, while also troubleshooting, repairing, and replacing power plants, hydraulics, flight controls, power trains, and general airframe components.

I am a skilled leader and administrator, proficient in training, evaluating, and supervising personnel, scheduling and tracking work orders, and processing forms, documents, and corresponding paperwork. I also gained a reputation as a safety-conscious worker, earning two respected safety awards and being named Fire Marshall. I was instrumental in implementing a repair information computer system, significantly increasing production and quality assurance level.

You would find me to be a hard-working and reliable professional who prides myself on giving 100% to every job I undertake. I can provide excellent references upon request.

I hope you will call or write me soon to suggest a time convenient for us to meet and discuss your current and future needs and how I might serve them. Thank you in advance for your time.

Sincerely,

Ivan A. Goode

Alternate last paragraph:
I hope you will welcome my call soon to arrange a brief meeting at your convenience to discuss your current and future needs and how I might serve them. Thank you in advance for your time.

IVAN ALAN GOODE

1110½ Hay Street, Fayetteville, NC 28305 · preppub@aol.com · (910) 483-6611

OBJECTIVE

To benefit an organization that can use a safety-conscious rotary wing aircraft mechanic who offers hands-on technical experience, production control, and personnel supervision, as well as excellent motivational, planning, and time-management skills.

AIRCRAFT EXPERTISE

Can repair, troubleshoot, maintain, disassemble, and assemble a wide range of helicopters and other aircraft, including CH-47 Chinooks, UH-60 Blackhawks, OH-58 Kiowa Scouts, AH-64 Apaches, and UH-1H Hueys; am proficient in troubleshooting, repairing, and replacing power trains, power plants, hydraulics, flight controls, and general airframe components on various helicopters.

EXPERIENCE

Advanced in the following track record of promotion with Sikorsky Aircraft Corporation, Stratford, CT:

HELICOPTER REPAIR SUPERVISOR. Sikorsky Aircraft Corporation, Stratford, CT (2000-present). Refined leadership skills after being rapidly promoted from mechanic to supervising four team leaders in the maintenance and repair of OH-58 Kiowa Scouts, UH-60 Blackhawks, CH-47 Chinooks, UH-1H Hueys, and other helicopters; control a $15 million tool room operation.

- Liaise with Production Control to schedule all job completions, in addition to reporting all unscheduled emergency maintenance.
- Train, evaluate, and supervise 30 mechanics responsible for a $2 million Aviation Ground Unit MEP 360A.
- Earned praise for utilizing technical expertise and excellent time-management skills to reduce maintenance and repair time.
- Use operational tests to certify the airworthiness of repaired aircraft.
- Appointed organization Fire Marshall, train 225 personnel in safety and fire prevention and received two awards for outstanding departmental safety record.

HELICOPTER REPAIR SUPERVISOR. (1999-00). Polished technical expertise while handling maintenance and repairs for OH-58D's in addition to supervising five mechanics and a ground support equipment inventory worth $4 million.

HELICOPTER REPAIR MANAGER. (1997-98). Rapidly promoted after being recognized by top-level management for my outstanding technical and managerial skills; served as team leader, ensuring quality assurance of all OH-58D helicopter repairs and maintenance.

- Trained, supervised, evaluated, and directed six mechanics.
- Controlled all departmental inventory management and parts ordering.
- Recognized by superiors for attention to detail and excellent decision-making.

HELICOPTER MECHANIC. (1994-96). Learned the importance of teamwork while performing maintenance and repairs for OH-58A helicopters and preparing aircraft for missions; earned over 100 flying hours as a flight crewmember. Utilized avionic information computer systems, significantly increasing maintenance production output; trained other employees.

EDUCATION

Completed a wide range of technical training and continuing education courses, including leadership, management, safety, and over 1200 hours in helicopter repair.

- Honor Graduate, Helicopter Repair Supervisor Course, 1996.
- Distinguished Graduate, Helicopter Repair Course, 1995.

PERSONAL

Am an enthusiastic, hard-working professional who believes in always giving 100%.

Date

Exact Name of Person
Title or Position
Name of Company
Address (number and street)
Address (city, state, and zip)

HELICOPTER
REPAIR SUPERVISOR

Dear Exact Name of Person (or Dear Sir or Madam if answering a blind ad):

With the enclosed resume, I would like to make you aware of my interest in exploring employment opportunities within your company in which my strong mechanical skills could be put to work for your benefit.

As you will see from my resume, I received a diploma in Auto Mechanics from a vocational school and worked as an Auto Mechanic prior to my employment with United Technologies Corporation. Even as an entry-level employee, my leadership abilities were recognized as I was named Team Leader and placed in charge of 10 employees. I graduated as Honor Graduate from Helicopter Repair School and was promoted ahead of my peers into management positions which placed me in charge of managing up to four individuals.

In my current position with United Technologies, I have become skilled in quality control, and I am known for my ability to train employees to perform complex trouble-shooting while continuously emphasizing the importance of a drug-free, safety-conscious, and clean work environment.

I am skilled at operating and repairing numerous types of equipment as well as in operating hysters, backhoes, bulldozers, and dump trucks.

I hope you will contact me to suggest a time when we might meet to discuss your needs and how I might help you. I can provide outstanding personal and professional references, and I thank you in advance for your time.

Sincerely,

Blake Starks

BLAKE STARKS

1110½ Hay Street, Fayetteville, NC 28305   •   preppub@aol.com   •   (910) 483-6611

OBJECTIVE

To contribute to an organization that can benefit from my skills as a maintenance mechanic as well as my experience in training and managing other employees.

SKILLS

Helicopter Repair: As an OH-58 Helicopter Repairer, skilled in performing and supervising maintenance on scout helicopters which includes removing and installing subsystem assemblies such as engines, transmissions, gear boxes, rotor hubs, and rotor blades.
Automotive Repair: Experienced in auto service center mechanics.
Equipment Repair: Skilled in troubleshooting and repairing mechanical equipment including small engines, lawn mowers, weed-eaters, and other equipment.

EDUCATION

Received a Certificate as a OH-58D Helicopter Repairer, United Technologies Aviation School, 1994.
- Was named **Honor Graduate.**

Received Certificates from Hazardous Materials Handling Course, Driver Training Course, and Leadership Course, Washington, DC, 1995.
Completed Auto Mechanics Diploma, Bowie High Vocational School, Bowie, MD, 1994.
Completed numerous college courses, University of Puget Sound, 1998-present.
Other training:
- Completed training as a parachutist and training in mountaineering and rappelling.
Equipment handling: Am skilled at operating and maintaining backhoes, bulldozers, dump trucks, tractors, and hysters.

EXPERIENCE

HELICOPTER REPAIR SUPERVISOR. United Technologies, Stratford, CT (1999-present). Supervised up to four mechanics while performing and supervising maintenance on helicopters; trained and managed employees while emphasizing safety consciousness and molding them into a highly motivated team.
- Removed and reinstalled subsystem assemblies such as engines, transmissions, gearboxes, rotor hubs, and rotor blades.
- Became skilled in quality control and quality assurance while preparing helicopters for extensive inspections and maintenance; performed comprehensive inspections and repairs.
- Performed operational checks of repair systems; troubleshot electrical malfunctions.
- Trained personnel on maintenance forms and records as well as in maintaining automated aircraft logbooks.
- Instructed subordinates on the maintenance and use of common and special tools and ground support equipment (GSE).
- Trained my subordinates to perform complex troubleshooting.

MECHANIC AND HELICOPTER REPAIR SUPERVISOR. Sikorsky Aircraft Corporation, Stratford, CT (1998-99). Was promoted ahead of my peers to mid-management while supervising three helicopter mechanics.

AUTO MECHANIC Larry's Auto Service, Downing, GA (1994-97). Performed mechanical maintenance on vehicles, tires, brake systems, and transmissions.
- Handled responsibilities for ordering parts and stocking parts.

PERSONAL

Excellent references on request. Skilled in removing and installing subsystem assemblies.

Date

Exact Name of Person
Title or Position
Name of Company
Address (no., street)
Address (city, state, zip)

**HYDRAULICS
SUPERVISOR**

Dear Exact Name of Person (or Dear Sir or Madam if answering a blind ad):

I would appreciate an opportunity to talk with you soon about how I could contribute to your organization through my technical expertise with hydraulic systems.

In my current position as Hydraulics Supervisor for Lockheed Corp., in Seattle, Washington, I have earned a reputation as a highly skilled technician who is able to quickly learn and apply new information. My experience in troubleshooting, repairing, and testing aircraft hydraulic components has also allowed me to become familiar with electrical wiring and reading schematics.

I earned rapid promotion to a supervisory position and now oversee a 10-person crew maintaining and repairing assigned C-130 aircraft.

I hope you will welcome my call soon to arrange a brief meeting at your convenience to discuss your current and future needs and how I might serve them. Thank you in advance for your time.

Sincerely yours,

Amos C. Andrews

Alternate last paragraph:
I hope you will call or write soon to suggest a time convenient for us to meet and discuss your current and future needs and how I might serve them. Thank you in advance for your time.

AMOS CHARLES ANDREWS

1110½ Hay Street, Fayetteville, NC 28305 • preppub@aol.com • (910) 483-6611

OBJECTIVE	To benefit an organization through my technical expertise in troubleshooting and repairing a wide range of hydraulic systems, my ability to quickly master new techniques, and my supervisory skills.
TECHNICAL SKILLS & KNOWLEDGE	Through training and experience, can troubleshoot, repair, and test hydraulic components. Skilled in rebuilding actuators, control valves, selector valves, restrictors, hydraulic motors, hydraulic restrictors, flow regulators, and other components. Have gained knowledge of the principles of electric equipment operation through working on equipment with electric motors. Read schematics and troubleshoot wiring connected to components.
AIRCRAFT EXPERTISE	Offer experience in maintaining hydraulic systems on aircraft including: C-130 Hercules C-141 Starlifter C-5 Galaxy

TRAINING   Excelled in more than 600 hours of training in the following areas:
- aircraft pneudraulic systems mechanics
- C-130 aircraft hydraulics
- C-141 aircraft hydraulics

EXPERIENCE   **HYDRAULICS SUPERVISOR.** Lockheed Corp., Seattle, WA (2000-present). Earned rapid promotion to supervise 10 people while conducting maintenance and repairs on aircraft manufactured by Lockheed.
- Perform inspections, bench checks, troubleshooting, repair, overhaul, and operational checks.
- Inspect maintenance operations to ensure quality of work performed.
- Prioritize and schedule work assignments.
- Was singled out for special praise for my technical expertise in handling numerous malfunctions quickly.
- Applied my troubleshooting skills to locate a faulty cannon plug on a C-130 wing flap selector valve and returned a C-130 to service.
- Maintain maintenance data using a computerized recordkeeping system.
- Control an inventory of repair parts and supplies which consistently received "outstanding" evaluations.
- Was cited as a "key player" in achieving a 100% successful aircraft availability rate during a special training project.
- Manufacture high- and medium-pressure hoses for hydraulic, pneumatic, oil, and fuel systems.
- Display a talent for locating difficult malfunctions and was often able to make the repairs in less than half the normally required time.

HYDRAULIC SYSTEMS TECHNICIAN. Boeing Aircraft, Los Angeles, CA (1993-99). Refined my supervisory skills and learned my capacity for working under pressure and time restraints while performing maintenance, inspections, and repairs of aircraft hydraulic systems.

CLEARANCE   Hold a Secret security clearance.

PERSONAL   Am known as a very dedicated hard worker who can be counted on to contribute to team efforts. Offer expert skills in rebuilding and testing hydraulic components.

Exact Name of Person
Title or Position
Name of Company
Address (no., street)
Address (city, state, zip)

**MAINTENANCE
ENGINEERING
DIRECTOR**

Dear Exact Name of Person (or Dear Sir or Madam if answering a blind ad):

    I would appreciate an opportunity to talk with you soon about how I could contribute to your organization through my leadership experience, problem-solving skills, and versatile management abilities.

    As you will see from my resume, I offer a proven ability to supervise people, develop and implement new programs, and manage budgets of varying sizes. While being promoted to the rank of GS-18 in the Department of the Army, I excelled in resourcefully managing budgets ranging from thousands of dollars to millions of dollars. I have been commended for my "knack" for instilling a sense of organizational pride in employees, and I have earned a reputation as a powerful motivator.

    In several jobs I have held I have "turned around" marginal operations. Once I transformed, in only one year, a maintenance program evaluated as "worst" into the one rated "best." My ability to "get things done through people" was the key to this dramatic transformation.

    While traveling worldwide to provide management and technical consulting, I had the opportunity to refine my ability to communicate with people from all backgrounds and at all organizational levels. You would find me to be someone who is equally comfortable conducting high-level presentations to top executives and coordinating the training and activities of entry-level personnel. I believe my greatest strength, and the key to my professional success, is my exceptional ability to relate to people and to come across as the kind of leader they want to follow.

    I hope you will welcome my call soon when I try to arrange a brief meeting at your convenience to discuss your needs and how I might serve them. Thank you in advance for your time.

Sincerely yours,

Andrew S. Mitch

Alternate last paragraph:
    I hope you will call or write soon to suggest a time convenient for us to meet and discuss your current and future needs and how I might serve them. Thank you in advance for your time.

ANDREW S. MITCH

1110½ Hay Street, Fayetteville, NC 28305   •   preppub@aol.com   •   (910) 483-6611

OBJECTIVE

To contribute to the overall effectiveness of an organization in need of a proven leader and problem solver with superior management, planning, and motivational skills.

EXPERIENCE

Excelled in the following track record of promotion to GS-18, Dept. of the Army:

Personnel Management

OPERATIONS DIRECTOR. Washington, DC (2002-present). Directed 3,000 personnel in six locations and controlled an annual budget of $8.5 million while developing/implementing policies and procedures for the largest tactical fighter wing in the Middle East.
- Developed, modified, and managed training, safety, and quality control programs.
- Was recognized for having the best maintenance, repair, and environmental programs in the Middle East. Directed resources supporting the war against terrorism.

Logistics Management

DIRECTOR OF LOGISTICS. Classified locations in the Middle East (2000-02). Coordinated movement of aircraft materials, including 2,800 tons of critically needed munitions, to and from locations throughout the Middle East in support of the war against terrorism.
- Contracted for and purchased over $50 million of food and supplies for 500,000 refugees.

Program Management

CHIEF OPERATING OFFICER. Washington, DC (1995-00). Supervised 1,800 maintenance technicians and ensured quality training programs while managing an annual operating budget of over $8 million.
- Directed maintenance of **$1.6 billion** in 72 F-15 fighter planes and assets.
- Through management, increased retention rate of key maintenance personnel 12%; through maintenance, increased aircraft availability 8%.
- "Turned around" a maintenance program in one year from "worst" to "best."

Budgetary Planning

MAINTENANCE ENGINEERING DIRECTOR. MacDill AFB, Florida (1990-95). Managed a budget of $300 million related to maintaining 1,800 aircraft while developing policy and reorganizing an international training facility.
- Monitored the modification and acquisition of defense assets.
- Served as logistics expert on weapons/aircraft systems program review.

Training Development

TRAINING DIRECTOR. NATO Headquarters, Belgium (1985-89). Was handpicked for this critical position establishing and implementing maintenance policy, procedures, training, and concepts for more than 40,000 employees while overseeing activities of 375 field personnel.

DEPUTY COMMANDER FOR MAINTENANCE. Washington, DC (1981-84). Earned a reputation as a resourceful planner while preparing a $5.3 million budget and advising the maintenance chief of a 980-person organization.

Other U.S.A.F. experience worldwide: excelled in "line" and "staff" roles.
- Planned strategy and managed airspace as Plans and Operations Chief.
- As Maintenance Chief, earned the highest rating in Europe in 18 years.

EDUCATION

M.A. degree in Asian Studies, University of Hawaii, Honolulu, HI.
B.S. degree in Management, Wentworth College, Wentworth, IA.
Graduated from the **Air War College** and the **Air Command and Staff College**.
Studied management and computer time sharing, A.F. Institute of Technology.

PERSONAL

Have a "knack" for instilling a sense of pride in employees. Hold a **Top Secret/ESI** security clearance. Logged 3,100 hours of flight time, including 1,500 as pilot-in-command.

Exact Name of Person
Exact Title
Exact Name of Company
Address
City, State, Zip

**MAINTENANCE
EVALUATOR**

Dear Exact Name of Person (or Dear Sir or Madam if answering a blind ad):

With the enclosed resume, I would like to make you aware of my interest in exploring employment opportunities with your organization and to acquaint you with my distinguished track record of achievements as a manager.

As you will see from my resume, I have excelled in positions requiring top-notch management, communication, and organizational skills while serving my country in the Federal Aviation Administration. I rose to one of the most senior ranks in my career field, and I was handpicked for jobs which required a resourceful problem-solver and astute decision-maker. In my most recent job as a Maintenance Evaluator and Consultant, I was officially evaluated as a "brilliant manager, leader, and technical expert" while overseeing quality control and training effectiveness for organizations throughout the world.

In my previous job, I was praised for totally revitalizing and rebuilding substandard training programs, and I was widely credited with improving the quality of academic and flight training for CH-47 aviators and maintenance test pilots throughout the country.

While becoming known as a technical expert in the aviation field, I have gained a reputation as an accomplished communicator with outstanding oral and written skills. In one job, I researched, wrote, and updated lesson plans for Army aviators, and in other jobs I performed with distinction as an Instructor and Consultant. I have also applied my technical knowledge in resourceful ways that led to superior bottom-line results. For example, in one position managing multimillion-dollar aviation assets, I maintained availability rates 15% above standards, and I found ways to significantly decrease downtime while decreasing repair parts expenditures. Needless to say, safety and quality assurance were always paramount concerns throughout my career, and I have become accustomed to operating in "no-room-for-error environments" in which an error in judgment can result in the loss of human lives and assets.

I hope you will welcome my call soon when I try to arrange a brief meeting to discuss your goals and how my background might serve your needs. I can provide outstanding references at the appropriate time.

Sincerely,

Adrian M. Jonathan

ADRIAN M. JONATHAN

1110½ Hay Street, Fayetteville, NC 28305   •   preppub@aol.com   •   (910) 483-6611

OBJECTIVE

To contribute to a company's growth and efficiency through a distinguished track record as well as through a reputation as an innovative, resourceful, and articulate military officer with top-notch abilities related to the management of human and material resources.

EDUCATION & TRAINING

Pursuing **Master of Applied Science in Counseling**, Ohio State University, Columbus, OH. **Bachelor of Applied Science,** Resource Management, Ohio State University, 1998. Extensive training with an emphasis on aviation maintenance management, instructional techniques, and test flight procedures for helicopter pilots.

EXPERIENCE

Advanced to a senior civil service position while building a reputation as one of the Federal Aviation Administration's most knowledgeable professionals:
MAINTENANCE EVALUATOR & CONSULTANT. Washington, DC (2001-present). Officially described as a "brilliant manager, leader, and technical expert," observe, assess, and evaluate active, National Guard, and reserve units throughout the world while providing guidance on maintenance test flight training and standardization for CH-47 aircraft.
* Consistently receive evaluations as a responsive, articulate, and intelligent professional who inspires confidence and loyalty in others while tackling the tough jobs.

SENIOR INSTRUCTOR, MAINTENANCE TEST PILOT, & MAINTENANCE EVALUATOR. Ft. Rucker, AL (1997-00). Earned the respect of my superiors for my technical expertise and flying skill which translated into an effective style of teaching and resulted in a 100% success rate for students attending the Army Aviation School.
* Researched, wrote, developed, and updated lesson plans and training aids.
* Planned, coordinated, and managed arrangements for relocating the maintenance test pilot school to this installation including conducting research into space requirements.
* Directed the work of seven mid-managers and a $1.2 million budget for a flying program.

MAINTENANCE PRODUCTION CONTROL MANAGER. Korea (1996-97). Managed logistical, administrative, and maintenance support for 16 aircraft valued in excess of $300 million; supervised and conducted academic/test flight training for a 2,850-hour program.
* Was described as the driving force behind the unit's success in maintaining availability rates 15% above standards, decreasing downtime by 24 days, and reducing repair part expenditures 25%. Supervised 40 aircraft repair specialists and three supervisors.

MAINTENANCE QUALITY CONTROL MANAGER. England (1992-96). Managed maintenance support for 16 aircraft valued in excess of $300 million while simultaneously acting as maintenance test flight evaluator; supervised eight people.
* Earned praise for my problem-solving and decision-making skills which allowed the unit to excel in providing air support in a hostile, inhospitable desert environment.

Highlights of earlier experience worldwide: Built a reputation as a talented, concerned professional with exceptional skills as an instructor, resource manager, and aviator.

AIRCRAFT EXPERTISE

Hold these certifications: FAA Commercial Instrument Helicopter Certificate; Maintenance Test Pilot (CH-47 and UH-1H); and Instructor Pilot (CH-47).
Have logged 2,700 flight hours in CH-47 Boeing Vertol 234 and UH-1H Bell 205 aircraft.

PERSONAL

Secret security clearance. Excel in developing and managing programs which achieve goals while reducing costs and man-hour requirements. Offer expertise in supply and logistics.

Exact Name of Person
Title or Position
Name of Company
Address (no., street)
Address (city, state, zip)

**MAINTENANCE
MANAGER**

Dear Exact Name of Person (or Dear Sir or Madam if answering a blind ad):

I would appreciate an opportunity to talk with you soon about my desire to become a valuable part of your organization through my experience in production/maintenance management, administration, quality/safety control, and personnel supervision.

As you will see from my resume, I have excelled in "hot-seat" jobs in which one error of judgement can result in multimillion-dollar liability. I am accustomed to working in environments in which nothing is "routine" during the day except an attitude of constant vigilance and attention to detail. While thriving on the challenge of such positions, I have cultivated an attitude in which I view every problem as an opportunity for improving internal operations, and I have always instilled in my associates a belief that "quality and quantity production result in customer satisfaction."

My resume provides some insight into my ability to boost productivity while cutting costs. For example, while managing aircraft maintenance in Europe, I saved $420,000 of a $1.6 million budget by carefully eliminating unnecessary items. My bookkeeping techniques have been adopted by other agencies, and I am proud of the money-saving initiatives proposed by junior employees I trained.

In aircraft maintenance, there's always "an accident ready to happen," so many of my achievements have to do with things that never happened! I am, however, proud of the fact that, on one occasion following an F-16 mishap, a toxic chemical was contained in only four minutes using a plan I authored for responding to chemical emergencies.

I hope you will give me the opportunity to meet with you in person. At that time I could tell you about other accomplishments related to solving refueling dilemmas, reducing downtime, troubleshooting vent tank malfunctions, diagnosing "impossible" problems, and continuously improving repair and maintenance techniques. Known as a vibrant supervisor who enjoys working with others and who believes in "leadership by example," I also enjoy handling paperwork (believe it or not!) and I am known for my meticulous attention to detail and enthusiasm when handling huge volumes of technical documentation.

I hope you will welcome my call soon when I try to arrange a brief meeting with you to discuss your current and future needs and how I might serve them.

Sincerely yours,

Rudolph Nestle

RUDOLPH NESTLE

1110½ Hay Street, Fayetteville, NC 28305 • preppub@aol.com • (910) 483-6611

OBJECTIVE

To offer my expertise in production management, maintenance, quality assurance, and inventory control to an organization that can use a seasoned cost-cutter and creative problem solver known for "making things happen" while developing highly productive workers.

EDUCATION

Completing Associate's degree, Webster University, Webster, MO.

Received diplomas for completing three separate executive development programs lasting nearly two years in **Supervision/Management**, Air University; 1990, 1988, and 1987.

Earned numerous certificates from training programs studying advanced maintenance techniques, state-of-the-art quality control methods, and supervision.

HONORS & PUBLICATIONS

Named outstanding **Production Superintendent** based on performance reports, 2001.

Received 21 prestigious medals for exceptional performance, 1982-present.

Authored and published Air Force Regulation "Maintenance Techniques & Processes."

EXPERIENCE

AIRCRAFT MAINTENANCE MANAGER. U.S. Air Force, Europe (2001-present). At one of the Air Force's busiest airlift centers worldwide, supervise 49 people and control $2 million in assets while managing safety programs and instilling in all employees the philosophy that "quality and quantity production result in customer satisfaction"; am known for my belief that every problem is an opportunity to improve operations.

- *Creative problem solving:* When the war on terrorism required enormous numbers of aviation maintenance professionals at a time when we were seriously undermanned, I personally designed staffing plans which increased maintenance capability by 50%.
- *Aggressive cost control:* Trained junior supervisors in cost efficiency, assisted financial experts in establishing budgetary guidelines, created a new "working group" to brainstorm about money-saving proposals, and saw my bookkeeping techniques adopted by other agencies.
- *Safety management:* Wrote and implemented a plan for responding to emergencies that outlines steps for disposing of toxic chemicals.

ASSISTANT SHOP CHIEF. U.S. Air Force, Washington, DC (1998-00). Was rapidly promoted after excelling in managing 49 people and a monthly budget of $135,000.

- *Prudent cost cutting:* Saved $420,000 of a $1.6 million budget.
- *Personnel development:* Became respected for my ability to train and motivate.

MAINTENANCE SHIFT SUPERVISOR. U.S. Air Force, MacDill AFB, Florida (1995-97). Supervised and evaluated 20 personnel while advising on technical problems, reviewing and editing computer input/output for accuracy, and scheduling/prioritizing work loads.

- *Maintenance know-how:* In formal presentations to as many as 400 people, demonstrated improved methods of repairing aircraft.
- *Troubleshooting ability:* Modified emergency evacuation plans.

QUALITY CONTROL INSPECTOR. U.S. Air Force, Locations worldwide (1984-95). Evaluated and inspected 117 personnel in performing jobs related to aircraft maintenance.

- *Safety management:* Developed a safety training module for semi-annual review by workers that increased employee safety consciousness and attention to detail.
- *Inspection expertise:* Maintained aircraft continuously "free of discrepancies."

PERSONAL

Offer exceptionally strong analytical skills and pride myself on my ability to quickly "cut to the heart" of a problem. Live by the highest personal and professional standards.

Exact Name of Person
Exact Title
Exact Name of Company
Address
City, State, Zip

**MAINTENANCE
MANAGER**

Dear Exact Name of Person (or Dear Sir or Madam if answering a blind ad):

With the enclosed resume, I would like to make you aware of my interest in exploring employment opportunities with your organization.

As you will see from my resume, I have excelled as a Maintenance Supervisor and Quality Assurance Manager with the U.S. Navy, and I have been described as a "meticulous manager" and "a master at motivating and molding subordinates." Considered an expert at troubleshooting and repairing aircraft systems, I am a skilled troubleshooter in correcting stubborn problems affecting electrical systems. At locations worldwide, I have trained and supervised junior technicians as well as mid-managers performing maintenance on a fleet of aircraft. During the war in the Middle East and in Afghanistan, I was specially selected as Troubleshooting Manager in charge of assuring that aircraft were ready to fly on time in a combat environment.

I am skilled in managing maintenance in work center environments. In my previous job as a Maintenance Manager in charge of aircraft maintenance and quality assurance activities, I performed testing for maintenance personnel and conducted audit inspections. I was repeatedly sought out by my peers when they needed help in solving complex and perplexing troubleshooting problems. A resourceful individual with a strong bottom-line orientation, I developed an innovative and time-efficient compass swing procedure which was evaluated for incorporation into SH-60B technical manuals.

If you can use an astute industrial manager who is accustomed to working in an environment in which there is "no room for error," I hope you will contact me to suggest a time when we might meet to discuss your needs. I can provide outstanding personal and professional references at the appropriate time.

Sincerely,

Dylan Fisher

DYLAN FISHER

1110½ Hay Street, Fayetteville, NC 28305　　·　　preppub@aol.com　　·　　(910) 483-6611

OBJECTIVE

To benefit an organization that can use an experienced technical problem solver who offers extensive experience in maintenance management and quality assurance along with a reputation as a superior leader, administrator, and supervisor with an ability to train, motivate, and develop other individuals.

SKILLS

A skilled aviation electrician and can expertly troubleshoot/repair electrical and electronic aircraft systems. A7-E, FA-18, SH-60B, and S3B aircraft.
* Skilled in cable repair and instrument repair.
* MC-1000 Operator; Proficient with compasses; FA-18 radar, weapons systems.
* Skilled in soldering, operating oscilloscopes, troubleshooting of RF Iff and power amplifiers.
* Proficient with solid-state power supplies.
* Licensed to operate numerous vehicles including tow tractors, forklifts, and buses.

EXPERIENCE

MAINTENANCE SUPERVISOR & QUALITY ASSURANCE MANAGER. U.S. Navy, NAS Jacksonville, FL (2000-present). Was handpicked for this position which involves managing 150 individuals involved in performing maintenance on a fleet of eight aircraft; prioritize workload, schedule work to be done, oversee ordering of spare parts and repair parts, and continuously train personnel in effective troubleshooting techniques.

DIVISION SUPERVISOR & QUALITY ASSURANCE MANAGER. U.S. Navy, FL (1997-00). Was evaluated as an "absolute top performer" while managing 11 senior aircraft maintenance managers involved in quality assurance activities. Conducted evaluations of work centers under my supervision, and performed testing for maintenance personnel. Was described in writing as "a master at motivating and molding subordinates."
* Was described as a "meticulous manager" after producing top-notch results in directing 15 comprehensive work center/detachment quarterly audits; maintained the highest standards of quality and safety.
* Developed an innovative and time-efficient compass swing procedure, which was evaluated for incorporation into SH-60B technical manuals; volunteered to work many hours of overtime hours in order to perform compass swings which guaranteed on-time missions.

AVIONICS-ELECTRONICS SUPERVISOR. U.S. Navy, FL (1992-97). While supervising 15 individuals, received a respected Navy Commendation Medal and was evaluated as "the single most important petty officer in this command" and a "masterful technician and manager who demonstrates the highest level of integrity and judgement."
* Was cited for unparalleled knowledge of the F/A-18 electrical/avionics and weapons systems. Was cross-trained in all areas of F/A-18 maintenance and quality assurance.
* Diagnosed complex malfunctions which threatened high-tempo flight operations.
* Supervised and directed comprehensive aircraft inspections; interpreted electrical and electronic schematics and drawings.

AVIATION-ELECTRICIAN I LEVEL TECHNICIAN. U.S. Navy, FL (1984-92). Performed intermediate-level maintenance, IMUTS 608 Technician/Operator.

TRAINING

Completed numerous college courses as well as extensive U.S. Navy training including: Basic Electricity and Electronics, Quality Assurance and Safety (numerous courses and hours)

PERSONAL

Dynamic leader known for integrity and absolute reliability. Excellent references.

Exact Name of Person
Exact Title
Exact Name of Company
Address
City, State, Zip

**MAINTENANCE
SUPERVISOR**

Dear Exact Name of Person (or Dear Sir or Madam if answering a blind ad):

With the enclosed resume, I would like to make you aware of my versatile background and technical abilities as well as my expertise in supervising and managing resources for maximum effectiveness and productivity.

As you will see from my resume, I have served my country in the U.S. Air Force and have acquired considerable knowledge related to electronics. Although I am highly respected for my technical, leadership, managerial, and mechanical skills, I have made the decision to leave military service and return to Texas where I grew up. I am seeking full-time employment and will be pursuing a degree in Electronics Engineering from DeVry Technical Institute in Irving in my spare time. I have received extensive training in the specialized field of aerospace ground equipment maintenance and repair while also completing programs in automated systems operations, quality awareness, and leadership development.

In my most recent job as a Maintenance Supervisor, I provided technical advice and guidance while overseeing, scheduling, coordinating, and participating in the activities of a 12-person team which inspected and performed maintenance on a $3.3 million inventory of aerospace ground equipment used in support of 33 C-130 aircraft. Consistently described as an innovative and resourceful professional, I have become known for my top-notch skills as a troubleshooter. On many occasions, I saved government funds and man-hours by troubleshooting and completing repairs which solved problems and reduced aircraft downtime for costly repairs and services.

If you can use a dependable, assertive, and creative professional who offers excellent resource management and supervisory skills, I hope you will contact me soon to suggest a time when we might meet to discuss your needs. I can assure you in advance that I can provide outstanding references and could quickly become an asset to your organization.

Sincerely,

Charles David Wills

CHARLES DAVID WILLS

1110½ Hay Street, Fayetteville, NC 28305 • preppub@aol.com • (910) 483-6611

OBJECTIVE

To contribute to an organization in need of an innovative and assertive leader with expertise in electronics technology and security systems along with a reputation as a meticulous and detail-oriented professional with proven managerial and supervisory skills.

EDUCATION & TRAINING

Pursuing **degree in Electronics Engineering** in my spare time, DeVry Technical Institute, Irving, TX.

Received extensive military training in aerospace ground equipment maintenance and repair as well as in automated systems, leadership development, and quality awareness programs.

Completed course work at DeVry Technical Community College (TX) and the University of Maryland.

EXPERIENCE

Advanced to manage and supervise aviation maintenance activities, U.S. Air Force:

MAINTENANCE SUPERVISOR. Fort Polk, LA (2000-present). Provide technical advice and expertise in troubleshooting while supervising and training a 12-person maintenance team inspecting and performing major and minor maintenance on 375 pieces of aerospace ground equipment (AGE) valued in excess of $3.3 million in support of 33 C-130 aircraft.

- Handled a wide range of actions which included planning and organizing maintenance schedules, establishing production controls and standards, interpreting and implementing directions, and making decisions on resource requirements and allocations.
- Utilized drawings, diagrams, schematics, and technical instructions while troubleshooting and resolving problems.
- Polished my computer skills while processing parts requests using the Standard Base Supply Systems (SBSS) and documenting discrepancies using the Core Automated Maintenance and G081 systems.
- Applied knowledge of automated systems to design an inventory system which streamlined the process of tracking parts and significantly improved accountability.
- Honored as **"Employee of the Month"** on several occasions and officially described as a superb performer, top-notch troubleshooter, and as extremely resourceful.
- Singled out for my contributions to the community, volunteered in numerous fire department blood drives and fund raisers.

ELECTRONICS/AVIONICS SYSTEMS MECHANIC. Germany (1996-00). Quickly gained respect for my self-motivation while applying technical and mechanical skills inspecting, testing, modifying, maintaining, repairing, and delivering aerospace ground equipment.

- Gained knowledge of the electrical, hydraulic, environmental, and mechanical systems which worked together to ensure the smooth operation of aircraft used worldwide.
- Was credited as a key factor in the unit receiving the highest possible ratings in a NATO evaluation because of my "meticulous attention to detail" in ensuring that more than 50 pieces of equipment were prepared and delivered on time.
- Selected for a special project in Italy, replaced parts which had been taken for other missions and brought equipment availability rate from a low of 49% up to 97%.
- Was cited as a key contributor in efforts which resulted in the 1995 **U.S. Air Force in Europe Maintenance Effectiveness Award.**

PERSONAL

Was entrusted with a **Top Secret** security clearance. Offer outstanding time and resource management skills and an ability to motivate others to achieve 100% production levels.

Bonneville Power Admin. Pers Spc-15
905 NE 11th Avenue
Portland, OR 97232

**REFUELING
SPECIALIST**

Dear Sir or Madam:

     Can you use a hard worker and team player who offers the proven ability to learn and absorb new information quickly along with strong mechanical skills?

     While serving in the U.S. Air Force I received extensive training as a Fuels Specialist and was singled out for my technical abilities. I maintained aircraft/ground equipment refueling equipment, conducted inspections, and operated bulk storage facilities as well as maintaining documentation of fuel transactions and maintenance performed.

     My military experience also allowed me a chance to develop supervisory skills while leading and overseeing the performance of employees on my shift in a Fuels Control Center operation.

     I hope you will call or write soon to suggest a time convenient for us to meet and discuss your current and future needs and how I might serve them. Thank you in advance for your time.

                   Sincerely yours,

                   Frederic L. Paris

FREDERIC L. PARIS

1110½ Hay Street, Fayetteville, NC 28305   •   preppub@aol.com   •   (910) 483-6611

OBJECTIVE

To benefit an organization that can use a hard-working young professional who learns quickly, works well with others, and offers strong mechanical skills along with experience in the specialized aircraft refueling field.

AREAS OF SPECIAL KNOWLEDGE

Through training and experience, am familiar with refueling equipment manufactured by Mack, Tri-State Refuelers, and Kovatch:

R-9	R-8	A2A	MH2B	C300
R-5	A-2	HSV	MH2A	C301

EXPERIENCE

FUELS BULK STORAGE AND HYDRANT SPECIALIST. U.S. Air Force, Washington, DC, and Afghanistan (2000-present). Operated and performed minor maintenance on permanently installed facilities for bulk fuel storage, conducted daily inspections of 30 pieces of refueling equipment, and maintained records on computers.
- Directed receipt, storage, issuance, and transfer of fuel products including jet fuel and other petroleum products.
- Was recognized as a highly skilled professional while working alone to maintain hydrants on what was usually the facility's busiest shift.
- Earned recognition for my technical knowledge and was placed in charge of maintaining 18 50,000-gallon fuel tanks, one 500,000-gallon tank, 82 hydrant outlets, and 12 lateral control pits.

FUELS CONTROL CENTER SHIFT SUPERVISOR. U.S.A.F., Europe (1991-99). Gained experience in leading and overseeing employees while planning, coordinating, scheduling, and directing fuel operations.
- Applied my mechanical skills and technical knowledge to keep multimillion-dollar facilities operating to avoid loss of service.
- Learned to use IBM computers to maintain records of all transactions.

FUELS DISTRIBUTION SPECIALIST. U.S.A.F., Lackland AFB, FL (1988-91). Maintained 22 items of refueling equipment used to issue approximately three million gallons of fuel a month to both aircraft and ground equipment.
- Conducted daily inspections of all refueling equipment to ensure compliance with safety regulations and performed any needed minor maintenance.

TRAINING

Completed a six-hour course for safety supervisors as well as two intensive technical training courses:
    249-hour "Fuels Specialist Course"
    Nine-month "Fuels Career Development Course" on-the-job training program

CLEARANCE

Was entrusted with a Secret security clearance.

PERSONAL

Work well with others to reach team goals. Am a fast learner in classroom situations as well as through self-study and "hands-on" training.

Exact Name of Person
Exact Title
Exact Name of Company
Address
City, State, Zip

SYSTEM TECHNICIAN   Dear Exact Name of Person (or Dear Sir or Madam if answering a blind ad):

With the enclosed resume, I would like to introduce you to my considerable technical and mechanical skills as well as to my reputation as a highly self-motivated and results-oriented young professional.

As you will see from my resume, I am serving my country in the U.S. Air Force where I have earned the respect of my superiors and peers for my ability to quickly learn and master new procedures and equipment. Currently assigned as an Aircraft Instrumentation and Telemetry System Technician, I was nominated for early promotion based on my job knowledge and leadership. I have been credited with playing a major role in the success of a unit which has won numerous honors including the President's award for "Quality in the Workplace," a high-level maintenance effectiveness award, and an "Air Force Outstanding Unit Award."

Selected for special projects and teams, I have participated in the development of aircraft modifications and earned recognition from the Undersecretary of Defense and the McDonnell Douglas Aircraft Corporation for my efforts.

If you can use a self-starter with excellent electronics and mechanical skills along with the ability to work independently or as a contributor to team efforts, I hope you will welcome my call soon when I try to arrange a brief meeting to discuss your goals and how my background might serve your needs. I can provide outstanding references at the appropriate time.

Sincerely,

Chad Walters

CHAD WALTERS

1110½ Hay Street, Fayetteville, NC 28305   •   preppub@aol.com   •   (910) 483-6611

OBJECTIVE

To offer well-developed electronics, troubleshooting, and mechanical skills to an organization that can use a quick learner who produces results while working independently or as a contributor to team efforts.

EDUCATION & TRAINING

Have completed training in technical schools and programs which included the following:
precision, high-reliability soldering
operation and troubleshooting of radar interfacing systems
formatting, troubleshooting, and programming advanced airborne test systems
ASE refrigerant recovery and recycling

TECHNICAL KNOWLEDGE

Ability to troubleshoot and repair to the component level electronic, mechanical, and electro-mechanical devices with analog and digital circuitry.
Operate test equipment including:
oscilloscope   DMM   hand-held bus monitor   power meter   TRD   spectrum analyzer
Offer additional skills in calibration, controlling COMSEC (communications security), DECOMM programming (converting bit stream into words and frames), and repairing and maintaining the Advanced Airborne Test Instrumentation System.

EXPERIENCE

AIRCRAFT INSTRUMENTATION AND TELEMETRY SYSTEM TECHNICIAN. Washington, DC and Afghanistan (2001-present). Cited for my technical knowledge and take-charge attitude, have advanced to perform maintenance, calibration, and operation as well as prelaunch and recovery checks on the instrumentation systems of 12 flight test center F-15 aircraft.

- Played a key role during the war in Afghanistan through my ability to solve complex instrumentation problems.
- Was cited as a key reason the air base was the winner of the President's "Quality Award for Quality in the Workplace."
- Have made direct contributions to the success of search-and-rescue flights for downed pilots by installing, operating, and maintaining Global Positioning Tracking Systems in 25 helicopters used by a joint services search-and-rescue test program.
- Interpret electrical and mechanical engineering schematics and drawings while installing and modifying complex instrumentation systems.
- Made contributions which led to the unit winning both a major maintenance effectiveness award and the "Air Force Outstanding Unit Award" in 2000.
- Developed expert knowledge of modifications to the aircraft's Visually Coupled Acquisition Targeting System which led to my selection as the instrumentation technician assigned to accompany the aircraft to other test locations worldwide.
- Received a Letter of Commendation from the Undersecretary of Defense for my contributions to the success of the joint search-and-rescue team.
- Was acknowledged by McDonnell Douglas Aircraft Corporation for my contributions and service during a radar update test program.

Highlights of earlier civilian experience:
As a Field Representative, had extensive public contact while inspecting buildings before and after demolition projects, Crayton Engineering, Middletown, MA, 1998-99.

PERSONAL

Was entrusted with a Secret security clearance. Earned a Joint Service Achievement Medal for "meritorious achievements" during a December 2002 training exercise.

Exact Name of Person
Exact Title
Exact Name of Company
Address
City, State, Zip

**TECHNICAL
INSPECTOR**

Dear Exact Name of Person (or Dear Sir or Madam if answering a blind ad):

With the enclosed resume, I would like to make you aware of my background as a versatile and experienced professional with a history of success in areas which include computer operations, logistics and supply, production control, and employee training and supervision.

As you will see, I am completing requirements for my bachelor's degree in Computer Science from Snyder College which I expect to receive this winter. I am proud of my accomplishment in completing this course of study while simultaneously meeting the demands of a career in the Federal Aviation Administration. In my current position as a Technical Inspector at Ft. Gordon, GA, I ensure the airworthiness of aircraft utilized by the 18th Airborne Corps which is required to relocate anywhere in the world on extremely short notice in response to crisis situations.

Throughout my career I have been singled out for jobs which have required the ability to quickly make sound decisions and have continually maximized resources while exceeding expected standards and performance guidelines. I have been responsible for certifying multimillion-dollar aircraft for flight service, training and supervising employees who have been highly productive and successful in their own careers, and applying technical computer knowledge in innovative ways which have further increased efficiency and productivity.

I offer a combination of technical, managerial, and supervisory skills and a level of knowledge which will allow me to quickly achieve outstanding results in anything I attempt. Known for my energy and enthusiasm, I am a creative and talented professional with a strong desire to make a difference in whatever setting and environment I find myself.

I hope you will contact me to suggest a time when we might meet to discuss your needs. I can assure you in advance that I could rapidly become an asset to your organization.

Sincerely,

Brad J. Frost

BRAD JACKSON FROST

1110½ Hay Street, Fayetteville, NC 28305 • preppub@aol.com • (910) 483-6611

OBJECTIVE

To offer a versatile background emphasizing computer operations, logistics, inventory control, production control, and security to an organization that can benefit from my experience as a supervisor and manager with a reputation for creativity.

EDUCATION & TRAINING

Will receive a **B.S. in Computer Science**, Snyder College, Snyder, GA, winter 2002. Selected for extensive training, including courses for security managers and computer operations and applications as well as technical courses in aircraft repair and maintenance, professional leadership development, equal opportunity practices, and Airborne School.

CLEARANCE

Was entrusted with a Top Secret security clearance.

EXPERIENCE

Earned a reputation as a focused and goal-oriented professional, Federal Aviation Administration:
TECHNICAL INSPECTOR. Ft. Gordon, GA and Afghanistan (2000-present). Officially cited for my in-depth knowledge of aviation maintenance and logistics issues, conduct technical inspections on 24 helicopters while also providing training, guidance, and supervision.
- Transformed a substandard quality control section into one which sets the example.
- Received the NATO Medal for Service for my contributions during operations in Afghanistan.

SUPERVISOR FOR AVIATION MAINTENANCE AND SUPPLY. Europe (1995-99). Made numerous important contributions while coordinating supply, maintenance, and readiness issues for units worldwide.
- Received a letter of commendation from a three-star general for my expertise as the Security Manager for the corps headquarters and for personally revitalizing the physical security program which received "commendable" ratings.
- Developed a database for managing aircraft maintenance histories which greatly increased the reliability of information about the organization's 968 assigned aircraft.
- Created and presented effective training on physical security and ADP operations.

MAINTENANCE SUPERVISOR. Washington, DC (1997-98). Provided oversight for a $6 million annual operating budget and ensured the quality and timeliness of all phases of support for a fleet of 104 aircraft while also reviewing daily/monthly status reports, coordinating supply up to the wholesale level, and recommending procedural changes.
- Consistently exceeded Department of the Army standards for aircraft availability and was singled out for praise for my expertise as a trainer, mentor, and leader.

MAINTENANCE SUPERVISOR. Germany (1992-97). Cited as directly responsible for a high level of achievement and productivity; collected and processed maintenance data on 123 aircraft while controlling flight safety information and support for four divisions.
- Selected to oversee a project during which new equipment and automation assets were integrated into use; achieved a smooth transition.
- Was a member of the team which first fielded the ULASS computer system which is a tool for managing production, maintenance hours, and supplies.

TECHNICAL INSPECTOR. Locations worldwide (1988-92). Cited for my ability to quickly master technical information, made determinations on aircraft serviceability and safety.

PERSONAL

Known for my enthusiastic style of leadership and reputation for unwavering ethical standards.

Delta Airlines
Attn: Dept 85
Fax number: 704-773-6035

CUSTOMER SERVICE   Dear Sir or Madam:

As requested, I am sending a copy of my resume prior to my appointment this week in Atlanta, GA. I have an appointment at 8 a.m. on March 8 to discuss possible employment with your airline as a Customer Service Representative.

As Customer Service Representative for the City of Sampson and Piedmont Hawthorn Aviation, I am currently excelling as a Customer Service Representative. In fact, I was promoted to Senior Customer Service Representative (CSR) a month ago, and I was selected to train junior CSRs in technical skills as well as in the overall ability to handle a complex, multi-task job. In my current position I serve a diversified customer base including Fortune 500 companies who fly into the city on private jets; it is part of my job to coordinate transportation, hotels, and other matters.

Responsible for extensive recordkeeping, I utilize a computer to input data daily related to aviation fuel and I use a two-way radio to talk with refueling personnel and incoming pilots. I began in my job with the City of Sampson, and then I was asked to continue with the company when a private contractor took over from the city.

My husband and I are in the process of relocating to the Atlanta area, and I am seeking an employer that can use my strong customer service background. On a daily basis, I utilize my outstanding written and oral communication skills, including my knowledge of English usage, spelling, grammar, and punctuation.

I can provide strong references at the appropriate time, and I would appreciate your contacting me to suggest a time when we could meet to discuss your needs.

Sincerely,

Kelly Stevens

KELLY STEVENS

1110½ Hay Street, Fayetteville, NC 28305　　•　　preppub@aol.com　　•　　(910) 483-6611

OBJECTIVE　　I want to contribute to the success of an organization that can use an experienced customer service professional with exceptional management, communication, sales, and organizational skills.

EXPERIENCE　　**CUSTOMER SERVICE REPRESENTATIVE.** City of Sampson and Piedmont Hawthorn Aviation, Sampson, MI (2002-present). Began as a Customer Service Representative and was promoted to Senior Customer Service Representative (CSR); was selected to train junior CSRs in technical skills as well as in the overall ability to handle a complex, multi-task job.
- Serve a diversified customer base including Fortune 500 companies who fly into the city on private jets; coordinate transportation, hotels, and other matters.
- Utilize a computer to input data daily related to aviation fuel; use a two-way radio to talk with refueling personnel and with incoming pilots.
- Began in this job with the City of Sampson, and then continued with the company when a private contractor took over from the city.
- On a daily basis, utilize my outstanding written and oral communication skills, including my knowledge of English usage, spelling, grammar, and punctuation.
- Refined my ability to handle a high volume of tasks simultaneously, and also refined my problem-solving skills while figuring out solutions for customer needs.
- Was frequently commended for my gracious style of interacting with the public.
- Resigned my position in order to relocate to Atlanta with my military spouse.

Was promoted in the following track record of accomplishments by a bookstore, Sampson, MI (1996-02).
MANAGER. (2000-02). Responsible for all aspects of store operation, supervised one assistant manager and four employees; oversaw the training of all employees.
- Opened/closed the store; handled bookkeeping and prepared bank deposits.
- Managed shipping and receiving; monitored incoming and outgoing inventory.
- Prepared weekly employee schedules as well as daily logs and store reports to track store sales and ensure a strong in-stock position.
- Ensured the highest level of customer service.
- Interviewed, hired, and disciplined employees.
- Monitored store security to guarantee safety of inventory and employees.

ASSISTANT MANAGER. (1996-2001). Co-responsible for store operation.
- Supervised four employees; assisted in training new employees.

Previous experience:
ELEMENTARY SCHOOL TEACHER. (1978-1996). Taught in schools in England and Germany, including six years in a military school. Additional responsibilities for English, basic computer skills, library service. Implemented curriculum guidelines,. Ordered books and equipment; distributed them and assessed their effectiveness.

COMPUTERS　　Proficient in utilizing a computer to enter credit card information, supply data, and fueling activities; working knowledge of Word and Excel.

EDUCATION　　**B.A. degree in History,** Wabash College, Wabash, IL, 1977.

PERSONAL　　Outstanding references available on request. Am a citizen of the United States.

CUSTOMER SERVICE AND TRAVEL PROFESSIONALS
Date

Exact Name of Person
Title or Position
Name of Company
Address (no., street)
Address (city, state, zip)

CRUISE SPECIALIST   Dear Exact Name of Person (or Dear Sir or Madam if answering a blind ad):

I would appreciate an opportunity to talk with you soon about how I could contribute to your organization through my experience and training related to the travel industry.

As you will see from my resume I offer extensive travel experience and am very knowledgeable of the upscale markets of the Caribbean. My product knowledge has allowed me to develop a reputation as an "expert" in marketing cruises, hotels, and vacation packages.

I have been given the opportunity to attend a training program for cruise and travel specialists sponsored by the Department of Tourism in Puerto Rico and another for "Caribbean Destination Specialists" sponsored by the Institute of Certified Travel Agents.

My sales and customer service skills as well as my extensive personal travel experience make me a professional with a great deal to offer your organization.

I hope you will welcome my call soon to arrange a brief meeting at your convenience to discuss your current and future needs and how I might serve them. Thank you in advance for your time.

Sincerely yours,

Serena R. Cruze

Alternate last paragraph:
I hope you will call or write soon to suggest a time convenient for us to meet and discuss your current and future needs and how I might serve them. Thank you in advance for your time.

SERENA R. CRUZE

1110½ Hay Street, Fayetteville, NC 28305 • preppub@aol.com • (910) 483-6611

OBJECTIVE

I wish to apply my experience in the travel industry to an organization that can benefit from my personal knowledge of the travel, cruise, and hotel products available to the traveler in search of the best available accommodations, particularly in the Caribbean.

TRAINING

Graduated from the Lucas Travel School, Atlanta, GA, 1991.
Received training in the following specialized areas of interest:
* extensive knowledge of Caribbean destinations — a 40-hour program sponsored by the Institute of Certified Travel Agents (ICTA)
* a Puerto Rican Department of Tourism week-long "travel expert" course
* SABRE computer training
* booking, selling, and marketing cruises — sponsored by the Cruise Lines International Association (CLIA)

CARIBBEAN KNOWLEDGE

In addition to formal training in the travel industry, offer a "hands-on" background of knowledge of the Caribbean islands:
* Have traveled to every island and stayed in or personally inspected most hotels.
* Inspected and maintained the most up-to-date information on every active cruise line in the market.
* Enjoyed extensive personal travel in the upscale markets of the Caribbean.

EXPERIENCE

CARIBBEAN AND CRUISE SPECIALIST. Georgia Travel, Atlanta, GA (2000-present). Sell potential customers on the comparative advantages of a variety of cruise and Caribbean vacation options.
* Book air travel, hotel accommodations, and vacation packages.
* Became the office's "resident expert" on the specialized Caribbean and cruise options by applying my personal knowledge of these areas.

SALES REPRESENTATIVE and **TRAVEL AGENT.** World Travel, New York, NY (1991-99). Worked with clients to assist them in planning business and personal travel arrangements and booked hotels, cruises, and other types of travel packages.
* Earned the confidence of the agency's discriminating clients who came to rely on me to provide expert advice on the cruise and Caribbean segments of travel.

SPECIALIST IN CARIBBEAN AND CRUISE TRAVEL. Best Travel, Dallas, TX (1988-91). Provided guidance to clients interested in the areas of Caribbean cruises and upscale travel vacations.
* Achieved high sales volumes through my personal knowledge of the areas in which customers displayed an interest.

EDUCATION

B.A., Psychology/Religion, The University of Texas, Dallas, TX.
A.A., Weymouth College, Weymouth, IN.
Completed 30 hours of graduate-level course work in Education and Counseling, Culver University, Culver, TX.

PERSONAL

Am flexible and available for frequent travel. Can provide an "expert" level of service and product knowledge. Remain open to new information and opportunities. Will relocate.

Date

Trust Company Bank
P.O. Box 4418
Dept. 139/RJ
Atlanta, GA 30302

GATE AGENT
Although this individual
has experience as a
Gate Agent, he is
seeking a career
change out of the
stressful world which
aviation has become.
He is making an
attempt to reenter the
field of computer
operations.

Dear Sir or Madam:

I would appreciate an opportunity to talk with you soon about how I could contribute to Delta Airlines through my experience and technical expertise in information systems, operations management, computer programming, sales, and public relations, as well as my excellent communication, planning, and organizational skills. Although I am excelling in my current position as a Gate Agent with Delta, I would like to explore opportunities for transitioning into the company's IT area.

As you will see from my resume, I have worked at a large university as a computer operator, refining my hands-on technical abilities. In addition, I became proficient at troubleshooting the system, mastering documentation techniques, and polishing my operations management knowledge. I am proficient in a wide range of computer software, languages, operating systems, and hardware.

Highlights of other experience include gaining valuable sales, public relations, and marketing experience while working as a realtor assisting in the buying and selling residential and commercial properties. I also discovered a knack for accounting and administration while working as an office manager and bookkeeper at Evans Engineering in Greensboro, NC.

You would find me to be a versatile professional who enjoys challenges and discovering innovative solutions to difficult problems.

I hope you will call or write me soon to suggest a time convenient for us to meet and discuss your IT needs and how I might serve them. Thank you in advance for your time.

Sincerely,

Esmerelda S. Root

ESMERELDA S. ROOT

1110½ Hay Street, Fayetteville, NC 28305 • preppub@aol.com • (910) 483-6611

OBJECTIVE To benefit an organization seeking a hard-working professional experienced in information systems, operations management, computer programming, and sales who possesses excellent communication, planning, and organizational skills.

EDUCATION **Bachelor of Science degree in Information Systems**, University of North Carolina at Greensboro, NC, 1996.
Areas of study included production management controls, marketing, microcomputers, and business communications.

COMPUTERS Proficient with a wide range of computer software, languages, operating systems, and hardware, including the following:
  Software: Word, Excel, PowerPoint, Lotus 1-2-3, SuperCalc, MAS90, many others.
  Languages: COBOL, BASIC, PASCAL, JAVA..
  Operating Systems: Microsoft Works, DEC VAX/VMS, UNIX, and Novell Network.
  Hardware: PCs and mainframes.

EXPERIENCE **GATE AGENT**. Delta Airlines, Atlanta, GA (2000-present). Provide exceptional customer service while accepting boarding passes and accommodating changes in seating requests.
  • Refined attention-to-detail skills while processing detailed documentation for aircraft departure.
  • Ensure compliance with strict regulatory guidelines.

  COMPUTER OPERATOR. University of North Carolina at Greensboro/Instructional and Research Computing Department (1997-00). Gained valuable "behind the scenes" knowledge of a large computer system accessed to over 1,000 terminals.
  • Distributed printouts to users and mounted and loaded tapes for Business faculty.
  • Answered and resolved all end users' questions and concerns.
  • Mastered documentation techniques and learned how important they are to users and programmers.
  • Gained expertise in operations management while developing practical programs.
  • Resolved problems in applications, programs, software, and hardware.
  • Installed and tested equipment and programs.
  • Studied, designed, programmed, and implemented complex batch and on-line projects.

  OFFICE MANAGER/ACCOUNTING MANAGER. Wyckliffe Engineering, Greensboro, NC (1990-96). Refined time-management skills while overseeing all office functions in addition to supervising personnel and handling a wide range of accounting procedures in this fast-paced company.
  • Administered monthly billing for 150 clients, processed accounts payable/receivable and payroll, and provided notary functions.
  • Compiled and wrote an office operations manual for use by support staff.
  • Acted as office "front-line," greeting customers, routing calls, and answering multi-line phones.
  • Prepared correspondence, memos, proposals, loan surveys, and legal documents.
  • Performed extensive data entry and processing.

PERSONAL Am a flexible, dedicated professional with a knack for problem-solving and decision-making. Enjoy challenges and finding creative solutions. Am fluent in Spanish.

Date

Exact Name of Person
Exact Title
Exact Name of Company
Address
City, State, Zip

**RAMP SERVICES
SPECIALIST**

Dear Exact Name of Person (or Dear Sir or Madam if answering a blind ad):

With the enclosed resume, I would like to make you aware of the skills and experience which I have gained related to supervising ramp services for commercial transportation of goods and materials, including hazardous materials.

As you will see from my resume, I am presently working for a commercial arm of Federal Express, and I am excelling in multiple supervisory and technical roles. While supervising up to 12 special cargo handling specialists and ramp services personnel, I have also recently been assigned to the additional duty of Explosive Safety Supervisor. This duty means overseeing personnel handling explosives and to provide them with training in critical safety measures for working with potentially dangerous cargo.

In a prior position in London, England, I advanced to supervisory roles ahead of my peers while overseeing special handling and ramp services activities in another of the military's major airlift hubs. I gained skills in training others on the operation of automated scheduling and cargo planning systems and in all aspects of safe, accurate, and timely cargo handling support operations.

If you can use a well-rounded and mature young professional who offers expertise in hazardous material management and inspection as well as a reputation for possessing high levels of drive, initiative, and energy, I hope you will write or call me soon to suggest a time when we might meet to discuss your needs and goals and how my background might serve them. I can provide outstanding references at the appropriate time.

Sincerely,

Jan Bogart

JAN BOGART

1110½ Hay Street, Fayetteville, NC 28305   ·   preppub@aol.com   ·   (910) 483-6611

OBJECTIVE

To contribute skills in scheduling, load planning, inspecting hazardous cargo and shippers declarations, and cargo handling to an organization that can benefit from my ability to supervise and carry out airport support operations.

EDUCATION & TRAINING

Completed course work in the Japanese language at the University of Maryland.
Completed training which included FedEx Air Transportation School, Dallas, TX.

TECHNICAL KNOWLEDGE

Certifications: HAZMAT certified and Load Planning certified, have a working knowledge **determining weights and balances of an aircraft and in certifying hazardous materials using AFJAM 24-204 (49CFR).**
Computers: am skilled in utilizing APACCS (scheduling) and CAPPS-2 (cargo planning) software systems – these databases are used while entering and retrieving data needed to analyze cargo loads and determine scheduling.
Aircraft: calculate load weights/balances and apply load restrictions for aircraft including:

        C-130   C-5   C-17   C-141   L-100

Material handling equipment and vehicles: am licensed to operate 4K, 10K standard, 10K all-terrain forklifts; drive 29-45 passenger buses, lavatory and water service vehicles, wide body loaders-Cochran, TA-15, TA-40; baggage conveyor, staircase trucks, bobtail, tug; 25, 40, and 60K loaders.

EXPERIENCE

Have advanced ahead of my peers to supervisory roles with the U.S. Air Force:
RAMP SERVICES SPECIALIST and **EXPLOSIVE SAFETY SUPERVISOR.** Federal Express, Industrial Materials Division, Tempe, AZ (2000-present). While excelling in multiple simultaneous duties at one of the world's busiest airlift hubs, supervise 12 people contributing to effective support services provided by a 20-person shift.

- Selected for the special duty of **Explosive Safety Supervisor,** oversee personnel handling explosives and provide training in proper safety.

SUPERVISORY SPECIAL HANDLING SPECIALIST. Federal Express Corporation, Explosives Handling Division, London, England (1997-00). Quickly earned a reputation as a knowledgeable, reliable young professional and was selected for a critical role inspecting hazardous cargo; accepted, loaded, unloaded, and provided security for shipments which included registered mail as well as classified and perishable items.

- Played a key role in my unit's recognition with the **"Outstanding Unit Award."**
- Inspected hazardous cargo and ensured each shipment was properly labeled, marked, and certified in accordance with all applicable international regulations.
- Contributed to the success of the inspection process as an average of 89 shipments with a total weight of 89 tons were airlifted monthly with no in-flight accidents.
- Led the unit to its fifth consecutive **"Explosive Safety Award"** for error-free transport.

SUPERVISORY RAMP SERVICE SPECIALIST. Diversified Packaging Services, Okinawa, Japan (1992-97). Was promoted to supervise six people; loaded and unloaded general and special handling cargo and mail; determined tiedown requirements and secured cargo.

- Performed operator maintenance, operated, and trained others on 31 pieces of material handling equipment valued in excess of $6.4 million.

PERSONAL

Will relocate. Offer knowledge of Japanese gained while living there for three years; have limited conversational ability and a goal to become fluent.

Date

Exact Name of Person
Title or Position
Name of Company
Address (no., street)
Address (city, state, zip)

**TERMINAL SERVICES
SUPERVISOR**

Dear Exact Name of Person (or Dear Sir or Madam if answering a blind ad):

I would appreciate an opportunity to talk with you soon about how I could contribute to your organization through my background of excellent performance in air terminal operations management including cargo handling, employee training and supervision, and resource management.

While working for U.S. Airways, I have consistently earned recognition for my planning and coordination skills as well as my expertise in overseeing the many and varied details of both air and ground transportation activities. I am the recipient of numerous cash bonuses and certificates for exceptional performance. I have completed extensive safety and counterterrorism training, and I have frequently been placed in charge of terminal services during emergencies and evacuations due to natural disasters and terrorist threats.

A self-starter, I work well with others in leadership roles and as a contributor to successful team efforts. I have refined my supervisory skills while earning a reputation for my dedication to putting in whatever time is required to guarantee that quality work is performed and that my employees achieve high standards of performance.

I hope you will call or write me soon to suggest a time convenient for us to meet and discuss your current and future needs and how I might serve them. Thank you in advance for your time.

Sincerely yours,

Chet J. Woodman

CHET J. WOODMAN

1110½ Hay Street, Fayetteville, NC 28305 • preppub@aol.com • (910) 483-6611

OBJECTIVE

To offer my abilities as a leader and supervisor as well as my specialized experience related to air terminal operations and freight handling procedures to an organization that can benefit from my excellent planning and coordination skills and reputation for dependability.

EXPERIENCE

Advanced in air terminal management roles, U.S. Airways, Atlanta, GA:
TERMINAL SERVICES SUPERVISOR. Atlanta Airport, Atlanta, GA (2000-present). Supervised as many as 80 employees while planning and scheduling air cargo and passenger movements and working closely with other airlines to ensure that people and goods were transported safely and smoothly.
- During relief efforts in the aftermath of a major hurricane, loaded 3,250 tons of cargo and 2,876 passengers onto 294 aircraft within one three-day period.
- Managed a 20-person team at an adjunct airport and loaded 30 air craft using "engine-running " loading procedures at a dirt landing strip.

OPERATIONS CENTER SUPERINTENDENT. Macon Airport, Macon, GA (1995-99). Excelled in meeting the demands of coordinating loading/unloading activities as well as passenger, fleet, and terminal services in a facility handling an average of 2,500 tons of cargo and 18,000 passengers a month.
- Was cited as being personally responsible for the terminal maintaining 100% transportation reliability for the most recent ten-month period.
- Displayed my ability to remain in control during an emergency situations when a jet plane crashed into a transport plane: relocated the operations center, accounted for all personnel and equipment, and established communications with higher headquarters.
- Compiled detailed operating procedures guidelines for load planning, consolidated aerial port operations, and related communications systems.

TERMINAL OPERATIONS MANAGER. Savannah Airport, Savannah, GA (1990-94). Earned rapid advancement from Shift Supervisor and Assistant Operations Manager to manage 30 employees, control funds, and establish and enforce policies in a terminal which handled 32,000 passengers and 4,000 aircraft annually.
- Revitalized a safety program which became recognized as the standard for others.
- Saved the organization more than $15,700 a year by building a piece of wide-body aircraft baggage-handling equipment and eliminated the need to rent one.
- Selected to receive special training in hazardous cargo handling, revamped information and procedures which made all concerned personnel more aware of special procedures.

**EDUCATION &
TRAINING**

Certified in Aerospace Management Logistics, FAA, 1994.
Excelled in training programs in operations management, cargo handling, and supervision.

**SPECIAL
SKILLS**

Am well-versed in on- and off-loading cargo and baggage from aircraft including Lockheed C-5, C-141, and C-130 (L-100 and L-1011); McDonnell Douglas DC-8, 9, and 10; and Boeing 747. Have well-developed knowledge of flight line safety and security skills.
Offer familiarity with various aircraft cargo and passenger loading vehicles to include: 4,000 to 15,000-lb. forklifts (Allis-Chalmers, Hyster, Case, Terex, Clark), Cochran elevator loaders, up to 40,000-lb. aircraft cargo loaders, and passenger staircase trucks.

PERSONAL

Nonsmoker and nondrinker, and can pass the most rigorous background investigation. Can provide outstanding personal and professional references.

Date

Reference: Job #GA-TSZ
TRAVELSPAN Human Resources
400 Fortune Parkway, NW
Atlanta, GA 30339

TRAVEL AGENT　　Dear Sir or Madam:

With the enclosed resume describing my considerable expertise in the travel industry, I am responding to your recent advertisement for a Sales Manager in your Atlanta office. I am single and willing to relocate, and I find the Atlanta location particularly appealing.

As you will see from my resume, I am currently excelling as Senior Travel Agent with a travel agency in Colorado. I offer advanced computer skills and am my office's "internal expert" on all matters of software and hardware technology, including troubleshooting hardware malfunctions. I have completed Datas II, Worldspan, and Advanced Professional Sabre courses and am very interested in teaching Worldspan software. I am also my agency's expert on advanced ticketing applications including ticket exchanges, coupon redemption, and group airline ticketing.

With a commitment to continuous professional training, I am always seeking ways to improve my knowledge in my spare time. I hold an A.A. degree in Liberal Arts.

Although I am equipped to book travel worldwide, I offer particularly strong knowledge related to most major U.S. cities, the Caribbean, Great Britain, Italy, Greece, and Bermuda. I have traveled extensively myself and am a former resident of St. Croix.

I can provide outstanding references from my current employer as well as from both corporate and leisure clientele. A hard worker who thrives on new challenges and who rapidly masters new concepts, I feel certain I could excel as a Sales Manager in your Atlanta office. I, of course, know of your company's fine reputation, and I would be honored to be associated with a company respected for its industry leadership and commitment to customer service.

I hope I will have the pleasure of meeting with you in person to discuss my strong qualifications for and interest in the position you advertised. I look forward to hearing from you soon to suggest a time when we can talk about your needs and my ability to meet them. Thank you in advance for your time.

Sincerely yours,

Frances Rothstein

FRANCES ROTHSTEIN

1110½ Hay Street, Fayetteville, NC 28305 • preppub@aol.com • (910) 483-6611

OBJECTIVE	To offer my experience to an organization that can benefit from my knowledge of domestic and international travel planning related to leisure travel, corporate accounts, and tour packages as well as my expertise related to travel industry computer technology.
LEADERSHIP	Am highly respected within the community in which I work, and serve as Chairwoman of the Board of Directors, Scottish Pilot Club of San Angelo.
EXPERIENCE	**SENIOR TRAVEL AGENT.** Travelers, Inc., San Angelo, CO (1990-present). Have become the top sales agent while gaining broad exposure in all aspects of the travel industry; have earned a reputation as a knowledgeable professional and serve a large repeat clientele because of my courteous service orientation and attention to detail.

- **Management:** Provide oversight and technical leadership to four other junior travel agents.
- **Advanced Computer Skills:** Am the office's "internal expert" on computer software and hardware, and am the individual who teaches software enhancements to office personnel while also troubleshooting hardware malfunctions; have excelled in the following courses:
  - **Datas II**, Atlanta
  - **Worldspan**, Atlanta
  - **Advanced Professional Sabre**, Dallas
- **Areas of Expertise:** Am equipped to book travel worldwide, but offer particularly strong knowledge of most major U.S. cities as well as the Caribbean, Bermuda, Great Britain, Greece, Italy, and most major cruise lines; am a former resident of St. Croix, US Virgin Islands.
- **Commitment to Continuous Professional Training:** In my spare time, am working on the Disney College of Knowledge Diploma; have attended several CLIA workshops, and have also attended two "See the Ships" seminars and Carnival Cruise Lines seminars in Miami; currently enrolled in a Microsoft Office course at Richmond Community College.
- **Advanced Ticketing Applications:** Am in charge of advanced ticketing applications from ticket exchanges, coupon redemption, and group airline ticketing.

Highlights of other experience: Polished public relations and office operations skills in earlier jobs including:

- **OFFICE MANAGER:** For a dentist office with four partners, was in charge of accounts receivable and billing; filed insurance claims and formulated payment plans.
- **DEPARTMENT SECRETARY:** Earned promotion based on my accomplishments and professionalism, Colorado University, Denver, CO.
- **ART INSTRUCTOR:** Taught art under ESEA Title I summer school program.
- **VOLUNTEER:** Volunteer within the public school system.

EDUCATION & TRAINING	Hold an **A.A., Liberal Arts,** Mount Vernon College, Washington, DC. Studied computer applications, Titusville Community College, Titusville, CA. Excelled in a word processing course related to Windows, Word, and Excel, San Angelo Community College, San Angelo, CO, 2002.
PERSONAL	Enthusiastic quick learner and self-starter. Accustomed to producing ongoing reports according to established schedule. Am single and willing to relocate. Excellent references.

Walt Disney World Co.
Salaried Casting Dept. LSTW50629
P.O. Box 10,090
Lake Buena Vista, FL 32830

TRAVEL AGENT   Dear Sir or Madam:

I would appreciate an opportunity to talk with you soon about how I could contribute to your organization through my experience and knowledge related to the travel industry along with my reputation as an enthusiastic and energetic professional who is known for a strong customer service orientation. With expert knowledge of cruise line operations, I am responding to your ad for a **Department Head, Corporate & Incentive Sales.** Although I am responding to a specific ad, in my capacity as a travel agent I have become such a fan of the Disney organization that I would be happy to be considered for employment in any area of the organization where my expert knowledge, creativity, and management skills could be utilized. I am single and will relocate according to your needs.

In my years with Travel Time, Inc. in Tampa, FL, I have applied my thorough understanding of the travel business in order to help the company increase profitability yearly and maintain excellent customer relations. Working for this company has given me the opportunity to deal with both foreign and domestic corporate and leisure travel. I have gained valuable experience while learning to accommodate the different needs of corporate clients and their families. I have become the agency's cruise specialist which involves dealing regularly with representatives of the major cruise lines: Princess, Royal Caribbean, Carnival, and Premier among others.

As a top sales agent, I have become very successful in applying my knowledge to help customers make decisions on the best values for their particular needs. My time management skills are finely tuned and allow me to handle multiple tasks simultaneously in a fast-paced office.

You would find me to be an enthusiastic self-starter with an eye for detail and with excellent instincts, acquired through experience, about what kind of "adventure" people might like in their leisure travel. I am skilled at using standard industry software and hardware and I enjoy keeping up-to-date on the latest innovations and changes which will help me provide fast, efficient, and friendly service. I can provide outstanding personal and professional references.

I hope to hear from you soon to suggest a time convenient for us to meet and discuss your current and future needs and how I might serve them. Thank you in advance for your time.

Sincerely yours,

Hope L. Bluebell

HOPE L. BLUEBELL

1110½ Hay Street, Fayetteville, NC 28305 • preppub@aol.com • (910) 483-6611

OBJECTIVE

To offer a strong base of travel industry experience to an organization that can benefit from my knowledge of domestic and international leisure and corporate travel planning as well as my outstanding skills in sales, customer service, and travel office management.

EXPERIENCE

SENIOR TRAVEL AGENT. Travel Time, Inc., Tampa, FL (1990-present). Have become the top sales agent while gaining a broad base of exposure in all aspects of the travel industry and earning a reputation as a knowledgeable professional with the ability to excel in both corporate and leisure travel.

- Specialize in handling the details of arranging cruises and regularly deal with the major cruise lines including Premier, Carnival, Royal Caribbean, Princess, Regency, and Holland America.
- Have attended advanced technical training programs becoming skilled in using Datas II, Worldspan, and Professional Sabre with Windows.
- Was chosen as acting office manager to handle agent inquiries, bank transactions, and computer operations during the owner's absence.
- Developed a solid understanding of airline operations, rules, and procedures while making arrangements and overseeing the details of global travel.
- Have become known for my service orientation and courteous, helpful manner.
- Provided the personal attention needed to satisfy the requirements of personnel from major corporations with their domestic and international business travel planning.
- Exhibited a special talent for finding answers — creatively used all available resources to ensure customer and agent questions were thoroughly and properly answered.
- Successfully built on an early interest in the travel industry which grew from childhood experience in traveling to medical conferences and on trips abroad due to my father's profession as a surgeon.

Highlights of other experience: Polished public relations and office operations skills in earlier jobs including:
REAL ESTATE AGENT: Became licensed by the state and sold residential real estate, Century 21, New York, NY.
RELOCATION SPECIALIST: During frequent relocations due to spouse's government job, have developed and refined versatile skills in organizing, scheduling, and handling finances while displaying adaptability and flexibility.

EDUCATION & TRAINING

A.A., Liberal Arts, Mount Vernon College, Mount Vernon, VA.
Studied computer applications, Tampa Community College, Tampa, FL, 1995: the course presented an overview of Excel and Lotus 1-2-3 for spreadsheets, Word for word processing, and databases.
Attended "See the Ships" seminars and several CLIA workshops.

COMPUTER SKILLS

Am familiar with word processors and in the use of the standard industry hardware and software; keep up with state-of-the-art systems in use.

PERSONAL

Am an enthusiastic quick learner who adapts easily to change. Volunteered extensively in various schools, churches, and social/athletic organizations while raising my children. Have excellent time management skills: can handle multiple tasks simultaneously. Will relocate and travel as extensively as is needed by my employer.

CAREER CHANGE

Exact Name of Person
Title or Position
Name of Company
Address (no., street)
Address (city, state, zip)

TRAVEL AGENT

Dear Exact Name of Person (or Dear Sir or Madam if answering a blind ad):

Can you use a resourceful quick learner who offers a background of travel throughout Europe including several years spent living and working overseas? I am interested in exploring opportunities to work as a Travel Agent with your company.

As you will see from my resume, I recently completed the Travel Agent I course at Grand Rapids Technical Community College. My maturity, talent for developing relations and communicating with others, and travels abroad led my instructor to recommend that I be hired to teach. I have been offered an opportunity to instruct the course Travel Agent I and Travel Agent III — Geography during the next term. While that offer is flattering, it is my desire to obtain full-time employment in the travel industry as a travel agent.

I offer a background strong in customer service and sales as well as an ability to easily and quickly become familiar with new computer systems and other types of office equipment. In every job I have ever held, I have been quickly promoted to handle management responsibilities, and I have become the "go-to" individual for the toughest customer service problems.

I hope you will welcome my call soon to arrange a brief meeting at your convenience to discuss your current and future needs and how I might serve them. Thank you in advance for your time.

Sincerely yours,

Terri M. Ticket

Alternate last paragraph:
I hope you will call or write soon to suggest a time convenient for us to meet and discuss your current and future needs and how I might serve them. Thank you in advance for your time.

TERRI M. TICKET

1110½ Hay Street, Fayetteville, NC 28305 • preppub@aol.com • (910) 483-6611

OBJECTIVE

To contribute to an organization that can use a resourceful quick learner who offers outstanding interpersonal relations, communication, and computer operating skills along with a background of extensive travel and years spent living in Europe.

SPECIAL INTERESTS & TRAVEL EXPERIENCE

- Traveled extensively on my own throughout Europe for approximately 5 1/2 years.
- Lived like a "native" while working in jobs including receptionist for a London record company; "au pair" in Eilat, Israel; and as a maid in a youth hostel in Munich, Germany, to earn the money to continue my travels.
- Have traveled and/or lived in countries including the following: Israel, Turkey, Greece, Yugoslavia, Spain, Portugal, France, Germany, Austria, Switzerland, Czechoslovakia, Poland, Sweden, Denmark, Belgium, England, Scotland, and Japan.
- Developed and refined the ability to establish communications with people of all nationalities and economic levels; am very effective in communicating even if my knowledge of the country's language is limited.
- Speak and understand the German language.

EDUCATION

Completed the Travel Agent I course, Grand Rapids Technical Community College, MI, 2002.
- Was singled out for my maturity, experience, and communication abilities to teach Travel Agent I and Travel Agent III - Geography.

Studied Hotel/Restaurant Management and French while attending college in Illinois and Wisconsin.

EXPERIENCE

Excelled in jobs requiring strong communication and customer service skills:
CUSTOMER SERVICE REPRESENTATIVE. Blockbuster Video, Grand Rapids, MI (2000-present). Apply my naturally outgoing personality while providing efficient service to customers checking out videos and handling additional actions including accepting payments, accessing a computer for item status, and ordering stock.
- Proved to be very effective at handling difficult customers and the pressure of long lines in a very busy and often hectic retail location.

RETAIL SALES ASSOCIATE. Hechts, Grand Rapids, MI (1995-00). Maintained an awareness of what items are available on sale and at regular prices in a ladies' clothing store doing approximately $6,000 to $7,000 in business a day.

ASSISTANT STORE MANAGER. London Fur & Leather, London, England (1991-94). Earned rapid promotion to this key management position while living in London; developed a strong repeat customer base while supervising two sales associates in an upscale location.
- Handled the details, including phone hookup and moving all merchandise and displays, for a relocation of the business.
- Displayed a knowledgeable sales style despite no previous experience in "luxury" sales.
- Maintained accountability for a $300,000 inventory, twice-daily inventories, ordering merchandise, control of layaway items, and paperwork after only one week of training.

SUPERVISOR. Fast Freddy's Convenience Stores, Syracuse, NY (1989-90). Supervised 12 filling station/convenience store employees while reconciling daily receipts and receiving/stocking merchandise.
- Gained valuable management and decision-making experience.

PERSONAL

Offer office skills including typing 50 wpm and operating any type of equipment.

FLIGHT ATTENDANT

Dear Sir or Madam:

I would appreciate an opportunity to talk with you soon about how I could contribute to Carnival Airline as a flight attendant through my proven skills in customer service and public relations which have been even further refined since joining EastWind Airlines as a Flight Attendant.

As you will see from my resume, after excelling in business courses and in training as a cosmetologist, I quickly distinguished myself in the cosmetology field, both in my performance in competitions and in rapid promotion to shop management positions. I am well known for my cheerful disposition, patience, and highly refined style of dealing with the public.

In every job I have held, I have contributed to the success and profitability of my employer by my ability to attract new customers and keep existing ones happy. I feel certain that my ability to handle people graciously and solve problems courteously could benefit Carnival Airline.

With a reputation as an enthusiastic self-starter with a proven ability to excel in anything I attempt, I would greatly enjoy the opportunity to meet with you to show you in person that I have the kind of professional skills and warm personality that could add value to your business.

I hope you will call or write me soon to suggest a time when we might meet to discuss how I might join Carnival Airline as a flight attendant. Thank you in advance for your time.

Yours sincerely,

Nancy E. Drew

NANCY E. DREW

1110½ Hay Street, Fayetteville, NC 28305   •   preppub@aol.com   •   (910) 483-6611

OBJECTIVE
I want to contribute to an organization that can use a dynamic self-starter with a strong service orientation and proven public relations skills along with a love of teamwork and travel; I am willing to relocate.

EXPERIENCE
FLIGHT ATTENDANT. EastWind Airlines, Winston-Salem, NC (2000-present). Ensure the safety, comfort, and enjoyment of airline passengers.
- Assisted any passengers with special needs: for example, minor children traveling alone or those with physical handicaps.
- Made announcements which kept the passengers aware of conditions such as take-offs, landings, or descents as well as where such things as reading lights, earphones, and rest rooms were located.

Previously earned a reputation in my community as a hard-working young professional with the ability to serve others in a gracious manner and build a base of satisfied customers whose "repeat" business was the foundation of the success and profitability of my employers:
BOOTH MANAGER. Super Star Beauty & Barber Salon, Charlotte, NC (1994-2000). Managed all functions involved in running a business including financial management, customer relations, marketing, and tax preparation while operating as a cosmetologist in a popular local salon.
- Was named **Stylist of the Year** because of my technical skills as in my field as well as my leadership and communication skills.

SHOP MANAGER. Umoja's Hair Innovations, Charlotte, NC (1989-93). Began in this business as a cosmetologist and was rapidly promoted to manage the shop because of my "common sense" and business knowledge.
- *Finances:* Handled accounts receivable and payable and assured that the business had a reputation for paying its bills on time and enjoyed excellent credit.
- *Inventory control:* Ordered and controlled an inventory of products; met with vendors and negotiated prices and contracts.
- *Advertising and marketing:* Established the marketing and advertising plan for this business, and generated new business through the innovative ideas I implemented.
- *Maintenance management:* Coordinated with the janitorial and other service personnel in a business which required careful handling/disposal of chemicals as well as attention to detail in routine cleaning activities.
- *Customer service:* Became the "voice and face" of this business, and was commended by the owners for increasing business by 25% through my ability to attract new customers and keep existing ones happy.
- *Imagination and creativity:* Became known for my creative approach to solving problems; took pride in earning the respect of people many years my senior.

EDUCATION
Business: Excelled in one year of college course work in business management, Winston-Salem College, Winston-Salem, NC, 1987-88.
Technical training: Earned a Certificate of Completion in Cosmetology, Wanda's Hair-styling Academy, Winston-Salem, NC, 1988-89.

PERSONAL
Am considered by others to be a refined and elegant young person who believes in the old saying that "you never get a second chance to make a first impression." Have refined my customer service and public relations skills in an industry which is highly competitive. Believe outstanding service with a smile is an essential ingredient to customer service.

CAREER CHANGE

FULL-TIME HOMEMAKER TO AIRLINE FLIGHT ATTENDANT

For some time, this devoted wife and mother made plans to make a career in the travel industry, once her children were out of the home. This cover letter and resume was used to approach numerous airlines. All she had to do was address each one personally to the appropriate person at each airline with the hiring authority for flight attendants. On the basis of this letter and resume, she became a flight attendant with a major airline.
Note: This is a very creative resume designed to make her look and sound as though she is a natural "fit" with the travel industry. If she were trying to re-enter the financial services field and resume the type of work she did 15 years ago, her resume would be written in an entirely different fashion.

Exact Name of Person
Exact Title
Exact Name of Company
Address
City, State, Zip

Dear Exact Name of Person (or Dear Sir or Madam if answering a blind ad):

I would appreciate an opportunity to talk with you soon about how I could contribute to your organization through my proven ability to serve the public and "bring out the best in people." I am interested in becoming a flight attendant for your airline.

Both in high school and in college, I was fortunate enough to be the recipient of many honors ranging from winning the pageant in my high school to becoming elected class president on my college campus. I am known as a self-starter with a high energy level and a true concern for others.

As you will see from my resume, I have excelled in jobs as a financial consultant and account executive/sales representative. During the period of that employment, however, I have pursued and excelled in studies related to travel, tourism, computer reservations, and the travel agent field. Through the extensive experience described on my resume, I have become a "professional traveler" and I am positive I have all the natural ingredients and acquired skills necessary to excel as a flight attendant.

You would find me to be a gracious and polished person who would enhance the image and reputation of any organization. I can provide outstanding personal and professional references, and I am willing to travel and relocate according to your needs.

I hope you will write or call me soon to let me know what the "next step" is with regard to my goal of joining your airline as a flight attendant. Thank you in advance for your help in this matter, and I look forward to hearing from you.

Sincerely,

Florence Martin

FLORENCE MARTIN

1110½ Hay Street, Fayetteville, NC 28305 • preppub@aol.com • (910) 483-6611

OBJECTIVE

I want to contribute to an organization that can use a dynamic self-starter with a strong service orientation and proven public relations skills along with a love of teamwork and travel; I am willing to relocate.

LIFESAVING SKILLS

CPR Certified; knowledgeable of first aid.
Am on a community lifesaver team.

TRAVEL

Offer a natural talent for establishing rapport with others and have become knowledgeable about other cultures through traveling to places including:

New York City, NY	Islands of Oahu and Maui, HI	Toronto, Canada
Washington, DC	San Juan and Dorado, PR	Richmond, VA
Lake Tahoe, NV	Orlando and Miami, FL	France
San Francisco, CA	Acapulco, Mexico	Switzerland
Atlanta, GA	New Orleans, LA	Omaha, NE

HIGHLIGHTS

Physical Appearance: Was selected as "Miss Autryville High School" over 350 other contestants; have judged beauty pageants and was chosen as official chaperone for the Queen of the Azalea Festival on visits to resorts and special events such as the Cotton Bowl.
Intellect: Was named a Marshall in my college studies based on academic achievements.
Leadership: Was voted Class President of my college campus because of my leadership ability.
Service to Others: Have become respected for my reputation as a "doer" and "giver" through volunteering my time to help others in organizations that include Meals on Wheels, United Way, and Junior League as well as my church, garden club, and the local hospital.

EXPERIENCE

ACCOUNT EXECUTIVE. Madison Avenue Communications, Autryville, SC (2000-present). In a part-time job for this communications company with diversified advertising, publishing, and public relations interests, played a key role in creating and publishing *The Autryville Newcomer's Guide for 2002,* a publication with a 25,000-person distribution that is the "bible" for area newcomers and travelers.
- After extensive analysis and research, produced a comprehensive profile of educational, cultural, religious, and business activities.
- Used my strong sales skills and public relations ability to sell advertising in the publication to businesses and other organizations.

Previous experience: Prior to working inside the home full-time while my children were at home, excelled in these positions:
FINANCIAL CONSULTANT. Optimum Planning Resources, Inc., Autryville, NC. After completing a rigorous course of study, earned my license to sell life, accident, and health insurance; worked with professionals from every field to create sound investment and insurance portfolios.
- Assisted many people in reducing their taxes and expanding their wealth.
- Analyzed risk tolerance of clients and made recommendations for repositioning assets.

BANK TELLER. Autryville National Bank, Autryville, NC. Was rapidly promoted to train other tellers while earning respect for my outstanding customer service skills.

PERSONAL

Excellent references on request. Outstanding reputation. In my spare time, enjoy dancing and aerobics. Am in excellent physical condition.

Date

Exact Name of Person
Title or Position
Name of Company
Address (no., street)
Address (city, state, zip)

TRAVEL CONSULTANT

Dear Exact Name of Person (or Dear Sir or Madam if answering a blind ad):

With the enclosed resume, I would like to make you aware of my background as a Travel Consultant and express my interest in joining your organization. My husband and I are in the process of relocating to your area because of his recent promotion, and I am seeking employment with a local firm that can use a dedicated, knowledgeable industry professional.

In my current position with a San Francisco travel agency, I am the designated office manager when the owner is out of town on frequent trips. In my capacity as a Travel Consultant, I have doubled my predecessor's monthly sales average, and I have aggressively prospected for new commercial accounts. In a previous position in the travel industry, I worked as a Travel Agent in San Antonio.

Early in my working career, I was employed as an Air Passenger Specialist for Midwest Airlines, and I gained valuable insight into the inner workings of airlines and airports. That knowledge has come in quite handy for me as an agent when I am choosing airports, routes, and travel destinations. In a position outside the travel industry, I worked for the well-known Bose organization as an Account Representative, and I excelled in all aspects of sales and customer service.

A self-starter, I am known for my ability to establish strong working relationships with co-workers, industry professionals, and customers. I have received numerous letters of appreciation from customers and from airline personnel for my exceptional attention to detail and problem-solving skills.

I hope you will call or write me soon to suggest a time convenient for us to meet and discuss your current and future needs and how I might serve them. Thank you in advance for your time.

Sincerely yours,

Samantha H. Tall

SAMANTHA H. TALL

1110½ Hay Street, Fayetteville, NC 28305   •   preppub@aol.com   •   (910) 483-6611

OBJECTIVE   To apply my extensive knowledge of the travel industry, outstanding customer service skills, and technical proficiency to an organization that can benefit from my office management experience, dedication, and helpful personality.

SPECIAL SKILLS
- Am experienced in using the Eastern Airlines System I computer as well as the United Apollo and Delta systems.
- Operate office equipment including a PBX switchboard, 10-key calculators, and adding machines; type 60 wpm. Strong computer knowledge with various software programs.

EXPERIENCE   **TRAVEL CONSULTANT.** AAA Travel Agency, San Francisco, CA (2000-present). Have taken the initiative to become familiar with all aspects of office operations in addition to my main responsibility of booking both domestic and international flights, car rentals, hotels, and vacation packages.
- Excelled in collecting data and preparing the detailed, critical weekly Airline Reporting Corporation (ARC) sales figures.
- Took care of ordering tickets, itineraries, and other forms which must be accounted for individually.
- Doubled my predecessor's monthly sales average.
- Completed the American Airlines "Fly Away Vacation Expert Program" on enhancing sales techniques for selling vacation packages.

ACCOUNT REPRESENTATIVE. BOSE Corporation, San Diego, CA (1998-2000). Earned a reputation as a "highly motivated, hard-working, and dedicated sales professional" while controlling inventory, merchandising, and demonstrating products for an account with a monthly average of $800,000 in sales.
- Increased market share from 25% to 47% and moved ahead of nine other top companies in tough competition for audio-video sales.
- Recognized for my judgment, successfully forecasted stocking requirements.
- Polished my communication skills making individual and group presentations.

TRAVEL AGENT. Air Fare Consultants, San Antonio, TX (1990-97). Became skilled in accounting and managerial skills unique to the travel industry while making reservations, collecting and processing payments, and preparing data for the Airline Reporting Corporation in a two-person office.
- Handled the details of typing invoices for billing purposes and company checks to make payment of bills. Attended Eastern Airlines' 40-hour training course and gained familiarity with the System I computer.

AIR PASSENGER SPECIALIST. Midwest Airlines, San Antonio, TX (1985-90). Earned a reputation as a customer-oriented professional while coordinating travel arrangements for corporate personnel and dealing directly with airline passengers using corporate services.
- Learned tact and diplomacy in dealing with VIP passengers.
- Worked closely with the Scheduled Airline Ticket Office (SATO) while making requests and receiving authorization for customers.

EDUCATION   Received certification as a Travel Consultant after completing a 1,580-hour program, Great Oaks Vocational School, Milford, OH.

PERSONAL   Excellent personal and professional references on request.

ABOUT THE EDITOR

Anne McKinney holds an MBA from the Harvard Business School and a BA in English from the University of North Carolina at Chapel Hill. A noted public speaker, writer, and teacher, she is the senior editor for PREP's business and career imprint, which bears her name. Early titles in the Anne McKinney Career Series (now called the Real-Resumes Series) published by PREP include: *Resumes and Cover Letters That Have Worked, Resumes and Cover Letters That Have Worked for Military Professionals, Government Job Applications and Federal Resumes, Cover Letters That Blow Doors Open,* and *Letters for Special Situations.* Her career titles and how-to resume-and-cover-letter books are based on the expertise she has acquired in 20 years of working with job hunters. Her valuable career insights have appeared in publications of the "Wall Street Journal" and other prominent newspapers and magazines.

PREP Publishing Order Form

You may purchase any of our titles from your favorite bookseller! Or send a check or money order or your credit card number for the total amount*, plus $4.00 postage and handling, to PREP, Box 66, Fayetteville, NC 28302. You may also order our titles on our website at wwwprep-pub.com and feel free to e-mail us at preppub@aol.com or call 910-483-6611 with your questions or concerns.

Name: _____

Phone #: _____

Address: _____

E-mail address:

Payment Type: ☐ Check/Money Order   ☐ Visa   ☐ MasterCard

Credit Card Number: _____ Expiration Date: _____

Check items you are ordering:

☐ $16.95—REAL-RESUMES FOR MANUFACTURING JOBS. Anne McKinney, Editor

☐ $16.95—REAL-RESUMES FOR AVIATION & TRAVEL JOBS. Anne McKinney, Editor

☐ $16.95—REAL-RESUMES FOR POLICE, LAW ENFORCEMENT & SECURITY JOBS. Anne McKinney, Editor

☐ $16.95—REAL-RESUMES FOR SOCIAL WORK & COUNSELING JOBS. Anne McKinney, Editor

☐ $16.95—REAL-RESUMES FOR CONSTRUCTION JOBS. Anne McKinney, Editor

☐ $16.95—REAL-RESUMES FOR FINANCIAL JOBS. Anne McKinney, Editor

☐ $16.95—REAL-RESUMES FOR COMPUTER JOBS. Anne McKinney, Editor

☐ $16.95—REAL-RESUMES FOR MEDICAL JOBS. Anne McKinney, Editor

☐ $16.95—REAL-RESUMES FOR TEACHERS. Anne McKinney, Editor

☐ $16.95—REAL-RESUMES FOR CAREER CHANGERS. Anne McKinney, Editor

☐ $16.95—REAL-RESUMES FOR STUDENTS. Anne McKinney, Editor

☐ $16.95—REAL-RESUMES FOR SALES. Anne McKinney, Editor

☐ $16.95—REAL ESSAYS FOR COLLEGE AND GRAD SCHOOL. Anne McKinney, Editor

☐ $25.00—RESUMES AND COVER LETTERS THAT HAVE WORKED.

☐ $25.00—RESUMES AND COVER LETTERS THAT HAVE WORKED FOR MILITARY PROFESSIONALS.

☐ $25.00—RESUMES AND COVER LETTERS FOR MANAGERS.

☐ $25.00—GOVERNMENT JOB APPLICATIONS AND FEDERAL RESUMES: Federal Resumes, KSAs, Forms 171 and 612, and Postal Applications.

☐ $25.00—COVER LETTERS THAT BLOW DOORS OPEN.

☐ $25.00—LETTERS FOR SPECIAL SITUATIONS.

☐ $16.00—BACK IN TIME. Patty Sleem

☐ $17.00—(trade paperback) SECOND TIME AROUND. Patty Sleem

☐ $25.00—(hardcover) SECOND TIME AROUND. Patty Sleem

☐ $18.00—A GENTLE BREEZE FROM GOSSAMER WINGS. Gordon Beld

☐ $18.00—BIBLE STORIES FROM THE OLD TESTAMENT. Katherine Whaley

☐ $14.95—WHAT THE BIBLE SAYS ABOUT... *Words that can lead to success and happiness* (large print edition) Patty Sleem

☐ $10.95—KIJABE An African Historical Saga. Pally Dhillon

_____ **TOTAL ORDERED (add $4.00 for postage and handling)**

PREP offers volume discounts on large orders. Call us at (910) 483-6611 for more information.

THE MISSION OF PREP PUBLISHING IS TO PUBLISH BOOKS AND OTHER PRODUCTS WHICH ENRICH PEOPLE'S LIVES AND HELP THEM OPTIMIZE THE HUMAN EXPERIENCE. OUR STRONGEST LINES ARE OUR JUDEO-CHRISTIAN ETHICS SERIES AND OUR BUSINESS & CAREER SERIES.

Would you like to explore the possibility of having PREP's writing team create a resume for you similar to the ones in this book?

For a brief free consultation, call 910-483-6611
or send $4.00 to receive our Job Change Packet to
PREP, Department SPR2002, Fayetteville, NC 28302.

QUESTIONS OR COMMENTS? E-MAIL US AT PREPPUB@AOL.COM

Made in the USA
Lexington, KY
17 November 2012